FLORIDA STATE
UNIVERSITY LIBRARIES

FEB 16 1995

TALLAHASSEE, FLORIDA

MY DAUGHTER, THE TEACHER

MY DAUGHTER, THE TEACHER

JEWISH TEACHERS IN THE NEW YORK CITY SCHOOLS

Ruth Jacknow Markowitz

RUTGERS UNIVERSITY PRESS

NEW BRUNSWICK, NEW JERSEY

F
128.9
J5
M28
1993

Library of Congress Cataloging-in-Publication Data

Markowitz, Ruth Jacknow.
  My daughter, the teacher : Jewish teachers in the New York City
schools / Ruth Jacknow Markowitz.
    p. cm.
  Includes bibliographical references and index.
  ISBN 0-8135-1974-8 (cloth) — ISBN 0-8135-1975-6 (pbk.)
    1. Jews—New York (N.Y.)—Interviews. 2. Women, Jewish—New York
(N.Y.)—Interviews. 3. Jewish teachers—New York (N.Y.)—
Interviews. 4. Women teachers—New York (N.Y.)—Interviews.
5. Public schools—New York (N.Y.)—History—20th century. 6. New
York (N.Y.)—Ethnic relations I. Title.
F128.9.J5M28 1993
974.7'1004924—dc20   92-37565
                                                                              CIP

British Cataloging-in-Publication information available

Copyright © 1993 by Ruth Jacknow Markowitz
All rights reserved
Manufactured in the United States of America

For Harvey, Juliet, and Michael

CONTENTS

ACKNOWLEDGMENTS

Because the debts of gratitude incurred in this project have been so many, it is therefore one of the pleasures of completion, at long last, to be able to thank those who have made it possible. First and foremost are the sixty-one former teachers who gave so generously of their time to provide the interviews that are at the core of this book, and without whom this work would not have been possible. Sadly, many of them are no longer alive, but I will always cherish the warmth, humor, interest, and assistance of this formidable and dynamic group. I am also grateful to those who located these women for me and persuaded them to participate. I am especially indebted to Stephen Rosenthal, Director of Teachers' Records, Division of Personnel, at the New York City Board of Education, who kindly allowed me to examine the teachers' personnel cards, going out of his way to facilitate my work there.

My research has benefitted from the competent and professional assistance of archivists and librarians. Thanks are owed to Richard Strassberg, Archivist at the Labor-Management Documentation Center of Cornell University; Lillian Lister, Archivist at Brooklyn College; William Omelchenko, Archivist at Hunter College; Jean Holliday at the Seeley G. Mudd Manuscript Library, Princeton University; and Fannie Zelcer, Archivist at the American Jewish Archives in Cincinnati. I am also obligated to the people at Special Collections at Teachers College: David M. Ment, Head of Special Collections; Kate Rousmaniere, Manuscript Curator; and Bette Weneck, Photo Curator. Lucinda Manning was a great help to me in my research in three different locations, first when she was Archivist of the United Federation of Teachers collection at the Robert F. Wagner Labor Archives of the Tamiment Institute at New York University; next when she served as Archivist at Barnard College; and then at Special Collections at Teachers College. The staff at the State University of New York at Stony Brook Interlibrary Loan Office has cheerfully performed services above and beyond the call of duty, including arranging for the loan of twenty years' worth of newspapers.

ACKNOWLEDGMENTS

I have been most fortunate to have had Wilbur R. Miller, chair of the history department at the State University of New York at Stony Brook, nurture this project from its inception as a dissertation. He has been generous with his time, providing cogent and useful criticisms, along with moral support, and has prevented my occasional lapses into pedagogical jargon. Nancy J. Tomes is responsible for suggesting I interweave the threads of my interests in women, immigration, and education into this topic. Her interest and thoughtful advice have contributed immeasurably to this work. I am also grateful to Ruth Schwartz Cowan and Judith Wishnia, who, from the very beginning, have offered sisterhood and colleaguehood, along with their vigorous criticisms. I have profited from the wisdom and useful criticism of a number of scholars who have either read portions of this work, offered comments at formal presentations, or just answered my many questions. They are Joyce Antler, Selma C. Berrol, Betty Boyd Caroli, Hasia R. Diner, Patricia Palmieri, David Reimers, Sally Schwager, and Harold Wechsler.

One of the greatest joys over these many years has been the support, friendship, and intellectual stimulus of an extraordinary group of women I met in Stony Brook's history department: Barbara Beresford, Antonia Booth, Floris Cash, Teresa Fetzer, Marie Fitzgerald, and Barbara Kelly. Doris Halowitch, a true comrade-in-arms, has aided this work in ways too numerous to cite here. Less tangible but equally valuable has been the contribution of friends who listened to me talk interminably about teachers, and gave me their shoulders to cry on. They offered suggestions and criticism, accompanied me to archives and conferences, provided me with luxurious accomodations while I was away conducting research, and amused and diverted me when I most needed it. Sincere thanks to: Marilyn Auster, Ronna Juliano, Hedda Kantor, Bentley Maxwell, Harriet Rosenberg, Marcy Seidler, Joel Shatles, Susan Shatles, and Francine Teicher. And special acknowledgment is due Virginia Sanchez Korrol and Roberta Schiller. They never flagged in their enthusiasm for this project, and they actually read the manuscript in its entirety. I am most appreciative of the patience and consideration afforded me by Marlie Wasserman and Marilyn Campbell at Rutgers University Press. This work was skillfully refined by the meticulous copyediting of Adaya Henis.

Heartfelt thanks to Michael Markowitz, who willingly tracked down hard-to-locate books and material, and nagged me into finishing. He has solemnly promised to read this work when it is issued by *Cliff's Notes*, or if I rework it into a screen comedy. Juliet Markowitz, my daughter, the lawyer, has been my staunchest supporter in all my endeavors. She has never wavered in her enthusiasm and belief that I could actually complete this work, and by her own achievements has been a source of inspiration. Above all, I am grateful to Harvey Markowitz. In addition to chauffeuring me to libraries and archives and serving as my personal thesaurus and proofreader, he has proved steadfast in his support and encouragement.

MY DAUGHTER, THE TEACHER

CHAPTER

 1

FROM MOTHER'S KITCHEN
TO TEACHER'S DESK

Education and Jewish Immigrant Daughters

A woman, strolling down a street, meets a friend who is holding her two small children by the hand.

FIRST WOMAN: *"What darling children! How old are they?"*

SECOND WOMAN: *"My son, the doctor, is four, and my daughter, the teacher, is two."*

Variation on an American joke

THE MOTHER IN THIS JOKE could only be Jewish, for "my son, the doctor" and "my daughter, the teacher" were among the most cherished phrases of Jewish immigrant parents, according to many observers of New York City's Eastern European Jewish community. This symbolizes the expectation of this group that the children's reach would exceed their parents', and illustrates how these two professions represented the pinnacle of immigrant parents' aspirations for their Americanized offspring. Supposedly, the attainment of these goals personifies the exceptionally successful socioeconomic adaptation of Jewish immigrants in

1

America. Although there is considerable evidence that "my son, the doctor" was more than a catchphrase for many, most studies indicate that this dream was a delayed one, at least for a generation or so. Although the sons of Jewish immigrants entered the professions in numbers far beyond their proportion to the rest of the immigrant population, for the most part, the earliest entrants into medicine, law, and teaching were the sons of German Jews who came to the United States well before the Jews of Eastern Europe. Contrary to social scientists who have invoked the Horatio Alger myth in portraying Jewish mobility, Eastern European Jewish mobility was "a two-stage, intergenerational phenomenon," as Stephen Steinberg has argued. The first generation, which possessed little formal education, used their occupational skills and cultural traditions to enter the marketplace, and were sometimes able to go into business for themselves. Usually, their sons followed them into the family occupation or business, and the great leap into the professions did not occur until the second generation was situated well enough to afford to educate the third generation.[1] To a great extent, these sons, or grandsons, did not become doctors until after World War II, when the combination of wartime prosperity and the lifting of restrictive quotas facilitated their entry into medical schools and other professional institutions.[2]

"My daughter, the teacher" was a far more realistic dream for immigrant parents, especially those living in New York City during the interwar years. If "my son, the doctor" was a dream deferred, the influx of daughters of Eastern European Jewish immigrants who entered the teaching ranks in the city's public school system during this period was a fulfillment of the second component of that dream. In 1920, Jewish women comprised 26 percent of the new teachers in New York City's public schools; by 1930 they made up 44 percent of those joining the teaching staff; and by 1940, 56 percent of the new teachers were Jewish.[3] During the interwar years, the preponderance of Jewish women teachers in the city's schools caused many New Yorkers to refer to teaching as "the Jewish profession," according to many informants. In the following two decades, Jewish women constituted the vast majority of all public school teachers in New York City, the largest public school system in the world, far more than the estimate of 50 percent provided by Nathan Glazer and Daniel Patrick Moynihan.[4]

The ever-increasing numbers of Jewish women who joined the teaching staff during the interwar years represent a new and unique phenomenon in Jewish and American history and in urban education, one that affected the women teachers, the Jewish community, and, most critically,

New York City's public school system. Because of the extraordinary number of Jewish teachers, the public school system of New York City underwent a major transformation during the period often characterized as the city's golden age of education. Yet the role played by these women during these important years has never been studied, as Joan Jacobs Brumberg and Nancy Tomes noted in 1982.[5] Although the women of the second generation set a new course for women in the public sphere, much as their immigrant mothers had done in their time, nevertheless the experiences and achievements of the daughters of Jewish immigrants have not received the attention historians have paid to the women of the first generation.[6] The second generation's role as classroom teachers has also been ignored. Female teachers, traditionally the focus of their students and the core of American education, have rarely been the subject of serious book-length studies, except for a recent book on primary teachers during the nineteenth century, a diatribe about the effects of feminization on teaching, or in biographies or sociological studies.[7] Female educators who are the subjects of biographies are always "woman worthies," as in all fields, and are usually involved in higher education. There are no entries in any of the four volumes of the biographical dictionary *Notable American Women* for any of the notable women activists in urban public education, save Julia Richman, who has yet to be the subject of a book-length study. Nor are there studies of teachers' union activists like Rose Russell, the legislative representative of the Teachers Union of New York City during its most critical years.[8] Sociologists tend to make the teacher the object rather than the subject of the study, barely acknowledging the significance of gender.[9] Recent scholarship has provided us with works on women in the professions, the semiprofessions, and in clerical and sales work, yet for schoolteachers we have only a reader and a composite portrait of the American woman teacher during the 1930s.[10] Despite the centrality of teaching in the lives of American women, as scholars have pointed out, "a good collective biography of the American 'school marm' has yet to be done."[11]

Unfortunately, what work has been done on schoolteachers often relies on the reports of school officials and schoolmen for information on the conditions under which women taught and learned. Yet the experience of teachers and their own viewpoints are not present in these reports or in the volumes that record the history and philosophy of education. And they cannot be found in the proliferation of teacher education texts or administrative handbooks or articles instructing teachers on how they should behave, for pedagogy is long on prescription and short on description. The typical research on teachers has concentrated on learning, rather than teaching, and has generally employed models and techniques at some distance removed from the realities of the classroom, leaving us with severely limited evidence about what teachers have actually done in their classrooms, and little about their perceptions.

This book is an attempt to rectify this situation, by studying the teachers themselves: who they were and what induced them to become teachers in such unprecedented numbers; how and where they prepared for their careers; and what was their experience as students and as student activists. The highly complicated process of securing a teaching appointment is scrutinized, as is the variety of experiences, both inside and outside the classroom. A quantified study of city teachers' maternity leave records proves that married women did not abandon the profession, but continued teaching until retirement age. This work also highlights the role of Jewish teachers in the union movement, and the anti-unionism and anti-Semitism they encountered, as well. Their story is brought into the decade of the fifties with its recrudescent anti-Communist hysteria, because so many of these women found themselves caught in the maelstrom of McCarthyism, losing their jobs and pensions. The aim has always been to keep the women themselves as the focal point. If this goal has been achieved it is because of the former teachers who provided the interviews that form the basis of so much of this work.

While the daughters of immigrants represented an innovation in the ethnic makeup of New York City's teachers, the very concept of female Jewish teachers was even more of a novelty, almost unthinkable in the Old World setting of immigrant parents. Throughout Jewish history, learning was not only of a strictly religious nature, it was reserved indisputably for males. Religious traditions informed women's lives, but because their obligations were home-centered, their education was geared toward this end. The only female who had a role as a teacher within the Jewish community of Eastern Europe was the wife of the boys' teacher, who sometimes taught girls to read and write a little Yiddish. This smattering of learning was deemed sufficient, because a girl's classroom was said to be her mother's kitchen.

Toward the end of the nineteenth century, the secular influences of the enlightenment movement, along with those of socialism and Zionism, slowly brought changes to the Jews of Eastern Europe, but their effect tended to filter down only to the daughters of the most modernized of the urban population, or to the daughters of adherents of the Jewish labor movement. Even for those who desired a secular education, fulfillment of this desire was extremely hard for Jewish children, and especially so for girls, since restrictive quotas were highly rigid, and school fees were prohibitive for most.[12] While education was seen as intrinsically valuable, it was also recognized as the key to economic and social success, even in the Old World. Although most Jewish boys received the rudiments of religious learning, only the wealthy could indulge in more advanced scholarship. Yet by the final decades of the nineteenth century, many who might have pursued such study recognized secular learning as a prerequisite of economic advancement. Hence, the literacy rate for Jews immigrating to the New World was one of the highest of all groups, for 50 percent of all Jews over the age of ten could read, and if women were excluded from consideration, because they were less likely to be literate, the literacy rate rose to 65 percent.[13]

Appreciation of education underwent a slight modification in the New World. In the Old World culture, learning had been the vehicle for mobility, community status, high-status marriage partners, and influence. In America, religious learning gave way to public school education. The Jews of Eastern Europe who immigrated to New York City were part of the new immigration that constantly swelled the city's populace. At the turn of the century, the city's foreign-born population was over one million, and by the second decade of the twentieth century, when most of the former teachers interviewed for this study were born, New York City's foreign-born population had more than doubled, constituting 33 percent of the city's almost seven million people in 1920.[14] Both the first and second generations comprised over 69 percent of New York City's total population, and an even higher percentage of the inhabitants of Manhattan and the Bronx.[15]

As the city's population increased in such extraordinary numbers, so too did the registers of its public schools. The immigration of Eastern European Jews was primarily that of families, and their children filled the schools to the bursting point, for it was said of this group that they "Land on Saturday, Settle on Sunday, School on Monday."[16] Clearly receptive to and accepting of schooling, and aware that further advances depended on education, Jewish parents embraced a school system that was hospitable and free of costs, making every effort to enable their children to continue school as long as possible. In 1908, according to the United States Immigration Commission, about one-third of New York City's schoolchildren were Jewish.[17] While Jews used the public schools more than other immigrant groups, their successes were greatly exaggerated. Selma C. Berrol, who has studied immigrants and education extensively, has debunked the great school myth by showing that educational achievement was the result of economic advancement for this group, rather than the cause of it. While scholarship was appreciated, the need for making a living took precedence. For the majority of the first generation and their children, despite their enthusiasm for schooling, it had little impact. Although Jewish students were more likely to be academic achievers, and were less likely to be truants or to be left back, as the Immigration Commission noted, few attended high school, and until 1916 or later, most left with only an eighth grade education, for their parents needed their earnings.[18]

Jewish males predominated over females in high school attendance during the first decades of the century because a higher premium was placed on educating sons. Since their sisters were expected to marry and raise families, immigrant families often considered their education wasteful. Therefore they were frequently withdrawn from school and were expected to contribute to the family economy until they married.[19] Yet the desire for an education was a common characteristic among Jewish immigrant women. The most remarkable aspect of the literature that deals with Jewish women from Eastern Europe, whether in the form of fiction, memoirs, or interviews, is the desire of these women for an education. Notably absent from most novels or oral histories of other immigrant groups who arrived at the same time as Jews from Eastern Europe is the same yearning for schooling. This absence is especially true among immigrants from Southern Italy, whose numbers in New York City approximated those of the city's Jewish population during the interwar years.[20] Although Octavia, the daughter in *The Fortunate Pilgrim,* Mario Puzo's novel of immigrant Italian life during Depression-era New York City, wanted to become a teacher, her mother, like most Italians, considered school superfluous for Italian women.[21] It took another generation before this traditional attitude toward women's roles changed and Italian-American women would be found in significant numbers among the city's teaching staff.[22]

This longing for an education, although born in the urban centers of Eastern Europe, had been a futile aspiration in the Old World, but was one of the most important appeals of the New World, where immigrants like Fannie Shapiro learned "you can get an education and you didn't have to pay for schooling." Like Anzia Yezierska, a Jewish immigrant writer, they dreamed of free schools and free colleges, but for most women of the first generation whose parents were too impoverished to forgo their daughters' wages, education was unattainable.[23] Many attempted to fill this void in their life by registering for the city's evening schools, where in 1908, 50 percent of their students were immigrants learning English and preparing for citizenship. However, because they attended after a full day's work, usually without time even for dinner, they were often so exhausted that they fell asleep and eventually dropped out. As Selma Berrol has pointed out, enrollment figures in night school were high, but attendance was erratic, since it took "an unusually able and determined student to utilize the evening schools for more than basic English literacy."[24]

The wish for more schooling remained a recurrent theme in the lives of immigrant women, even decades later. Forty-one out of the forty-six respondents in Sydney Stahl Weinberg's *The World of Our Mothers: The Lives of Jewish Immigrant Women* expressed their regret at not having had enough education. This was also the case with all the immigrant mothers of the former teachers interviewed for this study, as each woman told of her mother's disappointment at not having the opportunity for education in the New World. Interestingly, only a few of the interviewees mentioned that their fathers had similar regrets at not being able to achieve the education they desired. The first generation of immigrant women had been forbidden religious education by their religion's traditions and had been shut out of secular learning by the restrictions of the Old World and the poverty of the New. They were in awe of the schools, which they viewed as sacred citadels, regarding teachers with an attitude bordering on reverence. Teachers possessed coveted learning, which they could transmit to immigrant children by instructing them in American ways of dress, speech, behavior, and middle-class conventions. This would strip their children of their alien status and transform them into Americans. According to their daughters, teachers were a special class who could do no wrong in immigrant mothers' eyes, and all their mothers' thwarted ambitions for education were transferred to their daughters.[25]

Armed with stability and greater economic security, and fortified by their mothers' determination that their American-born daughters receive the education denied them, growing numbers of second-generation Jewish women remained in school through high school and beyond. However, for some of their daughters, timing was crucial when it came to their schooling. Although Sydney Stahl Weinberg noted this trend among the immigrant women she studied, birth order still made a difference among second-generation daughters. The order of their birth had an essential impact on what opportunities were afforded daughters of immigrants, with the greatest advantages going to those who were either the youngest in their families or who were born once their families were somewhat secure financially.[26] For many families, their poverty often necessitated the strategy of sacrificing the older children's education for the benefit of the younger ones, a tendency noticed in all by investigators of the backgrounds of New York City high school students, who found that the offspring of immigrants who remained in high school were likely to be the youngest in their families.[27] The observation of immigrant Mollie Linker that "It's the older ones in every family that have to help out" was replicated in the next generation. Attending the fiftieth reunion of Brooklyn College's Class of 1933, Irene Shapiro Goldenberg, who taught in the city's schools for thirty-four years, recalled that as the youngest of four, she was the only one to attend college. "Everyone did for me what they couldn't do for themselves," she explained.[28] The same was true of more than half of the sixty-one women interviewed for this study, who were the youngest in their families. Some of them had older sisters who were born in the old country and arrived in New York at a time when their earnings were desperately needed, so these young women worked, usually in garment factories, turning over their wages to their families. Other interviewees had sisters, or even brothers, whose adolescence occurred at a time when the family had not attained any degree of economic security, so that it was impossible to continue their education beyond the minimum. Many of these older siblings transferred their unattainable desires for an education to their younger sisters.

Yet others among the informants were the oldest in their families. Often their families made long-term economic plans, determined that no sacrifice was too great to enable the oldest child to remain in school, to achieve an education that would enable her to obtain a secure, well-paying position. The educated daughter, usually a public school teacher, was then expected, in turn, to contribute to the family economy, thus enabling younger siblings to obtain an education. Yet timing was not the only consideration to be factored in when the decision was made as to whether to educate a daughter. Mae Cogen claimed that coming from a home without sons allowed her aspirations to be fulfilled, claiming that she saw too many young women of her generation "sacrificed to pay for the brothers' schooling."[29]

The education received by these immigrants was intended to "teach them English, uplift their morals, improve their manners, erase their first language" and bring them "into the mainstream of life as it was lived in New York."[30] Like Myra Kelly's fictional teacher of Lower East Side children, public school teachers wanted to turn "little aliens" into "little citizens" as quickly as possible.[31] Certainly such an objective meant that encounters between immigrant children and American schools often were of a less than positive nature. Some pupils resisted the Americanization process or found it unpleasant or demeaning; others were recalcitrant or troublesome students.[32] Surely many of their experiences, as writer Irving Howe has suggested, were "a little less rosy and more abrasive than most memoirists acknowledge."[33] However, the Americanization process does not necessarily imply a devaluation of immigrant culture and values. Although far too many educators were disdainful of Old World traditions and showed their contempt, there were those who accepted them and even demonstrated their appreciation, as attested to by several of the interviewees.

How educators interpreted Americanization and the degree to which it was implemented in the schools remains problematic. But it is crucial to understand what the concept of Americanization meant for many immigrants, especially for Jewish women who had already rejected traditional roles and religious beliefs. While Americanization usually connotes an implicit and sweeping acceptance of American customs, institutions, and beliefs, along with a total repudiation of immigrant culture, in actuality this rarely occurred. According to the women interviewed, however, their objective was to become modern Americans, a target designated as "modernity" by Susan A. Glenn. In *Daughters of the Shtetl: Life and Labor in the Immigrant Generation* she distinguishes "modernity" as a receptivity toward change, which for female immigrants "meant breaking down traditional negative stereotypes" and extending their "presence and voice beyond the customary spheres." As Glenn notes, "America offered various opportunities to step into the modern world," recognizing that immigrants "embraced these opportunities selectively and adopted them within a largely Jewish social and cultural orbit."[34] According to those interviewed, both the first and second generation were able to maintain what several described as "a happy balance" between what they termed "old-fashioned" and "modern American" ways, without sacrificing their identity as Jews. For example, many changed their names, not to hide their Jewishness, but rather to be more "up-to-date," more "stylish," and more "fashionable." While Esther and Dvorah became Estelle and Dorothy, they usually remained Cohen and Levy.

The immigrant daughters who moved through the city's school system from kindergarten through high school, and on to its teacher-training schools or colleges, tended to be among the best and brightest of its students. Educators found Jewish pupils, and especially the girls among them, to be highly motivated, attentive, studious, and eager to please, because this was the group aspiring to be modern young Americans. If their teachers were determined to Americanize them, this was just fine with their parents, and it was equally acceptable to their offspring who were like Mary Antin, an immigrant writer who wholeheartedly embraced American schooling. They, too, were anxious for the schools to make them over into "Yankees."[35] Acknowledging that some immigrant children's school experiences were not as agreeable as theirs, nevertheless the daughters of Jewish immigrants who later taught in city schools have very pleasant memories of their school days, and of most of their teachers. Usually model students themselves, they took to schoolwork and glowed under the encouragement of their teachers. Lily Gordon insists she cannot recall any girl being a behavior problem in elementary school. "We all vied for the lavish praise of our teachers. We literally basked in it," she related. Ethel Cohen remembered with pride being held up to the class as an ideal student, "even though it was 1920. Third grade. I can still see Miss Jensen. She was my ideal." Their teachers were significant role models, "representative of a different, ineluctably more attractive way of life. They touched a nerve, these beautiful young women" among the immigrant girls who would later emulate them in their own classrooms.[36] They looked up to their teachers, considering them paragons of good taste, manners, speech, and deportment. "I remember how I admired them," Rachel Berkowitz stated, "for I loved the way they dressed and the way they spoke. I wanted to be just like them." Like Ethel Cohen, most of the respondents cited one special teacher as their inspiration, detailing some particular speech or dress characteristic that remained vivid in their memories after so many years had passed.

When these women recalled their teachers they, like most Americans, meant female teachers. Public school teaching in the United States, previously dominated by males, had been almost completely feminized before the Civil War. The spread of the common school movement in the early nineteenth century caused a greater demand for teachers than men could meet. Agriculture required male labor, and there were more lucrative opportunities in trade and business enterprises opening up to them. By 1830, education reformers like Horace Mann encouraged women's entrance into the field, stressing their supposed nurturing qualities and moral superiority, along with the economies resulting from women's willingness to accept lower wages.[37] Young women, out of economic necessity, religious zeal, intellectual curiosity, and a desire for a modicum of independence began making teaching a woman's field. In the words of Catharine Beecher, an antebellum advocate of teaching as a proper role for women, they not only were available to take jobs men had left for better pay, but became the "cheapest guardian and teacher of childhood."[38] By 1870, 61 percent of the nation's public school teachers were women, and from 1890 to 1920 their numbers doubled as school systems expanded in this period, with their proportion increasing to 86 percent by 1930. Although their numerical supremacy fell to 79 percent by the late thirties, nevertheless the teaching field had not only undergone a rapid and dramatic feminization, but was the number one profession among American women.[39]

Long before the daughters of Jewish immigrants entered the ranks of the New York City teaching staff, daughters of another immigrant group found it an attractive profession. As early as 1870, 20 percent of all city teachers were Irish women, and as the century progressed, teachers with Irish names began replacing Yankee ones. Offering steady employment and untouched by the vicissitudes of the economy, teaching became for the second generation of Irish women what domestic service had been for the first. Irish strength in urban politics gave these women easy access to jobs because the public schools in the late nineteenth century were part of the cities' political apparatus, under the control of the Irish. By the first decade of the twentieth century, Irish women constituted the largest group of non-Yankee teachers in New York City, comprising over one thousand of its total teaching population of seven thousand women. The preponderance of daughters of Irish immigrants on city teaching staffs was replicated in Chicago, San Francisco, Albany, and many other major American cities. By 1920, teaching ranked fifth among occupations of first- and second-generation women, employing almost 8 percent of such women.[40]

Although historians have examined the experience of females who taught in frontier and rural schools, and have studied the northern women who taught freed people in the South during Reconstruction, the urban female schoolteacher has not been the subject of a serious book-length study.[41] Yet American cities led the way in the increasing proportion of women teachers. In 1840, twice as many women as men taught in Cincinnati, and in 1851, women vastly outnumbered men teaching in Brooklyn and Philadelphia. By 1888, only 63 percent of all American teachers were women, whereas more than 90 percent of all urban teachers were women.[42] However, the experiences of urban teachers have been examined only within the context of their relations to teachers' union

11

movements, usually with little emphasis being given to the subject of gender.[43] Moreover, it was in the cities where those immigrating to the United States tended to settle that teaching became an important source of upward mobility for young women of immigrant background but, as Sally Schwager has noted, almost nothing is known about the experience of first- and second-generation immigrant women teachers.[44]

By 1914, the numbers of Jewish teachers began to diminish the previous Irish predominance. In that year, 22 percent of all teachers entering the city's public school system were estimated to have been Jewish; and by 1920, they constituted about 26 percent of all new teachers.[45] However, few of these women of the pre–World War I era were of Eastern European origin, but rather were German-Jewish, part of an earlier and more assimilated immigrant group. Often great cultural gaps existed between the children of immigrants and their teachers, even their Jewish teachers. Like Julia Richman, who rose from the teaching ranks to become a district superintendent before World War I, these German-Jewish teachers were uptowners who disdained their downtown working-class pupils for their parents' religious orthodoxy or socialist politics.[46] Pupils in the schools of the Lower East Side, Brownsville, and other Jewish neighborhoods were staffed with Jewish teachers, for the New York City Board of Education attempted to match the ethnicity of teachers and pupils. However, their pupils were seldom aware of this, believing only that their teachers were American. Few of those who attended city schools prior to the 1920s could recall having had Jewish teachers, but remembered teachers who were the very "models of Americanhood."[47]

Even before these daughters could formulate their own admiration of teachers and their own desire to follow in their footsteps, their mothers began planting the seeds of possibility in their heads. "Becoming a teacher was drummed into me by my mother at an early age," explained Goldie Cohen, who claimed she could not recall a time her mother was not exhorting her to "study, study, so you can become a teacher." Writer Kate Simon's mother began lecturing her ten-year-old daughter to study, learn, and go to college to become a schoolteacher because teaching was a "respected, privileged breed."[48] Although they recognized other acceptable paths of female mobility, such as stenography and typing, teaching was preferred because it combined economic security with a status highly valued by immigrant mothers. It was seen as "an American vision," one well worth sacrifice, which their daughters eagerly embraced.[49]

Immigrant mothers, who had spent their youth sewing in the sweatshops and yearning for an education, often grasped the advantages of a teaching career more readily than did immigrant fathers. In many instances, it was the mother who supported the idea of her daughter's becoming a teacher in face of opposition from her husband, serving as a mediating force between his Old World attitudes and the opportunities the New World offered her daughter. Interviews reinforce the strong influence of mothers in steering their daughters into the teaching profession. Fathers tended to be more opposed to careers for daughters, although several respondents emphasized that their fathers' reluctance was not rooted in Old World beliefs, but was in keeping with the American acceptance of marriage and motherhood as the proper female spheres. "Papa thought like most American fathers then," Sarah Rothman explained, "that his daughters should work only until they married. He figured that an education for his girls, and all the sacrifices that went along with it, would be wasted when we married," adding how fortunate she was that her mother did not agree. Nor did Frances Klein's mother, who interceded with her father on her behalf.[50] A considerable segment of the interviewees attributed to their mothers' encouragement their success in becoming teachers, for they often encountered disapproval from their fathers. "It was the only time I could remember my mother taking a stand against my father," Myn Silverman related. Her father did not want her to continue her education and go on to teach, but her mother was adamant that she pursue this goal. Unlike many of the female college students in the rest of the country, who seldom had vocational objectives in mind, immigrant daughters rarely had the luxury of attending college to obtain a general cultural education, for the prestige, or for the social life.[51] Their parents were not in a position to indulge a desire for education without a utilitarian purpose, and those who agreed to their attending schools of higher education were sold on the idea of a teaching career.

Though the persuasion of their mothers and the example of their teachers were powerful inducements for young Jewish women to become teachers, other factors influenced their decision. Some of their motives differed little from those that attracted non-Jewish women to the profession, especially those from blue-collar or lower-class families, for whom it offered upward mobility into white-collar, middle-class work, and a predictable income that would insure their economic stability. Accessible to women, teaching was congruent with feminine socialization, work styles, and family roles. Others, like Lillian H. Rosenberg, looked on the profession as their calling. She claimed she had wanted to be a teacher from the time she was born; when other little girls wanted to play house, she wanted to play school. She eventually taught in the city for forty-eight years.[52] But above all, schoolteaching was so attractive because its security, status, and training cost so little in a city that offered its citizens free education through college.

The profession was especially appealing to young Jewish women because it was a means to escape the oppressive labor of factory work or confinement in family businesses. It gave them a chance to climb from positions of subservience into positions of relative responsibility and esteem.[53] However, this did not mean that the profession was used by the second generation as a means of achieving complete independence from family constraints. In contrast, Catharine Beecher and so many college-educated women of white Anglo-Saxon Protestant backgrounds found that teaching served as a mode of liberation from the restrictions of familial obligations. Living at home was the norm among single Jewish women, as it tended to be among most teachers in urban areas, and after matrimony, Jewish women continued to live in close proximity to their families.[54] The decision to educate a daughter for the teaching profession was often part of long-term planning for the family's future. According to the interviewees, salaries were deemed part of the family economy, whether the teacher was single or married; this was characteristic of America's teachers during the years between the wars. A composite study of schoolteachers in the 1930s noted an amazing number who supported relatives, helped out in financial crises, and paid for the education of younger siblings.[55]

Teaching was neither a vehicle for total independence, nor was it a viable alternative to marriage for Jewish women. They were not like nineteenth-century Yankee women, who had been encouraged to become schoolteachers because teaching provided women with a respectable alternative to marriage, as Catharine Beecher had stressed.[56] Becoming a teacher did not exempt a Jewish daughter from her parents' or her own expectations that she would marry and raise a family. Old maid schoolteachers or career-minded women who would choose to remain single rather than give up their profession were untenable in the culture of immigrant families. Because New York City's teacher-mothers were allowed to continue in their classrooms after bearing children, teaching was compatible with marriage and motherhood.

Another important consideration in career planning for these women was the paucity of other avenues open to Jews. The presence or lack of occupational choice for young women always plays an integral part in how they prepare for future employment. When the white-collar sector expanded and opportunities increased for young women in the last decades of the nineteenth century, New York City's Jewish women prepared for these careers by studying typing and bookkeeping in the commercial high schools, so that by 1905, they had increased their participation in clerical jobs by 7.5 percent.[57] The new professions of nursing, librarianship, and social work, all of which had been feminized quickly and conspicuously, did not appear to have been viable career choices for a large segment of the city's Jewish immigrant daughters. While librarians commanded the respect afforded teachers, most of the former teachers interviewed claimed that openings in this field within the city were not sufficient to merit their undergoing the education required for this profession. To these women, nursing and social service did not have the cachet of teaching, nor did they pay as well as teaching.[58] Many of the informants said that Jewish parents considered nursing somewhat menial and therefore not an acceptable position for their daughters. In addition, they believed that the nursing profession was the bastion of Irish-American women, who controlled entrance into both nursing schools and hospitals.

By the 1920s however, opportunities for clerical work for Jewish women had decreased.[59] During the 1930s, unemployment was higher among the city's Jewish population between the ages of sixteen and twenty-four than among gentiles. Undoubtedly, their high unemployment rate was in part attributable to discriminatory hiring practices that were so blatantly anti-Semitic that newspapers openly advertised positions for gentiles only. New York City's largest employers, its public utilities, banking, and life insurance companies, rarely hired Jews during the interwar years. Placement agencies admitted that it was a waste of time to send Jewish women to the New York Telephone Company and to the large insurance companies. One woman said it was common knowledge "that the phone company was part of the Catholic Church."[60] For Jewish women, their only chances for clerical work were severely limited to Jewish-owned firms and department stores, scarcely enough to absorb all who aspired to white-collar status.

In other cities, "my daughter, the teacher" may have been the American dream for immigrant families. But this dream was not as easy to achieve in most American cities as it was in New York City. Where alternative opportunities were to be found, teaching was not always the favorite choice of careers. Because a sizable number of Jews in Portland, Oregon, owned their own businesses and most of that city's department stores, they provided ample jobs for Portland's unmarried Jewish women as clerks, as sales personnel, and as stenographers. Few of these women taught school; they would have had to leave their jobs when they married, since married women were excluded from the teaching force. Unmarried Jewish women did opt for the security of a teaching career during the Depression years.[61] In Los Angeles during the 1930s, there were enough white-collar positions to employ more than 75 percent of its Jewish women. Because they had sufficient employment in clerical and sales jobs, they constituted only a minority of that city's schoolteachers.[62] In all likelihood however, the main determinant for achieving "my daughter, the teacher" was the existence of free and accessible teacher training. It was one thing for immigrant parents to be able to afford to forgo their daughter's economic contribution while she attended teacher-training school or college, and quite another to be able to afford the cost of her education.

The daughters of Jewish immigrants who entered New York City's teaching staff during the 1920s joined an expanding system, offering women a chance to join a profession that was in need of their services. The city's schools had an enrollment of over one million in 1925, which increased by another quarter million in the next seven years, representing a registration that exceeded that of all other public schools in the state combined; it was nearly as many as that of Chicago, Philadelphia, and Detroit combined. In fact, New York City's student population would have made it the sixth largest city in the United States.[63] Pupils were housed in more than 1,000 buildings in schools ranging in size from P.S. 2 on Staten Island, which was a typical one-room rural school with one teacher and fourteen children, to New Utrecht High School in Brooklyn with 347 teachers and 9,965 pupils. Besides regular day classes in elementary and junior high schools, the city also maintained vocational, commercial, technical, industrial, and academic high schools; along with part-time continuation, evening, and Americanization classes. There were also classes for the handicapped; classes in day camps, convalescent homes, hospitals, and institutions; and home teachers provided for the infirm. Although Jewish women aspiring to teach would have a more difficult time securing a position during the Depression decade, those who were successful joined a teaching staff of approximately 39,000 by 1938.[64]

The experience and contribution of second-generation Jewish women who entered the New York City school system in such overwhelming numbers during the interwar years is particularly unique. In many respects, they were an especially fortunate group of young women, fortunate to come from families sufficiently secularized to appreciate that education and a teaching career would open paths of social and economic mobility. They were lucky, too, that their families were comfortable enough to keep them in school in a city that had a free and open system where they could flourish under the tutelage of the teachers they so admired. They benefited also from the timing of their birth, growing up in the post–World War I period, which encouraged what Alice Kessler-Harris has termed the "acquisitive individualism on the part of achieving Americans." Here in the New World, Jewish daughters could entertain ambitions and aspire to professions that were now possibilities for them, as well as for their brothers.[65] While their entrance into the profession transformed the ethnic makeup of the city's teaching staff, a more radical alteration took place. Jewish girls' learning moved from their mothers' kitchens to public school classrooms. Their own educational experience underwent yet another change as they provided education for other city children, thereby realizing the dream of "my daughter, the teacher."

CHAPTER

 2

SUBWAY SCHOLARS AT
CONCRETE CAMPUSES

Daughters of Jewish Immigrants
Prepare for the Teaching Profession

SPURRED ON BY THEIR PARENTS' dreams of "my daughter, the teacher," and by the opportunity to achieve middle-class and professional status through a career that offered intellectual stimulation and a comfortable, secure living, thousands of young Jewish women set out to become teachers in the New York City public school system in the decades between 1920 and 1940. To attain their goal, they first had to pursue a course of study that would lead to certification by both the state and city of New York, and thence to an appointment by the city's Board of Education. This could be accomplished by attending a private or public institution, or by graduating from a normal school or a liberal arts college. The required courses could be completed in only three years at a normal school, four years at a liberal arts college, or could take as long as eight years if they attended evening sessions at a municipal college.

Private colleges in New York City providing teacher training, such as Barnard College or New York University, graduated few Jewish women, whether they planned to teach or not. Even if Jewish women overcame the restrictive admission quotas at these schools, few of their parents possessed the economic means to educate their daughters at such expensive colleges.[1] While the Manhattan location of these colleges would permit New York City residents to avoid the expense of room and board, tuition and school fees were still beyond the reach of most parents, especially during the Depression years when the cost of attending Barnard amounted to more than $450 per year.[2] While Teachers College of Columbia University, located in Manhattan, was considered the most prestigious school of education, it had ceased providing undergraduate teacher training in 1926.[3]

Growing numbers of the city's middle-class Jews attended colleges outside New York State during the 1920s and 1930s such as the University of Wisconsin, the University of Chicago, and the Berkeley and Los Angeles campuses of the University of California. Among New York City's Jewish students studying out of state, however, the great majority were Jewish men, who went away much more frequently than did their sisters and went greater distances, to an even larger extent than did their Christian counterparts.[4] Undoubtedly, Jewish parents were much more willing to invest in their sons' education than in their daughters', and were far more reluctant to have their daughters living away from home. Moreover, many rationalized the decision to keep their daughters at home by emphasizing the free education they could obtain while living at home and commuting to the concrete campuses of a city institution, whether a liberal arts college or a teacher-training school.

These students attended the three teacher-training schools or the two four-year colleges, all maintained by New York City and supported by taxpayers' money: all-male City College of New York and all-female Hunter College, where would-be teachers could obtain training in pedagogy while obtaining a bachelor of arts degree. Teacher-training schools were also operated by the state of New York but were chosen by few New York City residents, because these schools were located a considerable distance from the city. In 1930 the city established coeducational Brooklyn College and, in 1937, coeducational Queens College,[5] which also provided teacher-training courses along with a liberal arts education. By far, the majority of those aspiring to teach in the city's elementary schools, which comprised the largest group of schoolteachers, attended either The Maxwell Training School for Teachers in Brooklyn,[6] The New York Training School for Teachers in Manhattan, or The Jamaica Training School for Teachers in Jamaica, Queens, until February 1933, when the three schools were closed as an economy measure.

Established in the last decades of the nineteenth century with the sole purpose of providing classroom teachers for the city's burgeoning educational system through a two-year curriculum, the teacher-training schools enjoyed a steady increase in enrollment, climbing to a total student registration of approximately one thousand in 1919. The greatest increase in enrollment figures occurred from 1923 to 1929, which coincided with a shortage of teachers in the city. The number of students increased during these years from approximately 2,300 in 1923 to a peak enrollment of 6,300 students in 1927.[7]

Although a considerable number of men entered the three teacher-training institutions in the early years of the Great Depression, students in the municipal schools were overwhelmingly female, reflecting the feminization of the teaching profession in the United States. This had already been established in the preceding century, and throughout the 1920s, women constituted from almost 92 percent to over 97 percent of the student body.[8] New York City women differed from those in teacher-training schools in the rest of the country, however, in that the majority of them were the daughters of immigrants, and were primarily Jewish. Whereas only 11 percent of all students training to become teachers in the United States belonged to the first generation, 61 percent of those attending the Maxwell School in Brooklyn had foreign-born parents; and more than 66 percent of the students at the Jamaica Training School were members of the second generation.[9] Had a survey been conducted at the New York Training School in Manhattan, as had been done during the mid-1920s at the aforementioned schools, undoubtedly the results would have been similar.

Moreover, one can state unequivocally that these daughters of immigrants were Jewish. Although the schools kept no records to indicate a student's religion, nor did the surveys provide this information, the names of every student-teacher assigned to the city schools were published in both the *Journal of the New York City Board of Education* and the *New York Sun's* "School Page," as were the names of each newly licensed teacher and each newly appointed teacher, along with the names of their training schools. Scrutiny of these names proves indisputably that the vast majority of the students at the three municipal teacher-training schools were Jewish. This fact was further borne out by examining the Teacher Personnel Cards, filed in the Board of Education's Bureau of Teachers' Records, which list teachers' birth and married names, as well as their training institution. The data contained on almost seven hundred cards of female teachers educated at the city teacher-training schools indicates that more than 70 percent of them were Jewish. Even if it is impossible to determine precisely what percentage of New York City's teacher-trainees were Jewish, the fact that Jews comprised only 3.5 percent of both male and female students enrolled in teacher-training schools in the entire United States is reflective of the low percentage of Jews in the American population, and causes one to realize how truly unique were these Jewish women.[10]

Prospective teachers at Hunter and Brooklyn colleges, as well, were predominantly Jewish, although it is difficult to estimate the exact number of Jewish students in any of New York City's colleges because such statistics were not maintained. A Hillel Foundation survey of Jewish college students, published in 1937, found that Jewish women constituted 52.1 percent of all women attending college in New York City. However, the figures are undoubtedly too low because they include enrollment at private, as well as public institutions, and fail to include enrollment in the evening sessions, which tended to have a higher proportion of Jewish students than did the day session.[11] Assertions that Jewish students at City College of New York and Hunter College comprised 80 to 90 percent of their populations, and that Brooklyn College students were overwhelmingly second-generation and 80 to 85 percent Jewish, are probably more accurate.[12] Moreover, the daughters of Jewish immigrants attended college in greater numbers than did their non-Jewish counterparts within the city, because 21 percent of the city's college-age Jewish female population were enrolled in college during the Depression, yet only 10.5 to 12.2 percent of all American women attended college, and only 9 percent of New York City's non-Jewish female population were enrolled in any college.[13] Those names of women graduates that were obviously Jewish, as observed in the yearbooks of Brooklyn and Hunter colleges during the 1930s, indicate that they comprised approximately three-quarters of the two colleges' graduates. Whatever their exact numbers, the majority of female students in the city colleges, like those at the teaching schools, were Jewish, the daughters of Eastern European immigrants.[14]

For these women intending to teach in the city's elementary schools, the three municipal teacher-training schools were the most attractive option available. Besides offering free professional training, the schools provided direct preparation for the examination for a teacher's license. Other advantages included being able to observe experienced and proficient teaching and classroom management in model schools, as well as practice teaching under the training schools' supervision and direction, while receiving paid remuneration as student-teachers. Undoubtedly, the greatest incentive for selecting a training school, rather than a four-year liberal arts college, was the prospect of prompt employment at a salary of about $1,500 per year during the mid-1920s in less time than it would take to graduate from a liberal arts college.[15] Interviews do not reveal significant differences in the socioeconomic backgrounds of those choosing training schools over four-year colleges. Some attended a training school because they wanted to begin teaching as soon as possible, a decision not always predicated on economic need, but sometimes merely indicative of a preference for spending less time in school. Others claimed that they selected a college because they wanted an education that would be broader than that provided by the training schools.

The course of study offered at the training schools from their inception until 1923 was a combination of theoretical and practical work. A thorough study was made of the methods of teaching employed in New York City's elementary schools. Students received a broad foundation in the principles and history of education, including the study of psychology and educational measurements. Observation of skilled teachers working with children in various grades of the city's schools began in the first semester and continued throughout the two-year course. Twenty weeks of practice in the elementary schools under the supervision of critic-teachers from the training schools alternated with theory work during the second year.[16] During the training schools' period of unrivaled popularity, the city's Board of Education replicated attempts by teacher educators throughout the nation to upgrade the teaching profession by raising standards of admission, revising the curriculum, and extending the years of schooling for teacher trainees.[17] In 1923 the Board introduced its three-year curriculum which was maintained by the training schools until 1929.[18]

A detailed listing of the courses required of students attending teacher-training schools in New York City during this time can be seen by examining the record of a 1928 graduate of the Maxwell School. During her first semester at Maxwell, the student studied English, health education, general psychology, sociology, music, drawing, nature study, penmanship, and arithmetic, and she spent one hour weekly observing in an elementary classroom. In her second semester she took English, library practice, health education, educational psychology, music, drawing, geography, and history. Her third semester was spent studying English, health education, psychology, handwork, history and civics, geography, nature study, arithmetic, class management, music, and drawing. The fourth semester was devoted to practice teaching. Student teachers were graded on discipline, preparation of lessons, skills in presentation, power of exciting interest, blackboard work, skill in drill, and executive ability.

The fifth and sixth semesters were spent back at Maxwell, taking many of the same courses as in earlier semesters and adding such pedagogical courses as kindergarten theory, experimental education, and integration of curriculum. Upon successful completion of this course of study, the training school graduate was permitted to take the examination for certification by the state and by New York City, which would then entitle her to apply for a teaching position in the public schools.[19]

Coupled with the Board of Education's desire to improve standards of teacher preparation by such methods as extension and modification of the curriculum was the realization that by 1927 an overabundance of teachers had been produced by the three training schools. Curtailment of immigration by 1924 meant fewer new students in the city's lower grades. Teachers resigned less often than in the past; and married women tended to continue teaching, even after having children.[20] Attempting to decrease enrollment in the training schools, in 1929, the Board of Education issued higher admission requirements. Besides completing a more comprehensive high school course with the required study of a number of branches of subject matter, applicants now had to have an average New York State Regents' Examination rating of not less than 75 percent. Added requirements were a satisfactory rating by the applicant's high school principal on the student's personality and use of oral English, and a physical examination.[21] At the same time, a further change was made to the curriculum: the number of courses taken per semester was increased and an optional fourth year of study was added, during which a student could specialize in a particular subject.[22]

Although enrollment dropped considerably by 1930, the higher standards of admission, the introduction of a broader and more difficult course of study, as well as an extended curriculum, failed to reduce significantly the number of applicants to the training schools. Moreover, a backlog of licensed teachers who had passed the test but failed to secure positions had developed, and it appeared that their chances for appointments were negligible. To further limit enrollment, the three teaching schools were reorganized as teacher-training colleges, instituting a four-year course and conferring upon its graduates the degree of Bachelor of Pedagogy.[23] This change reflected the current nationwide trend, stimulated by educators dissatisfied with the low standards in teacher training that had prevailed during their efforts to provide a sufficient number of teachers for the rapidly growing public schools. As the supply of teachers now exceeded the demand, educators no longer needed to sacrifice quality for quantity, believing improvements in quality could be accomplished best by transforming normal schools into teachers colleges. In 1920, there were 46 teachers' colleges and 137 state normal schools in the United States; by 1928, there were 137 teachers' colleges and 69 normal schools; and by 1933, 146 teachers' colleges and only 50 state normal schools. A similar change occurred in city normal schools, which decreased from 33 in 1920 to 16 in 1933; and in that same year, nearly one-third of all elementary teachers were university or college graduates.[24]

A distinct departure from the usual teacher-training course of study, the new curriculum emphasized academic subjects in the first two years and professional subjects in the next two. With the exception of a course providing an overview of teaching, one on juvenile literature, and another on penmanship, first- and second-year studies were quite similar to the freshman and sophomore years in most liberal arts colleges. Professional subjects were taught exclusively during the third year. In the first term of the fourth year, students were assigned to elementary schools as student teachers, returning to their colleges once a week for two pedagogical courses. The final term of their fourth year was devoted to professional studies and preparation for the licensing examination.[25]

The compulsory four-year course and stringent admission standards succeeded in drastically reducing the number of applicants to the municipal teachers' colleges, which in 1932 graduated the smallest classes in their history. Educators were pleased with the result, citing higher scholarship standards exacted and better qualified teachers graduated than in the past.[26] Yet the crisis in teaching appointments escalated to five thousand teachers on the eligible lists awaiting appointments. At the maximum rate of appointment, which was five hundred per year, it would be ten years before these could be absorbed, without even considering new graduates. Therefore, the Board of Education felt justified in no longer maintaining six colleges when three could suffice, and abolished the three teacher-training colleges in February of 1933.[27]

The Board of Education thereby turned over the training of most of the city's women teachers to the education departments of Hunter and Brooklyn colleges. Training more and better female teachers to meet the needs of the city's elementary schools had been the reason for Hunter's establishment in 1870 as the Normal College of the City of New York. To honor its founding president, Thomas Hunter, its name was changed to Hunter College of the City of New York in 1914. In 1926, as Hunter College affiliated with City College of New York, its official name became Hunter College of The College of the City of New York, and by the 1930s, it was the largest women's college in America. Initially offering a three-year training program, its course of study for the first two years was academic, and the third year was spent on pedagogical and professional subjects. Nine years after its founding, a four-year curriculum was instituted, and by 1902, Hunter was a full-fledged liberal arts college.[28] Brooklyn College of The College of the City of New York was established in 1930 as a four-year liberal arts college, and from its inception, it also offered courses designed to qualify students to serve as teachers in the city schools.

Because the training schools produced teachers qualified for the elementary school level only, and because elementary school teachers constituted more than two-thirds of all teachers in the school system, most of the city's teachers had been trained at one of the three teacher-training schools; whereas women teaching in the high schools, for which a college degree was a requisite, had trained primarily at Hunter College.[29] After the 1933 closing of the training schools, the vast majority of women teachers at all levels of instruction in New York City's public schools would receive their training at either Brooklyn or Hunter colleges.

Preparation for a teaching career at Brooklyn or Hunter colleges entailed following a course of study like that at any liberal arts institution. Educators at both colleges discouraged students from majoring in education, although significant numbers of students continued to do so. These educators strongly believed that the principal concern of its students should be with the subject matter in which they were to teach and that they should take only those pedagogy courses required by the state.[30] Students met all college requirements, as well as those decreed by the department in which they had declared their major. In addition, they took the requisite pedagogical courses, which consisted of courses in general and educational psychology, history and principles of education, and two methodology courses.[31]

A semester of student teaching in one of the city's schools, probably the most popular segment of teachers' education, was also mandatory. Supervised by the faculty of the department of education, students' work in the classroom was observed. Weekly conferences were held at the colleges to analyze the lessons they both observed and taught.[32] Although student teaching was often approached with trepidation, most students, like Dora Fein, looked forward to their semester of student teaching. Finding the theoretical and methodological courses "dry as dust," she recalled "counting the days until we could get into a classroom and face real, live children. Classroom teaching was our reality. That was what we prepared for," she said, adding that "for the first time we really felt like professionals, like real teachers." Sometimes student teaching could be the turning point in a young woman's life, as it was for Bel Kaufman, Hunter College Class of 1934, and daughter of an Eastern European immigrant, the Yiddish writer Sholem Aleichem. Kaufman was a public school teacher in New York City who later wrote *Up the Down Staircase,* a best-selling novel about teaching in the city's school system. She became a teacher "quite by accident"; because her friends took education courses, she "went along" and took them too, including the required student teaching. The first time she stood in front of a class "and saw all those pairs of eyes—fixed on me, waiting, I knew my goose was cooked. I was *fated* to be a teacher," Kaufman wrote in her reminiscences of her Hunter College years.[33] Students were usually assigned to the most experienced and competent teachers, who volunteered for the task and who taught the student teachers "the tricks of the trade," as Ruth Davidson put it, further stating that it was "one thing to read about maintaining discipline and quite another to have to quiet down a classroom of noisy children." Sylvia Rudzinsky asserted that it was during the semester of student teaching that "we learned, through trial and error, what teaching was all about." The experience was so positive for most teaching candidates that many called upon the schools to extend the length of time spent as student teachers and to decrease the number of courses dealing with the principles of education.[34]

Yet opportunities for student teaching were limited because there were not enough faculty supervisors to meet the need, nor were there sufficient teachers willing to expend the time necessary to serve as cooperating teachers. The situation was acute enough for a former Hunter College administrator to allege that because student teaching was so restricted, 90 percent of Hunter seniors expecting to teach were "poorly prepared in this respect."[35] With the closing of the training colleges in 1933, and the transfer of their students to Brooklyn and Hunter colleges, the problem was further exacerbated. As teaching jobs became more scarce and requirements for a license became more rigorous, would-be teachers were advised to arrange for as much observation and student teaching as possible, to give them an edge in securing a teaching position.[36] Students like Dora Fein took matters into their own hands. She went to the Brooklyn elementary school from which she had graduated and "badgered" the principal and teachers into letting her observe, finally persuading her former fifth-grade teacher to serve as her cooperating teacher. Later in the decade, the problem abated somewhat as all assignments were made by the Board of Education, which also created more student teaching opportunities by opening up the junior high schools (in addition to the kindergartens, elementary, and high schools) to student teachers.[37]

Jewish women preparing for teaching positions, whether attending a teacher-training school or a liberal arts college, did not reside in dormitories or attend classes in ivy-covered buildings, but were subway scholars at concrete campuses located in New York City. The three teacher-training schools, situated in busy sections of Manhattan, Brooklyn, and Queens, all necessitated daily travel to and from the schools by public transportation. When Hunter College moved into its own building on Manhattan's Park Avenue at 68th Street in 1873, the area was a remote, barren neighborhood where wild goats roamed, but by the 1920s, it was the location of a canyon of apartment houses, churches, and hospitals.[38] By 1929, Hunter College had an additional building at Lexington and 68th streets, annexes scattered in several midtown Manhattan locations, and evening sessions held in each borough, and had grown so large a second campus was opened next to the site of the Jerome Park Reservoir in the Bronx.[39] Students who attended the Bronx campus vividly remember the long cold trek to the college from the subway through snow and sleet, with an icy wind blowing over the reservoir. Women were not permitted to wear slacks to class and it "took some of us a good half-hour to thaw out in class," recalled a Hunter alumna.[40] After a fire destroyed the Park Avenue building in 1936, classes were held in a series of rented buildings. Former students like Rose Jacobi recalled having to scramble from classes in a loft on 32nd Street to classes in one of the annexes. Students at Brooklyn College found themselves emerging from the depths of the subway, dashing across traffic-congested streets, and riding elevators as they attended classes in the college's original location in a business section of Brooklyn. When the college relocated to its present site in 1937, students found they had to negotiate wooden planks stretched across muddy fields in Flatbush.[41]

Brooklyn College alumna Rae Lieberman spent more time commuting to college than she did in her classes, a recollection underscored by a Hunter College survey that found that its students spent more than half as much time on the subway as they did in classes, lectures, and labs. For example, a Hunter student living in Brooklyn, as many did, had to spend forty minutes in trains, buses, and trolleys for every sixty minutes spent in class. Students reported that they tried to do homework while in their underground campus, although they often failed to obtain a seat. Rae

27

Lieberman said she, like many of her fellow students, mastered "the art of studying while straphanging."[42]

These subway scholars, whether enrolled in a teacher-training school or a college, came from very similar socioeconomic backgrounds. Although dispersed throughout New York City, the daughters of Eastern European immigrants still lived with their parents in Jewish enclaves.[43] The slow but steady ascent many of their parents made toward middle-class status during the 1920s proved tenuous, not lasting through the Depression. The fathers of the former teachers interviewed for this study were small shopkeepers, skilled or semiskilled workers in the garment industry or the construction trades, peddlers, and salesmen. Manuscript schedules of the 1925 and 1930 censuses for Manhattan, the Bronx, and Brooklyn, indicate that only 14 percent of Russian Jewish men were in the professions or other white-collar occupations; and that most were in manual occupations, which had the highest unemployment during the Depression. Although white-collar occupations tended to survive the Depression fairly well, these were positions held by the second generation, for the most part. As Jewish youth educated in America, the brothers of the women training to be teachers were those qualified for white-collar jobs, and therefore held more attractive jobs than their parents.[44] Many of the mothers of those interviewed were housewives; yet a number worked in garment or light industry factories; and all whose families kept small stores worked in the stores. If their families had made some inroads during the 1920s, by the 1930s most, like the rest of the country, experienced a considerable economic downturn. Virtually every woman interviewed classified herself as poor during the 1930s, when 12 percent of Jewish household heads in New York City were unemployed. A detailed study of Brooklyn College students found that 7 percent of their families were on home relief and a little more than one-third of their families had a would-be wage earner out of work.[45]

Aspiring teachers who entered either the training schools or Hunter College during the twenties did so with a sense of privilege and optimism. They considered themselves highly fortunate that their parents were well-situated enough financially to forgo their wages from either the factory work or blue-collar jobs that had been the occupations of many of their older siblings. Moreover, their future as teachers was full of promise, as the need for teachers in the city's school system far exceeded the supply, and the adoption of standardized testing for teacher appointments assured them of nondiscriminatory hiring practices. In addition, New York City teachers in the 1920s would find teaching conditions far more pleasant and rewarding than ever before. New schools were erected in unprecedented numbers: from May 1924 to September 1929, the Board of Education constructed 130 new school buildings.[46] The decade was one in which teachers enjoyed a considerable increase in salary. In 1920, elementary school teachers earned a minimum salary of $1,500 and a maximum one of $2,900; while high school teachers earned a minimum of $1,900 and a maximum of $3,700. By 1928, elementary teachers were earning from $1,600 to $3,500; and secondary teachers from $2,040 to $4,200, thus affording teachers middle-class status. The decade also saw a willingness by the Board of Education to allow teachers to teach in schools located in their home neighborhoods, rather than causing them to travel great distances.[47]

By the following decade, their brimming optimism had greatly dissipated in the face of the adversities of the Great Depression and their ever-deepening pessimism about their chances of obtaining a teaching appointment. As economy measures, the Board of Education closed the teacher-training schools to reduce the number of new teachers and later promulgated a complete ban on all new teaching appointments in the city schools from 1932 until late in 1934, when 165 teachers received appointments. The number of positions peaked at 475 in the 1936–37 school year, then dropped off during another hiring stoppage that lasted from September 1939 until the following September.[48] Yet among the ranks of those who managed to secure teaching positions in this period were increasing numbers of Jewish women. Although the outlook for receiving teaching certificates was particularly bleak, women doggedly prepared for teaching careers, even during the complete ban on hiring, as shown by the seven hundred Hunter College graduates, constituting the greatest number from any institution, who filed applications for the June 1932 teaching license examination conducted by the Board of Examiners of the city's Board of Education.[49]

Acknowledging that in most years, the majority of its graduates turned to teaching, and alarmed because of overcrowding in the profession, Hunter College prepared a pamphlet entitled "What to Do in the World's Work" in which 275 positions in 165 fields were identified as alternatives to teaching.[50] Although widely distributed among the student body, the pamphlet apparently did little to deter students from pursuing a teaching career, as indicated by student polls conducted periodically by both Hunter and Brooklyn colleges during the 1930s, which further attest to the popularity of teaching as the career goal of its students. At the height of the hiring freeze, 564 of the incoming freshmen in a class of 876 at

Hunter declared their intention to teach, a 20 percent increase over the previous year.[51] The following year, while teaching jobs continued to be unavailable, Hunter reported that more than half of its new students planned to teach, and Brooklyn College also reported that the majority of its women graduates would seek teaching jobs.[52] Further polls continued in this vein, with teaching eclipsing all other careers as the choice of Brooklyn and Hunter women throughout the decade.[53]

Although Jewish women in ever-increasing numbers continued to enroll in Brooklyn and Hunter colleges with the intention of becoming teachers throughout the Depression years, feelings of privilege vanished along with roseate outlooks. Their education could no longer be viewed as an indulgence by their parents because for many young Jewish women, there were no other prospects. Confronted with rampant unemployment, which in New York City was higher for young Jewish women than for their white gentile counterparts, they were also the victims of job discrimination in a city where want ads stipulating non-Jews proliferated more than ever in history, and even a Jewish-owned newspaper like the *New York Times* advertised jobs "For Christians Only."[54]

While changing their names or wearing crosses around their necks might have enhanced their chances for obtaining good jobs, most Jewish women found these subterfuges too painful, and greatly preferred the opportunity offered by a teaching career in the public schools. Subtle forms of anti-Semitism were manifested occasionally through the oral examination required of all aspirants for a city teaching license; nevertheless, Jewish candidates were protected by law against unfair discrimination. The competitive licensing examination was the chief instrument of selection, unlike the hiring process at private schools, which also refused to employ Jews. Therefore, Jewish women elected to take their chances and train to become teachers in the New York City public school system. Although many shared Irving Howe's feeling of being "adrift" in the 1930s, they still went to college "because there was nothing else to do"; yet thousands of other Jewish women attended college because it was free, thus enabling them to cling stubbornly and tenaciously to their dreams for a while, before facing a future that appeared so grim.[55]

Even though education at the city's schools was free of charge, most students held jobs to pay for books, carfare, and some spending money, turning the rest of their earnings over to their families. Evening-session students led double lives, working at full-time jobs during the day and attending classes at night. Day-session students worked both on and off campus: on-campus jobs included working in the libraries, lunchrooms, and laboratories, or serving as tutors; off campus, their jobs ran the gamut from clerical work to movie ushering and cashiering, to modeling.[56] "I did all sorts of work in order to get through college and be able to help out my folks," recalled Ida Levinson, who did typing, mimeographing, waiting on tables, and sales work. Macy's department store provided employment for great numbers of women students because of its policy of hiring part-time salespersons and cashiers for Saturdays and Thursday evenings, although it was not a simple task to obtain such jobs. In order to be hired, one had to pass an examination that Bel Kaufman remembers as being "almost as difficult as my Master's." Yet she and a legion of other students successfully passed the test; in fact there was such a profusion of Hunter women employed at the store that the Hunter yearbook referred to Macy's as "the Saturday branch" of Hunter College.[57]

Even with such part-time employment, many women still could not even afford to buy the books they needed for their courses. To alleviate this situation, the schools often established student loan funds that granted interest-free loans for such purposes as the purchase of texts or payment of laboratory fees. Some lacked even carfare, as was the case with one student whose family could only afford to allot her five cents a day for transportation, which meant she had her choice of riding to school and walking home, or vice versa. Others suffered such severe economic deprivation that they were not only poorly clothed, but often so malnourished that it was not unusual on campus for a student to faint from hunger.[58] An "Ode to Higher Education," which made the rounds during the thirties, summed up their plight:

> I sing in praise of college,
> Of M.A.'s and Ph.D.'s,
> But in pursuit of knowledge
> We are starving by degrees.[59]

It is little wonder then that the process of obtaining an education while constantly scrimping and saving and enduring the often makeshift conditions at their subway schools, without much hope for a viable economic existence, left a bitter taste in the mouths of many of the young women who attended college during the Depression. Many resented not being able to attend an ivy-covered college away from home, feeling "cheated out of a rich college experience on some more pleasant and fashionable campus," believing their Alma Mater to be a "drab, proletarian place."[60]

31

Herman Wouk's Marjorie Morningstar, heroine of his novel of the same name, attended Hunter College a decade later, yet still harbored resentment because her parents could not quite afford to send her to a college out of town. Wouk describes Hunter College as a "concentration camp of . . . dreamers . . . forced by lack of money into the mold of subway grinds."[61] Others became cynical or pessimistic because they despaired of ever finding a place in the economy, and felt sorry for themselves as part of a "surplus generation," who would be out in the "cold cruel world, hunting in vain for a job or working for a pittance."[62] Some believed their training had not made them fit to meet present economic conditions. When asked if she was satisfied with her college education, Juliet Eisenberg angrily snapped, "Certainly not," stating that her education would not benefit her in the way she wished. "Very few of us are going to get the opportunities we've been looking forward to," she added.[63] A Hunter College official admitted that students frankly expected their education to be of "utilitarian value, and so help them get jobs which would relieve the stark misery in which many of them live."[64]

College life may have been a make-do existence with but a dim expectation of better days to come, but not all women brooded about being underprivileged. "Underprivileged!" exclaimed Rebecca Tisch. "It was a privilege. We were grateful to be there. . . . Imagine, it cost only a nickel for the subway each way," further explaining that her older sisters had to work in sweatshops when they were her age, so she was always "immensely, immensely grateful." "We were the children of peddlers, tailors, first-chance Americans, and everybody pointed to the city colleges and said, 'This is your opportunity, take it,' " related a 1934 graduate of Brooklyn College. Another Brooklyn graduate said she never thought about her college years as anything but "a glorious experience, something that was so wonderful that I could never see the seediness or hear the noise of the trolleys."[65]

Many may have been embittered by the sour circumstances under which they received their education, believing it did not prepare them for the world they faced. However, the majority insist they did not feel this way. Even though their memories are refracted through the prism of time, they assert that they received fine educations from outstanding faculty members. For many, what they were basically interested in, as recounted by a graduate of Brooklyn College, "was the intellectual level of the people whom we would be associated with, and the caliber of the staff."[66] As Bel Kaufman wrote: "We knew we were poor; we did not know how rich we were," explaining that their education was excellent and their teachers "great; at least some of them were. They were scholars in the days when scholarship was admired, authority was respected. High standards were expected, were demanded of us." Writer Kate Simon, who attended Hunter College during the 1930s, concurred in this assessment, asserting that she was given "what might be called a quality education." Herman Wouk did have his fictional Marjorie Morningstar, who "never liked the school," admit that she could get a good education at Hunter College where the competition for marks "was keen" and the girls "brighter than average."[67]

Although most women appreciated and admired their instructors, and respected the intelligence of their fellow students, their relations with college deans and other administrative officials, and some faculty members, was often less than amiable. The prevalent belief that college officials ought to oversee the deportment and guard the morals of women students, combined with the cultural prejudices often displayed by faculty and staff toward Jewish students, caused much friction between the two generations. Officials seldom took pains to conceal their belief that these daughters of immigrants were "raucous and gawky," displaying "only a rudiment of good manners."[68] Often the officials took a benign interest in imparting such good manners to students. Many first- and second-generation Irish-American women were on the faculty and staff of the Maxwell Training School, according to Leah Boroff, one of its graduates. These teachers were the daughters or granddaughters of women who had served as domestics in some of the "finest homes," Boroff related, "where they learned the oh-so-proper manners they taught the teachers at Maxwell," who, in turn, "tried to teach us the same. In the spirit of *noblesse oblige*. . . . We were forever invited to their genteel tea parties. . . . We who drank tea from a glass at home, trying to lift our pinkies, like our teachers," she explained, adding that they were constantly reminded that "to be a teacher meant one was a lady" and that "we should learn how to be ladies by emulating them . . . implying that we Jewish women had no idea what being a lady meant and needed their help in this way."

The women themselves were cognizant that the underlying reason for their instructors' perception of them as unladylike was rooted in anti-Semitism, but most tended to shrug this off. "That's just the way it was. It was all around you in those years," Etta Ginsburg stated. "You couldn't let it get you down," she added, "for we had too many other things to concentrate on. We didn't make too big a deal of it." While a number of informants seconded her statement, several others compared their relations with anti-Semitic instructors with walking a tightrope. "You didn't want to antagonize them," Dorothy Blau explained, "but at the same time, you couldn't let them get away with anything too blatant." Yet most of the interviewees agree that the anti-Semitism manifested toward them was of the more subtle variety. Considering their position as students, they felt they had to let it ride.

Although they acknowledged the existence of anti-Semitism, most of the women who attended the teacher-training schools saw their problems with faculty members as stemming from generational, rather than religious or cultural differences. They considered themselves modern young women, shaped not only by the new roles their mothers had carved out for themselves in the workplace, but shaped just as much by the media. Speaking for almost all of the interviewees, Dorothy Blau recalled how anxious she and her cohorts were to be "modern and up-to-date," avidly studying film actresses and fashion magazines to accomplish this, in the same way their immigrant mothers had attended movies to learn about American culture.[69] But to their instructors at the teacher-training schools, many of whom were "still stuck in another century," according to Blau, their dress, their language, their use of makeup, and their assertiveness all bespoke unladylike behavior. "Some of the old dears were relics of another era, fossils if you will, who actually still wore high button shoes," she added. But Blau and her cohorts saw no contradiction between their modern style and their perception of themselves as ladies, which they equated with a professional demeanor. "The one concession we did make was to give up our use of slang, which we were always told was unladylike. We realized that it was unprofessional for a teacher to resort to slang," Blau explained.

Teachers at the Maxwell Training School were not alone in their belief that Jewish students lacked refinement, but were joined in this impression by administrators and faculty at American colleges where Jewish students were in attendance. The interwar years saw ever-increasing numbers of Jewish students enrolled in colleges and universities at a time when quotas were instituted against Jewish students at Ivy League schools, not because these students were Jewish per se, as Henry L. Feingold argues most persuasively, but because they represented a "new kind of Jewish student. . . ." As Feingold points out, the elite schools had found nothing objectionable about the previous wave of Jewish students, for they were the cultivated, well-to-do, and acculturated offspring of German Jews, "hardly distinguishable from the non-Jewish majority."[70]

But the new Jewish students were distinctively different, with their unmistakably Eastern European style and manner. Younger than most college students, they were also brighter than the average student. Because their parents fully accepted education as the path to social mobility, they had been encouraged, and usually expected to succeed academically, a necessity for gaining entrance into the city's free colleges, which had extremely high admission standards. Moreover, these students took their education seriously, giving their studies their highest priority, which showed in their academic performance. They were in school not merely to train as teachers, but to learn, which in the classroom translated into eagerly raising their hands to answer questions and just as enthusiastically to question, not blindly accepting what they were taught as the ultimate wisdom handed down by their professors. This was behavior not normally seen before, as they "unknowingly . . . violated taboos against showy scholarship."[71] Undoubtedly, some students, like writer Kate Simon and her friends at Hunter College, derived a sense of excitement from attempting to "stump the professors as nastily as we could," to wrap "the Olympians in discomfort."[72]

But most were like Fanny Stein, who genuinely wanted to learn and asked questions "respectfully and with the utmost respect for the professor," yet was often resented by those she called "some of the real 'fuddy-duddies' " who made it clear that her questions were only annoying. Nor were these students content to receive "gentlemen's C's," but often protested a grade if they believed it to be undeservedly low. Stein, who attended Hunter, recounted the time when she approached a professor about an essay she had written, for which she was graded with a B, the first time she had failed to receive an A in any schoolwork. When she requested that her professor explain what was wrong with the paper, Stein said, the professor was "absolutely shocked that anyone would even want to discuss her marking. She told me I had no sense of propriety, that I was a rude and impolite girl, like all the others who pestered her with questions in class."

Besides posing questions in class, these students were more critical-minded than most students. Often exposed at home to ideas not within the mainstream of American society and unrestrained in their thinking by their family and community, they possessed open minds and critical attitudes toward just about everything they encountered, both in and out of the classroom. Morris R. Cohen, who taught philosophy at City College for many years, observed that his students were "not as prone to accept the authority of textbooks (or any other kind of authority) as are students elsewhere."[73] Historian Gertrude Himmelfarb, who attended Brooklyn College in the 1930s, is of the same opinion. After graduating from Brooklyn, she attended Oxford University and noted that students there were "more insular and provincial in spirit and intellect" than those at Brooklyn College. She found the English students more reverential toward authority, "not a failing of which my generation at Brooklyn could be accused." Brooklyn College students were "too suspicious of authority and guidance," she claimed, adding that Brooklyn students did not suffer in silence. Her fellow student at Brooklyn College, writer Norman Rosten, concurred, explaining that Brooklyn students "were a student body with a mind."[74]

As students who displayed little deference for authority, they were also perceived as nonconformists, in variance with the college community and the traditions of collegiate culture. In an attempt by the state legislature to produce conformity, all students entering colleges of the city of New York were required to sign a pledge of loyalty, whereby they agreed, in gratitude for the free education being given them, to abide by the schools' disciplinary codes.[75] However, a conspicuous segment of the student bodies of these colleges refused to accommodate to those rules, as was demonstrated by those participants in the student movement of the Depression decade.

Yet to many faculty members and most of the colleges' administrations, it was not the studiousness, skepticism, and noncompliance that vexed them most, but rather the fact that they perceived these Jewish students as being uncultured, clamorous, and rude; totally at odds with their accepted notion that college students always had been and should continue to be cultivated and refined—and not members of an exotic and alien culture. Jewish students were considered unpleasantly aggressive and unduly contentious, their manners the almost constant subject of faculty meetings throughout the 1920s and 1930s, when many professors considered their crudeness the "chief evil" that colleges needed to correct.[76] That Jewish students failed to meet the image of the conventional American student is underscored by the report of the Strayer Commission of the New York state legislature. Describing the students at City College, the report first determined that they were almost 80 percent Jewish, and that most of the freshmen entering in 1938 were second-generation Jews. The report then listed what the colleges' counselors identified as the students' "social handicaps": that they lacked social skills, could not get along with people, could engage in conversation only in an argumentative fashion, and were frustrated by financial difficulties and by their immaturity. The report then stated that their high scholastic achievement prior to college, along with "the constant pressure placed on them by their parents to succeed scholastically," resulted in "an over-emphasis on intellectual values to the detriment of other vital areas of personal development."[77] Eileen Eagan, in her study of college students of the 1930s, summed up the Strayer report quite succinctly and to the point: "In short, they were poor, smart, and obstreperous."[78]

College administrators and faculty rarely took pains to hide the fact that they considered these Jewish students crass and coarse. If the presidents of Hunter and Brooklyn colleges did not go as far as calling the students "guttersnipes," as did City College president Frederick B. Robinson in a celebrated incident during the 1930s, dissenting female students were denigrated by being referred to as minors and told condescendingly by Hunter's president that he "was seventeen once too."[79] Class and ethnic antagonisms surfaced often at Brooklyn and Hunter. Rachel Kalman, a former Brooklyn College student, recalls that after delivering a speech in class, she was told by her professor that she would be given a low grade for excessive gesturing, "like some immigrant from the Lower East Side." While berating some students, another professor, at Hunter, reminded them that they were called, "and properly, 'Hunter girls,' " while Radcliffe, Barnard, and Bryn Mawr professors taught "women."[80]

Beyond being at odds with the class and ethnic makeup of the student body, officials at Hunter College also felt constrained to act as moral guardians. Kate Simon described Hunter as still retaining "the faint tinge of a semicloistered female academy (or was it nun's school?)" with its deans' looking into the "*moral faiblesse*" of anyone rumored to be leading an "irregular life." Deans, once called "lady superintendents," viewed their duties as largely disciplinary, monitoring students' conduct. Any student who appeared in an "unladylike pose," anywhere on campus offended against the proprieties of the day and was summoned before a dean, an appearance Kate Simon termed "an inquisition." Even after almost forty years, the very name of Dean Hannah Egan of Hunter "touches me with fear: What have I done *now*?" Bel Kaufman wrote in 1970.[81]

Hunter College's staff not only was concerned with its students' demeanor but also was inordinately preoccupied with students' personal appearance, which was not the case at the men's City College, nor even at coeducational Brooklyn College. A former Hunter official commented that its faculty thought students "unattractive and vulgar. Some of them probably were," he added, further stating that Hunter students were "afflicted with acne . . . and deplorable hairdos."[82] Bel Kaufman related an incident in which a student came to school wearing an organdy blouse and was then summoned to a dean who sternly warned her that "such unseemly attire might inflame men's passions."[83] Ethel Cohen recounted a similar episode when Dean Egan came up to her in the student lounge and admonished her for wearing "a too-skimpy sweater." Faculty, as well as deans, seemed unduly concerned with the physical image portrayed by Hunter women, as frequent articles in Hunter's newspaper attest. For example, Professor Isabelle Green of the education department praised students' "style and chic as a whole," but then went on to lecture them on the "appropriateness of their dress . . . and neatness and grooming."[84] Staff and faculty even formed a committee for students to deal with problems in personal appearance, offering consultations on posture, appropriate clothing, "wise" use of cosmetics, care of skin, hair, hands, and the "ever present question of extra pounds."[85] According to the interviewees, students took such ministrations as a personal affront or reacted with complete indifference.

Collegiate life for many, however, was more than a series of skirmishes with deans or a daily struggle to obtain their education. There was an extracurricular side to their schooling, and each subway school, whether training school or college, offered a rich variety of clubs and organizations, as well as a full range of social activities for its students. Because many students had to hold down jobs along with a full course load, even during the relative prosperity of the 1920s, they were unable to avail themselves of any extracurricular activities. Others had the added burden of responsibilities at home, which precluded them from participation. "I never had the time," Rae Lieberman said with regret. Besides her schoolwork and various on- and off-campus jobs held during her school years, "I had to help with the cooking and cleaning...to help my mother who worked in our store," she stated. Still others had no interest in such activities, preferring other forms of activism or socializing. Rose Jacobi elected to spend her free time with her own family and friends, asserting she had "a very full social life—more than I could handle." Yet other students disdained campus activities, as did Fanny Stein, an ardent and active member of the Young Communist League, who expressed scorn for the "frivolous doings on campus. With thousands of people unemployed, ill-fed, and homeless, Hunter held their soirées at fancy hotels," she sneered. For others who would have liked to participate, such events were beyond their pocketbooks, as were the sororities that flourished at Hunter, and were spoken of wistfully by many of those interviewed who could not afford to join.

But there were sufficient numbers of women who had the time, the wherewithal, and the interest to participate in the plethora of extracurricular activities to be found at the training schools and colleges, as their yearbooks and student publications illustrate. Further evidence of the wide range of clubs and social events at these schools throughout the 1920s and 1930s can be found on the "School Page" of the *New York Sun,* which regularly reported on such activities. Each school had math clubs, science clubs, language clubs, and so on, in addition to student government and student publications, plus religious organizations like the Newman Club and the Menorah Society. There were also theater and choral productions, boat rides, and dances, which were indeed held at "fancy hotels," as Fanny Stein asserted.

These aspects of the extracurricular remained constant during the halcyon years of the twenties and the turmoil of the thirties. But interspersed with the extracurricular was the ferment of student activism, previously unseen in America, which sprang up on city campuses during the Depression years, at which time students became politically and socially involved with seeking solutions to the myriad problems confronting their society, an activism which would bring a certain fame or notoriety to their campuses. At the forefront of this student activism, passionately involved in the full spectrum of the causes it encompassed, were the daughters of Jewish immigrants who were pursuing careers as teachers by taking teacher-training courses at the very centers of campus activism.

CHAPTER

 3

PAMPHLETS, PETITIONS,

AND PICKETS

The Experience of New York City
Women as Student Activists
during the Depression Decade

AT PRECISELY ELEVEN O'CLOCK on a balmy April morning, college students in New York arose from their seats and filed out of class. Within minutes, most of the city's colleges, and especially its municipal colleges, were virtually deserted as the students paraded along the streets. Marching with a group from Brooklyn College was seventeen-year-old Esther Rubin, carrying a placard that bore the slogan "No More Wars!" Reaching her destination, she found a sea of humanity—six thousand college students from the Brooklyn area who had gathered to denounce war. A similar scene took place in Manhattan, where another six thousand students, two thousand from Columbia University alone, demonstrated for peace. At Hunter College, five hundred students paraded, chanting "Strike against war!" and "Abolish ROTC!" These women were participating in the peace strike despite the college administration's threat of disciplinary action against students who walked out on strike.[1]

This is not an account of an antiwar demonstration of the 1960s. It is a description of the first student antiwar strike, held on April 13, 1934, and thereafter an annual event for the next six years. Student activism during the 1960s, and more specifically, the antiwar movement, generated a number of scholarly studies of the national student peace movement of the thirties, many of them comparing and contrasting the activism of the two decades in an attempt to understand the far-reaching student movement of the sixties.[2] Scholars came to realize that college students are often "the most neglected, least understood element of the American academic community," and that the most "sensitive barometer" of what is occurring at a college, the "instrument of change," with which students make known their interests and values are the extracurricular activities in which they engage.[3]

Studies of the peace movement, a major aspect of the extracurricular activities of the college student of the 1930s, acknowledge the high percentage of women students who participated in the decade's antiwar movement and often cite prominent women activists, as did Eileen Eagan in her study of the national student peace movement of the 1930s, *Class, Culture, and the Classroom,* in which she states that the women's colleges became a "major force in the student peace movement." Eagan also acknowledges the very strong ties to the peace movement that prevailed among both students attending teachers' colleges and those enrolled in education programs.[4] Of course, during the Great Depression, as is true today, most students preparing for careers in education were women. Nevertheless, the focus of Eagan's book, as with most of the other studies, is Columbia and Harvard universities. In addition, the voices of those who participated in student activism during the 1930s are invariably those of men.[5] Although a great deal of literature has added to our knowledge of twentieth-century women in the years since Leila J. Rupp noted historians' neglect of twentieth-century women, a full agenda still remains.[6] The public was introduced to a Communist female student of working-class origins, active in the thirties antiwar movement at an unnamed college campus, when Barbra Streisand portrayed such a young woman in the popular film *The Way We Were.* Yet in the public mind, radicalism and campus agitation have been endemic only in all-male colleges, despite the significant contribution of women activists who attended either all-female colleges or coeducational institutions. Much in the same way as in the 1960s, the experience of women activists in the 1930s was eclipsed by that of their male counterparts.[7]

In addition to this disregard of women activists, the activist role played by working-class Jewish women, many of whom were in college preparing to become teachers in the city's public school system, has been largely ignored. Jewish women were involved in collegiate activism throughout the country; however, outside New York City, their numbers were relatively small, especially at the more prestigious women's colleges, which kept Jewish enrollment low through discriminatory admission policies.[8] Jewish students enrolled in private colleges during the Great Depression tended to be members of the middle or upper classes, since theirs were the only parents who could afford the cost of these colleges. Furthermore, Jewish students studying outside New York City were primarily males who attended out-of-town and out-of-state colleges in greater numbers than did Jewish females, whose parents' educational priorities were higher for their sons than for their daughters and who were loath to have their daughters living away from home.[9] Therefore, the overwhelming preponderance of working-class Jewish women engaged in student activism in New York City's municipal colleges represented a new and unique contingent.

The colleges attended by these women during the 1930s were quite unlike the traditional colleges of the period, for their students rode the city subways and buses to classes at concrete campuses. This was also the case for the Jewish women from New York City who attended Barnard College, located in Manhattan. Despite the fact that most of these women were middle-class, the native New Yorkers among them usually resided at home with their families. At Hunter and Brooklyn colleges, the student bodies themselves were very different from those of any other college except City College of New York in that approximately 80 to 90 percent of their students were the sons and daughters of Eastern European immigrants.[10] Most significantly, not only were more women enrolled in the city's municipal colleges than anywhere else in the world, since Hunter was the largest women's college, but Jewish women attended college in greater numbers than did the non-Jewish population.[11]

Another dissimilarity between these New York City colleges and others in the United States was that city students were more politically involved than on campuses elsewhere. During the 1920s, most American college students throughout the land had been an isolated group preoccupied with private rather than public concerns. The decade was dominated by an image of the college student as a flapper or raccoon-coated, hip-flask-toting flaming youth, full of optimism, seeking only fun and self-indulgence, and, above all, escaping from the serious cares of the world.[12] As noted by Helen Lefkowitz Horowitz in her study of campus culture, college rebels have been present since at least 1910, but during the 1920s, college rebels took two forms: those who withdrew from politics to seek "inner psychic freedom" and those who continued in a political vein, attempting to place collegiate issues within a broader national context.[13]

Although there had been a few antiwar organizations, several underground student newspapers, and some students who attempted to continue the reform impulse of the previous era's progressives, nevertheless, students were, for the most part, politically conservative.[14]

Virginia Crocheron Gildersleeve, dean of Barnard College, who had decried students of the twenties as being marked with "blasé indifference, self-indulgence and irresponsibility," noted that students of the thirties, influenced by the changes in their world, were not only more serious toward their college work, but were more interested in student government and in issues of the outside world, assuming more responsibility for trying to solve current-day problems.[15] Now profoundly affected by the Depression, facing unemployment at the completion of their college studies, and haunted by the specter of war, American students shed their apathy as they became more serious-minded, socially aware, and politically liberal than were their predecessors. Unprecedented numbers of college students would engage in a decade of student activism of a scope and intensity previously unknown in American society.

In this era of highly charged, incipient political activism, student activism was considered strongest in New York City.[16] Moreover, prominent student activists of the period, such as Hal Draper, assert that the students at New York's municipal colleges were "the most politicized in the nation," a point echoed by a former Hunter College official, who noted that its students followed congressional hearings "with an eagerness generally associated with a World Series."[17] New York's students were only too well aware of their distinctiveness, as when the Brooklyn College yearbook wrote that at an American Student Union convention, editors of campus newspapers ordered their reporters to "cover the dances," but were gratified that Brooklyn College editors ordered their reporters to "cover the strikes." The yearbook added, "with pleasure," and somewhat smugly, that Brooklyn College had "social consciousness."[18]

Well represented among its most committed activists were the women of Brooklyn, Barnard, and Hunter colleges, especially those who would eventually go on to teach in New York City's public schools. Evidence of student activism can be found in college archives, which contain student newspapers, magazines, yearbooks, and surveys in their collections. Most college newspapers usually recorded only those motions carried or defeated by student organizations, without discussion of the issues and events, as observed by Lynn D. Gordon, who has suggested college archives as a relatively untapped source for the study of twentieth-century students.[19] However, the newspapers published by these three colleges printed lively accounts of debates that raged within the various groups and provided full coverage of campus events, as well as an abundance of letters to the editor on a wide variety of subjects that interested and affected students. On several occasions, the city's daily newspapers were moved to report the existence of many women officers of Brooklyn College clubs, especially those in a political vein, such as the American Student Union, the Karl Marx Society, the Current Problems Club, and the Politics Club.[20]

College publications, as well, recognized that women activists were an integral part of campus life. In a 1934 profile of the Hunter College activist, the school's newspaper noted the difference between the Depression-era variety and her predecessor. While her mother and grandmother contributed to the poor under the name of charity, attempted to enter the political world by demanding the vote, and joined the business world, her daughter or granddaughter had "her finger on the pulse of everyday affairs." To further their interests in current issues, Hunter's students studied the fine arts less than in the past and now concentrated on courses dealing with government and the social sciences. Observing the effects of modern times on their outside activities, the paper stated that present-day students dabbled less than previous students had, feeling their time could be spent more profitably in "aiding government to provide a better world for human beings to live in."[21]

These women activists supported a wide spectrum of causes that reflected the most crucial issues of the day. The Hunter College profile of a student activist observed that a list of organizations to which a typical activist belonged included the Women's International Peace League, the Organization for the Rebirth of the Ukraine, The Cooperative in Government Corporation, the Pan-American Student League, and the Labor Zionist Organization.[22] But it was the peace movement that most attracted students in New York City, as well as on campuses throughout the country, to become politically active. Their involvement was especially visible during the annual antiwar strikes such as the one in which Esther Rubin marched during the first strike for peace. College students, along with women's organizations and the clergy, constituted the three moving forces in the peace effort of the thirties.[23] The extraordinary depth of student opposition to war was revealed in numerous polls and surveys taken during the period, one of which showed that 39 percent of America's students would not participate in any war, and that 33 percent would do so only if the United States were invaded.[24] Two major tactics employed by students in the antiwar struggle were the administration of the Oxford

Pledge to thousands of students who stated they would refuse to support the United States government in any war it might conduct, and the anti-war strike.

Increasingly popular and highly visible, the strikes, which escalated from twenty-five thousand student participants in the United States in 1934 to half a million in 1937, were organized, coordinated, and supported to a significant extent by women members of the American Student Union.[25] Women were well represented in all branches of the American Student Union, as well as in the national organization where two of its four officers were women. Moreover, ten out of twenty-five members of its National Executive Committee were women, and the publications of the city's colleges reveal an active female membership, as well as leadership, in the organization.[26] Although its national membership was never large and it never enrolled more than twenty thousand students, the ASU was the largest student organization at Barnard, Brooklyn, and Hunter; and the Brooklyn College chapter was the largest in the nation.[27] Besides the ASU, other peace groups, with women in the forefront, proliferated on city campuses. One such organization was Hunter's Peace Council, one of the most active at the college, which James Wechsler, a keen observer of the Depression-era student movements, called the "spear-head of anti-war agitation."[28]

Through their involvement in the peace movement, New York City's college students realized they had many interests and concerns in common with students throughout the country, and that results could best be obtained by acting in concert. Seeking unity with other student organizations, New York City students participated in the National Conference on Students in Politics and joined the National Students Federation of America.[29] Many women activists from the city were among those involved with such groups. When a Model League of Nations was held at Vassar College in 1936, the Government Department at Brooklyn College selected the college's delegates on the basis of their background and general knowledge of international relations, as well as for their speaking ability. In addition to two male students, the college's delegation consisted of Sarah Rappaport, Harriet Krieger, and Beatrice Orent.[30] Brooklyn College also sent three women students to represent the school at the Third National Negro Congress held in Washington, D.C., in 1940.[31] Participation in conferences held outside the city often entailed great difficulties for these students, yet they persevered in their determination to be actively involved. On one occasion, one hundred Brooklyn College students chartered a bus to attend the American Youth Congress in

45

Washington, D.C. Unable to afford the bus trip, three women and two men borrowed a car, and after nine hours, three blowouts, and some hitchhiking, they finally made it to the conference.[32]

As peace advocates, these women quickly recognized the threat posed by fascism, vociferously protesting its rise throughout the decade; and as Jews, they were immediate opponents of Nazism, constantly publicizing and decrying the persecution of Jews in Germany and elsewhere in Europe. As early as 1933, women students were among the more than one thousand students who clashed with police during a three-hour demonstration at Columbia University, objecting to the campus visit of the German ambassador.[33] The following year, women at Hunter College held a conference on antifascism and were among the nine hundred city college students who denounced the treatment of Jews in Germany.[34] Among city students who demonstrated and marched to protest the spread of Nazism was Bella Abzug, later to become a congresswoman from New York City, who attended Hunter College from 1939 to 1943.[35] Their demonstrations followed the march of fascism abroad, with students protesting en masse.[36] Outraged at Japan's invasion of China, women from Barnard, Brooklyn, and Hunter were among the city's students who picketed the Japanese consulate, burning their silk garments and boycotting Japanese goods, especially silk stockings. Throughout the last years of the decade, committed women students could be seen wearing lisle instead of silk stockings.[37]

Staunch supporters of the Loyalist forces in the Spanish Civil War, students were active in protesting the Spanish Falangists, as well as raising money to aid the Loyalist cause, and sending clothing and an ambulance to Spain.[38] Often their demonstrations approached the level of street theater as, on one occasion, a "brigade" of women from Brooklyn College, led by a young woman in Spanish garb acting as La Pasionaria, the Loyalist heroine Dolores Ibarruri, took part in a mass fund-raising rally.[39] La Pasionaria appears to have captured the imagination of women activists of the thirties. Several interviewees cited her as their role model during their college years. Fanny Stein, recalling how she and her fellow activists worked "*No Pasaran!*" into every speech and pamphlet, said "Forget Joan of Arc! La Pasionaria was our idol."

Another graphic illustration of world events was the day Hunter College's student council attempted to portray to the student body what it would be like attending college in Nazi Germany. The complete suspension of extracurricular activities demonstrated the limited opportunities in German universities, emphasizing the importance of such activities and showing what would result from their curtailment, as had happened in Germany. All activities were closed in all four Hunter buildings, including publications, club meetings, the college ticket agency, its library, and the student council. All bulletin boards were covered and the college newspaper was issued in blank edition. Lunchrooms operated by the student council served only bread and milk.[40] Participation in the experiment by some of Hunter's faculty helped impart a lasting impression of life under totalitarianism, as Hannah Austerman remembered her anthropology professor, "normally a receptive and liberal person," pretending to promulgate Nazi racial theories in the classroom and refusing to brook any discussion or disputation by irate students on that day.

Aware, also, of the possibility of totalitarianism at home, students protested the rise of demagogues within the United States. Hunter College's Social Science Club frequently featured discussions of this topic, and at an Open Forum meeting there, Millie Futterman and Harriet Reines criticized Huey Long and Father Charles E. Coughlin.[41] Even closer to home, students could not help but notice labor strife within the city itself, as they passed striking workers each day, and often had family members on the picket lines. A number of Brooklyn College alumnae who were interviewed recalled how students from that school joined striking cafeteria workers from a favorite local eating place. Dora Fein remembered how the students made so much noise while picketing in front of the cafeteria that the police soon arrived, taking the strikers and students away in a patrol wagon. Recorded on the police blotter after this arrest were such fictitious names as Arthur Schnabel, Becky Sharp, and Titus Andronicus.[42] Anita Levy explained that not giving one's correct name to the police upon arrest was a common ruse during the period, for if the college learned of a student's arrest, the student usually was punished. "We tried to be creative," she stated, recalling that when she was one of a group of students arrested for joining picketers at a Manhattan department store, she gave her name as Emma Bovary. And this Emma Bovary spent twenty-four hours in a New York City jail because she refused to pay the five-dollar fine levied, lest she "contribute to the wealth of the establishment."

The *cause célèbre* of the decade for many students, though, and the one that, while remaining in the news almost constantly, seemed to cut across all political shadings, was the Scottsboro case, in which nine southern African-American youths were convicted of raping two white women in Scottsboro, Alabama, in 1931. This blatant example of racism and obvious miscarriage of justice galvanized countless students into spending many years working on behalf of the defendants. One student newspaper, typifying so many that appeared during the thirties, wrote that the entire judicial system was being tested, and that given the influence of prejudice, any pretense of a fair trial was "a farce." The constant reportage in all college publications of fund-raising drives and petition signings being held by students to benefit the accused attests to the importance of this case to the students of the thirties. When author Bel Kaufman, in her memoir of her student years at Hunter College, recalled raising money for "the Scottsboro boys," she joined virtually everyone interviewed for this study in singling out the Scottsboro case as one of the most visible and emotionally involving causes of the Depression era.[43]

Besides seeking freedom for those unjustly accused, students sought academic freedom, which was threatened both on and off college campuses during the thirties. One such incursion was the passage by the New York State legislature of the Nunan Loyalty Oath bill, which provided for a compulsory oath of loyalty to state and federal constitutions to be taken by all students attending educational institutions supported by public funds. Women from Brooklyn College were among the student delegation who traveled to the state capital to protest this bill.[44] During the McNaboe probe of alleged radicalism in New York's public schools and colleges, Beatrice Gomberg, editor-in-chief of Brooklyn College's newspaper, addressed an audience of students and denounced the investigation as "a witch-hunt." At the same meeting, Jeannette Blumenthal of the school's student council reminded those assembled that all students who protested militarism in the schools, who fought for democracy in education, or who participated in antiwar strikes would become targets of the investigation.[45] Brooklyn College students also held a mass rally to voice their objection to the denial of free speech on campus when Earl Browder, head of the Communist party, was banned from speaking there.[46] Their fight for academic freedom was extended to faculty as well as students; when a professor was dismissed because of political beliefs and activities in the Teachers Union, students held a demonstration and sit-in in the college president's office.[47]

Far more serious to students at the municipal colleges, however, was the threat to their free education that surfaced early in the Depression decade, when the New York City Board of Education proposed the imposition of tuition at the city's institutions of higher learning. To a student body extremely hard hit by the Great Depression, tuition costs, no matter how nominal, would mean the end of their education and the cessation of any hope they might have for their future. Therefore, students at the city's colleges joined together and worked overtime to prevent fees from being charged. Petitions of protest were presented to the Board, and students demonstrated throughout the city.[48] A series of public meetings was held to voice their opposition to tuition charges. At one held at Hunter, more than five hundred students were present.[49] At another rally held at Brooklyn College, Thelma Kahn, a Hunter student who was the featured speaker, informed those assembled that only 18 percent of Hunter's students would be able to remain in school if the fees were imposed. Kahn described the fees as "clearly discriminatory," because they would force out those students of lower economic standing, stating that students "must prevent higher education from becoming the exclusive property of the privileged wealthy minority."[50]

Kahn's statements were taken from a pamphlet prepared and distributed by students who based their research on surveys conducted by the colleges. In this pamphlet, the students claimed that the parents of 34 percent of all students were unemployed and that 50 percent of all undergraduates held jobs that were necessary for their families' sustenance. James M. Kieran, then president of Hunter College, along with faculty members, challenged the accuracy of the figures produced by the students.[51] Yet published surveys of Hunter's senior class of 1933 and of the freshmen entering the college in 1933 confirm the statistics submitted by the students.[52] While the percentages of unemployed parents changed over the decade, annual surveys throughout the 1930s indicate that about 50 percent of all students at the municipal colleges had to have employment in order to attend school. In a detailed study of its students in 1933, Brooklyn College found that 7 percent of its students' families were on relief, more than one-third of students' families had an unemployed member, and one-fourth of its students had part-time jobs, contributing their earnings to their families.[53] By coordinating their efforts in a protracted fight against the Board of Education, the municipal colleges remained tuition-free for many more years.

There were several reasons why these women were motivated to expend so much time, energy, and emotion as student activists during the 1930s. For some, the origin of their involvement was connected to the historical Jewish commitment to social betterment. For many others, their activism was rooted in the heritage of their families' commitment to social and political causes, since a sizeable number of their immigrant parents had brought from Europe a radical tradition that was still the central principle of their lives. Most of the parents of the sixty-one women interviewed for this study were working-class Eastern European immigrants, a majority of whom had been members of the Jewish Labor Bund in Russia, and now belonged to leftist political parties and to labor unions. Both parents of more than half of those interviewed were members of the Socialist party; both parents of ten others were members of the Communist party; several others claimed their parents were either "fellow travelers" or Trotskyists; and the rest reported their parents as "Roosevelt Democrats," with not a Republican in the group. More than half of the women said their parents had been members of a garment workers' union at some time, and several others had parents who had once been members of other trade unions. Socialism and the labor movements were powerful strains in Jewish immigrant culture and undoubtedly established a tradition of social and political involvement by both men and women that many of their children sought to emulate.

Most student activists did attribute the example of their parents' activism as the inspiration for their own. Bella Abzug, a student council president at Hunter College, cited the influence of her father, a Russian immigrant.[54] Sarah Ann Weingart, one of Abzug's predecessors as student council president, said that she was born into a family that had "fought tirelessly against social injustice."[55] Still another Hunter alumna, Fanny Stein, said she had been an activist before she could even walk, for her mother had carried Stein in her arms during a rent strike demonstration. For many, political and social involvement began well before college; while still high school students they did volunteer work at institutions like the Home for Hebrew Infants and neighborhood settlement houses. A considerable number attained positions of leadership at an early age, serving as officers of organizations such as student governments or as editors of their high school newspapers.[56] Jewish women participated in forms of activism far more than did young women high school students who were Christian. A 1935 study of a cross section of New York City's youth found that twice as many young Jewish women than others were members of some political or civic club.[57] Shirley Horowitz explained her activism, which began at a very early age, as "inevitable, because it was something everyone in my family did and we were encouraged to do so, to take an interest, to care, and to try to make a difference."

Student activists not only followed in the footsteps of their parents, but sought their counsel and guidance in their undertakings. Because their parents were members of the working class who had been active in the Bund or the Workmen's Circle, students of the thirties do not appear to have been alienated from either their parents' political beliefs or their class background. Moreover, the thirties seem to have been characterized by a distinct absence of a generation gap like the one that existed between student activists of the sixties. During the sixties, the parents of student activists tended to be liberal and generally in accord with their offsprings' goals, but they differed over tactics and methods, and strongly objected to all vestiges of youthful counterculture. However, during the thirties, students had a definite connection with the political attitudes of their parents. Students affiliated with the youth groups of left-wing political movements took their cues from the adult groups and those without connections to such organized adults still "looked to our elders for advice," as Fanny Stein observed. In part, the lack of intergenerational conflict stemmed from the fact that the world of their parents was still an integral part of the daughters' lives and would remain so throughout most of their adult years. But equally important is the fact that their political and career goals were completely in tune with those of their parents, whose influence extended to the students' perceptions of the colleges, as well, for these students had been taught to respect knowledge and education. Despite their critiques of Depression-era society, college faculty members received very little criticism from student activists; and although the students of the 1930s were willing to confront the colleges on issues of academic freedom, they never considered having any control over either faculty or curriculum.[58]

For those whose families had little or no connection with politics or social activism, the all-pervasive effect of the Depression, which was the central reality of their lives, impelled students to respond to the economic crisis. Oscar Handlin, who would become a historian of the American immigrant experience some years after attending Brooklyn College, noted that when he was a student there during the 1930s, it was difficult to walk the streets of downtown Brooklyn between classes and forget the kind of world he lived in.[59] The same observation was made by the college's yearbook, which wrote "No sequestered nooks here! No protected oasis of learning," adding that there was little opportunity to forget the outside world.[60] Another Brooklyn alumnus, writer Norman Rosten, recalled "unemployment marches, picketing, evictions, police clashes," all of which took place "under our very noses," which students could no more shut out than they "could stop breathing." Rosten claimed this "constant brushing against the facts of life" awakened a sense of responsibility in students.[61] The unemployment marches, picketing, breadlines, evictions, and labor strife were everyday encounters that left indelible impressions and fostered a desire to improve conditions in the world.

Along with familial influence and the Depression atmosphere, the environment at New York City colleges propelled many women into activist roles. Events on the campus itself often served as a catalyst to their becoming activists. When college administrators punished students for distributing leaflets or for participating in demonstrations, or when they censored student publications or barred speakers from campus, many women reacted to such suppression of students' rights by seeking to amend these infringements through activism. Certainly most students lacked the time, stamina, or inclination to be campus activists, yet it would have been impossible for them to avoid absorbing the climate of ideas that pervaded the city's colleges. "We had to think; we learned to act; we signed petitions, joined organizations, clamored for redress of grievances," recalled Norman Rosten, who further stated that his fellow students were involved in the "maturing process of social experience."[62] Constant exposure to the burning issues of the day is what stands out most vividly for Rae Lieberman when recalling her collegiate experience of some fifty years ago. "We could not shut the world out," she explained, "because the other students wouldn't let us. They besieged us with petitions, recruited us for their organizations, demanded we take a stand."

And many did more than take a stand. There were long hours spent on picket lines or churning out pamphlets for a series of different causes. Picket lines were such an integral part of student life at Hunter College that its yearbook staff, wishing to provide an honest record of campus life, sought to include in the 1935 issue of the yearbook photographs of students picketing. This was definitely not the image that Hunter officials wished to convey, however, and the photographs were censored. When the editor of the yearbook resisted, she was suspended, and the picture of picketers never appeared.[63] For Fanny Stein, "a constant battery of pamphlets" symbolizes her student activism. "It seems I was always either writing them or thrusting them into others' hands," she recalled. The ubiquitous pamphlets were a continual source of contention in Shirley Siegel's family. While her parents ardently supported her political activities, they strongly objected to the perpetual clutter of pamphlets stored in their already cramped apartment. Yet another Hunter student also recalled her parents complaining, not about her politics, but about undistributed literature being "piled up high" in her home.[64] Pamphlets were apparently so omnipresent that a Brooklyn College professor, testifying before a congressional committee investigating un-American activities on campus, complained that professors and students alike were deluged with what he termed Communist propaganda, which allegedly littered stairways and sidewalks in accumulations of at least half an inch thick.[65] Many of these activists were Communists or Socialists: some joining the ranks of the rapidly increasing student membership of the two parties' youth groups because of the economic crisis; others, because they came from left-wing homes where it was as natural to belong to the Young Communist League or the Young People's Socialist League as it was for other young women to join a college sorority or the Junior League.[66] Obstreperous campus voices who were said to have made a noise that "seemed at times to drown out the roar of traffic outside," they were responsible for much of the agitation that gave Brooklyn and Hunter colleges a "Communist coloring in the public eye," or, as a New York City newspaper headline screamed: "Brooklyn College is Red Party Hotbed."[67] This talented and disciplined group controlled student organizations, publications, and activities and gave a radical tone to the city colleges.[68] Because these students were convinced that the disastrous Depression vindicated their belief in the imminent demise of capitalism, their involvement in Marxist movements imparted a sense of passion and commitment. This conviction is what sustained them through long, grueling hours speaking in grimy halls and on freezing street corners to mostly indifferent and frequently hostile audiences.

Yet membership in these organizations added extra pressures to their already overburdened days and nights. An extraordinary amount of energy was needed to be a student, a campus activist, and a Socialist or Communist. For nineteen-year-old Fanny Stein, whose days began at five A.M., it meant traveling, often great distances, by subway to classes that started at eight A.M. and ended at two P.M. Whatever time this member of the Young Communist League had between classes was spent distributing leaflets or collecting signatures for a petition. She also worked five hours a week in the psychology laboratory, and one weekday evening and all day Saturday at Macy's department store. In addition, there were countless meetings, rallies, and demonstrations; studying her required schoolwork, and lessons in Marxist dialectics. Every Wednesday night she was stationed outside a movie theater, selling the *Daily Worker*. After a student member of the Young Communist League complained of having no time for studies because of overwork in the party and meetings that ended at twelve P.M., a *Daily Worker* columnist admitted this was a problem. Activity in the YCL did not mean that schoolwork should be overlooked, he wrote. "Spread the work around," the column advised, suggesting that meetings should last no longer than two and a half hours. Yet most women involved in the radical movements were so devoted that they did whatever they were asked to do and more.[69] A small segment of the Marxist students attended college merely to do political work rather than to receive an education, and attended meetings, not classes.[70] However, for those seriously considering the teaching profession, classes were as important as organizing, according to those interviewed.

Despite the dedication of these young women, male students proved insensitive to and unappreciative of their endeavors. In its coverage of a campus demonstration, the Brooklyn College newspaper referred to the women participants as "gorgeous damsels" and "pulchritudinous pickets," concluding with the observation that "Never did more humble sandwich boards contain more tempting fillers," thus trivializing the contribution of women activists of the thirties by the same sexist attitudes and behavior women activists would encounter in the sixties.[71] Nor were women activists treated as equals by their male comrades within the radical movements, for even the *Daily Worker* commented on the physical appearance of women strikers and picketers.[72] Even though there were a few prominent women in the upper echelons of the Communist and Socialist parties, as well as many in important posts on the local level, none of the women interviewed could recall any women in leadership in the youth groups of either party.[73] Although Marxist theory advocated full equality for women, those in the Young People's Socialist League and the Young Communist League found themselves relegated to a subordinate status in these male-dominated organizations.[74] Women members were usually given duties reflective of the sexist bias of male members, such as typing, passing out leaflets, addressing envelopes, and serving coffee. In addition to their talents being underemployed, women in the Marxist organizations often found themselves subjected to sexual harassment from men in the movement, for many of them looked upon their female comrades in a sexual context only.[75] Those members involved in sexual liaisons were probably a small minority, viewed as freewheeling Bohemians by the majority. Betty Perlman, an active member of the YCL during the thirties, insists that those involved in sexual arrangements were few because of the circumstances of their time and their backgrounds. "Most of us were raised in an age when this was greatly frowned upon. We may have been political and economic radicals, but in that respect, we were conservatives, nice Jewish girls who wanted husbands."

Often resenting the roles to which they were confined during the 1930s, they seldom articulated these feelings at the time. These young women fully expected to work after graduation, and refused to consider choosing between family and career. Indeed, the subject had been argued and the point won by Hunter College's debate team, which emphasized that the increased number of married women who were working because of economic necessity had no bearing on the topic, despite government discrimination against married women in the job market during the decade.[76] Yet, as Barnard's dean Virginia Crocheron Gildersleeve stated, they were not feminists, scarcely knowing the word.[77] Serious considerations of feminism were deemed irrelevant because women of the Left believed their problems would be solved with the creation of a Marxist society. From their viewpoint, as Mildred Herman put it, "capitalism was the enemy, not the male chauvinists in YPSL." Esther Rubin stated that a feminist movement during the Depression "would have been a luxury we could not indulge in. There were far too many serious matters and threats to one's very being."[78] Still others interviewed insist gender discrimination was far less invidious than the racial and religious bigotry so prevalent in the 1930s. With the organized women's movement dormant during this period, gender-related consciousness could find little support. Although their capabilities were neither fully appreciated nor utilized within the Marxist groups, young women activists could console themselves with their vision of a better future.

CHAPTER

 4

REPRESSION AND
PUNISHMENT

The Reaction to Student Activists

THE WOMEN ACTIVISTS AMONG New York City's college students had to contend not only with the general hostility of those opposed to their political and social beliefs, but also with continual conflict with college administrators and faculty members who branded the women's endeavors as obnoxious, vulgar, and hysterical. Although much of this criticism stemmed from college officials' ideological disaccord with student activists, it also reflected their belief that students were not behaving in an acceptable manner. A primary objective of higher education in general was to socialize students to conduct themselves as members of an elite class, and female students were to be inculcated with the social graces.[1] Since the majority of students at the city colleges were of Jewish working-class origins, college officials, of a different background, considered these students "too crude, too serious, too ungrateful, and too radical."[2] Although it was assumed that most poor and ethnic students were radicals, those who had definite ties to the radical movement did little to dispel their image as firebrands, "always ready for confrontation and battle, at least verbally."[3] Betty Perlman, a former activist, recalls a faculty member's referring to her fellow demonstrators as firebrands. "Mama really got a kick out of that, remembering that was what people termed the shopgirls when they protested working conditions," she explained, referring to her mother's union activities decades earlier. Perlman admits to arguing endlessly, using the classroom as a forum, and inserting Marxism into classroom discussions and assigned papers, the sort of behavior that caused a Brooklyn College professor to insist that his students could not get along well with others, especially with those of differing opinions.[4]

Although officials and faculty members at City and Brooklyn colleges considered male students equally disputatious, they deemed such behavior by women most unladylike and utterly objectionable. Therefore, women collegians paid a higher price for their participation than did male student activists. Sanctions were employed by the colleges far more frequently and with far greater severity against women than men. Certainly City College reacted to the antiwar and antifascist activists among its students with wholesale expulsions and suspensions in the first several years of the 1930s, but such repressions did not continue as long or with such rancor as they did toward women students.[5] Furthermore, according to several former Hunter students, City College men punished for activism often were reinstated, which rarely occurred at Hunter.[6] The standard practice of City College officials seems to have been to inflict swift and harsh penalties on activists, and then, after a cooling-off period, to place the students on probation for a semester. Myn Silverman's brother was among those expelled for activism at CCNY. After a few weeks, he and the other men penalized by the college were called before officials who, after a long harangue on the errors of their ways, informed the men that their expulsion would be lifted because the college did not want to jeopardize their lives as "future breadwinners" by denying them an education. The man who would later marry Belle Aronoff, a Hunter alumna, was also a City College student ousted for antifascist activity and later readmitted under probation because officials did not want to see him "unemployed and unable to provide for a family in later years."

This attitude was not one taken by officials at Hunter College whose administration, apparently not perceiving its female students as future breadwinners, was especially repressive. Hunter was the site of an ongoing battle between students and administration throughout the thirties for student autonomy in extracurricular affairs and for the right to engage in antiwar activity. James Wechsler, writing about his involvement in campus activism, noted that Dr. Eugene Colligan, who became president of Hunter College in the spring of 1933, not only suspended students with impunity, but began an assault "on every vestige of self-assertion at Hunter College," warning that control of what he alleged to be an "organized minority" over student affairs "would have to be broken."[7] Backed by the faculty, who unanimously expressed their confidence in his "attitudes and methods" in providing "proper guidance" of students, Colligan ran roughshod over Hunter students.[8] He imposed faculty advisors, chosen by him, on all college clubs and publications, which resulted in what the student council called a complete nullification of student self-government.[9] Colligan subjected student activists to petty harassment such as that inflicted upon the junior class president and antiwar activist, Margaret Wechsler (no relation to James Wechsler). Wechsler, who was born in Canada, was the daughter of naturalized citizens, a fact duly recorded on the innumerable applications and official forms filed with the college during her three years at Hunter. Yet after a confrontation with Colligan, that concluded with Wechsler's suspension, Wechsler's father received a letter stating that an inspection of her records showed that Wechsler was not born in the United States, and that evidence of her parents' naturalization was required if she was to remain a Hunter student.[10] Colligan also waged a campaign of slander, often casting aspersions on student activists, claiming to possess "certain nauseating facts" about their private lives.[11]

When such libelous tactics failed to daunt Hunter's activists, Colligan resorted to even more extreme measures in an attempt to quell their antiwar efforts. After he suspended five students who participated in the antiwar strike of 1935, Hunter's Peace Council attempted to hold a protest meeting on campus. This meeting was halted by Dean Hannah C. Egan, who was backed up by city detectives called in by Colligan.[12] He then suspended Theresa Levin and Millie Futterman, who had called the meeting, branding their behavior "hysterical" and "unladylike." Three other students, who had gone to Colligan's office to request reinstatement for the suspended students, wound up with suspensions as well.[13] Still unintimidated, the Peace Council tried to hold yet another meeting, and again Colligan employed the police to prevent the meeting and to forcibly remove the guest speaker, an antiwar activist and clergyman from Union Theological Seminary. The police prevented students from leaving the room, while Dean Egan wrote down the names of those present, and then insisted they appear in her office, along with their parents. Strenuously objecting to the administration's bullying actions, a Hunter student wrote in the college newspaper that such demands to bring one's parents to school were unworthy of a school that purported to teach college women, and "smacked of dictatorship." The student argued that women activists were not "dangerous lunatics," nor were they "radicals or communists," but rather, liberal, intelligent, public-spirited, and peace-loving college women who resented the hectoring of the administration and the suspension of students for working in behalf of peace.[14]

To further restrain student activism, the college also employed economic sanctions. Frequently students were fired from campus jobs, including those federally funded through the Federal Emergency Relief Administration, established in 1933 to provide work-study projects on college campuses, to encourage young people to remain in school, and to reduce the number of untrained and unemployed. As the centerpiece of the New Deal's youth policy, the FERA was transferred in 1935 to the National Youth Administration, where it remained through the decade.[15] FERA grants were highly selective, and recipients were usually outstanding students who, despite long hours spent on work-study jobs, still managed to rank among the highest academically.[16] Yet if these students participated in campus activism, even if it was conducted off campus, college officials reacted by taking away their jobs, as was the case with Beatrice Shapiro, when it was learned that she had been distributing antiwar and antifascist leaflets outside the college and off school property. Although Shapiro was a scholarship student, a college dean pronounced her "unteachable" and ordered her to bring her parents to school. Her parents were told by a college dean that their daughter's conduct was unladylike and that her parents should teach her to be loyal. Her removal from her FERA job was then justified by the dean, who said that good character was a major qualification for FERA employment.[17]

Another student subjected to reprisals from Hunter officials was Ruth Rosenthal, who, while on a leave of absence from Hunter College because of family difficulties, attended the 1933 Columbia University rally opposing the appearance there of the German ambassador. The demonstration, which culminated in clashes between a large squad of police and over one thousand protesters, also resulted in the arrest of Rosenthal for distributing antifascist literature in front of Columbia's auditorium. Although Rosenthal was immediately released from custody because it was determined that she had broken no laws, she was identified to newspaper reporters as a Hunter College student. The next day, when her name appeared in the newspapers, she was summoned before a Hunter dean and chastised for her involvement.[18]

Two months later, when Rosenthal resumed her studies at Hunter, she was placed on probation for wearing a tag that called for the support of the Liberal Club, an organization of five hundred students devoted to discussions of social, political, and economic problems. The dean was also angry that Rosenthal had discussed the club in her speech class, saying she had heard that the speech was antiadministration. In addition, Rosenthal was forbidden to engage in any extracurricular activities for the term of her probation and would have to resign as a representative of the dramatic club. The following semester, Rosenthal was unanimously elected Bronx chairman of the Peace Council. She was then summoned by a dean who informed Rosenthal she was empowered by the New York City Board of Higher Education to regulate, suspend, or discontinue the extracurricular activities of any student "in the interest of the college." She then advised Rosenthal that although her behavior and studies were satisfactory, her probation was extended another term. The dean further announced that Rosenthal had to resign from the Peace Council or be denounced to Albany, where her refusal to accept the conditions of her probation could be viewed as "non-cooperation," and her state scholarship removed. The dean also threatened to report her to the authorities in the FERA who would then revoke her work-study job. Rosenthal acquiesced because her financial situation was such that she could not afford to attend college without the money she received from her scholarship and the FERA. When the Peace Council refused to accept Rosenthal's resignation, she was called before the faculty Conduct Committee, which said that the college president had intimated that Rosenthal's conduct was repugnant to his ideas of social action, and he had further claimed she had stuffed circulars in students' lockers and solicited funds for various organizations, both of which were strictly forbidden at Hunter. Despite the questioning of both Rosenthal and her father for two hours by the committee, Rosenthal denied the charges. They were never proven, but she remained barred from all extracurricular activity.[19]

Rosenthal's case was not unique, for several other Hunter students, prominent in antiwar and antifascist activities, on and off campus, were also threatened by college officials, according to a letter appearing in the Hunter College newspaper and signed by members of the Student League for Industrial Democracy.[20] Awareness of the consequences of student activism upon their FERA jobs often deterred students from full participation. Florence Rossi, who held a library position while attending Hunter, knew that she could not afford to get arrested while protesting, because it would have cost her her job, so when the police appeared at a demonstration, she "slunk away."[21] It was also charged that Hunter and Brooklyn colleges often used their influence with the FERA to prevent activists from receiving work-study jobs. Esther Rubin said she was told by a Brooklyn College official that her antiwar activity was instrumental in her being denied a grant from the FERA, and Rebecca Tisch insists she, too, was turned down, despite an impeccable scholastic record and a well-documented need for such assistance, which were supposed to be the FERA's only criteria for awards. Yet it was such common knowledge that the colleges interfered with FERA jobs that Hunter College's student council included their belief that there should be no political discrimination in the distribution of FERA jobs as a plank in its 1934 platform.[22]

As serious as these punitive measures were to students, however, college officials possessed an even more drastic sanction that they could employ against student activists who had incurred their displeasure: withholding their endorsement of teacher aspirants, which would, in effect, prevent them from teaching in the city's public schools. Newly graduated jobseekers have always been required by would-be employers to provide recommendations from their colleges. In most cases, one submits a faculty member's letter of reference one safely expects will be highly favorable. However, the New York City Board of Education mandated a detailed evaluation from college deans, thus presenting college officials with yet another form of punishment for student activists, one with the gravest consequences. Potential teachers' records, including their transcripts and endorsements, were forwarded to the New York City Board of Education's Board of Examiners, who passed judgment on all teacher candidates, screening them for subversive views. In 1934, subversive views were defined as those advocating violence as a means of influencing governmental policy and advocating use of the classroom as a means for transmitting social or economic doctrines inconsistent with standard constitutional doctrines, which was translated by the Examiners to mean those views held by candidates with radical or activist backgrounds.[23] Unless an applicant's activism was well publicized in the popular press, which occurred only occasionally, the only way the Examiners could learn of the applicant's so-called radicalism was through the college evaluation, resulting in a thorough investigation of the candidate. The Examiners asserted that if the activist's radicalism was deemed to be part of a maturation process, and if the candidate appeared to possess the "capacity for constructive service," the candidate was passed; but if the applicant appeared to present a "potential threat to the school system," a license was denied.[24] The Examiners further claimed that after five years of such scrutiny, not one candidate had been rejected for subversive beliefs.[25]

However, the Board of Examiners was not forthright in its claim, for candidates certainly were denied licenses because of student activism, although the reasons for denial were disguised, couched in such rhetoric as "insufficient and unmeritorious service," and college officials definitely were to blame for their decisions. Although there is no documentation that officials at either Brooklyn or Hunter college utilized such a sanction on their student activists, Joseph P. Lash, a leader of the 1930s student peace movement, reported that Eugene Colligan, Hunter's president, threatened any student who participated in the antiwar strike with a refusal to recommend her for a teaching position.[26] Moreover, several former students insist they that had first-hand experience with such intimidation. Esther Rubin was cautioned by a Brooklyn College dean to "tone down" her activism or the dean would find it impossible to write a reference attesting to her "good character." Mae Cogen, another activist at that college, was told by the same dean that "Everyone knows how Hunter's president keeps his students in line." The dean then hinted that if Cogen did not "show better manners" than she had in her role as a peace activist, she, too, could be denied a good evaluation. Three other former Hunter College activists also state that they were given similar warnings. In addition, many of the women interviewed claim to have secondhand knowledge of such sanctions either threatened or carried out against friends or fellow students. Whether or not recommendations were withheld from student activists with any frequency, the implicit threat existed; besides, college students of the thirties were only too well aware of the notorious case of Gertrude Epstein, who was denied a teaching license because of her activism while a student at Barnard College.

Not much is known about Gertrude Epstein's background beyond her student activism while at Barnard College, her views on war and fascism while editor of the college newspaper, and her fight to become a New York City public school teacher. Nor can much be learned about her life, as she refused to be interviewed, stating that her case was "well documented," and that she preferred to "let the facts speak for itself."[27] Judging by her name, though, she probably is Jewish, and presumably from a rather prosperous family, since she attended an expensive private college during the height of the Great Depression. A group photograph of the *Barnard Bulletin* staff in the college yearbook is further indication of her possible affluency, as she is shown, along with almost every young woman in the picture, wearing what was obviously a very fashionable and very costly overcoat with a large, luxurious fur collar.[28] While a Barnard student, Epstein worked on the college newspaper, becoming editor-in-chief in September 1933. She represented her college as its elected delegate at an antiwar conference held at Columbia University, and was the only woman elected to the executive committee of the Permanent Committee of the Columbia Antiwar Conference.[29] Epstein was one of the founders of *University Against War*, a monthly peace magazine published by Columbia University students. Besides contributing articles to the publication, she served as its publicity director, and was eventually elected its editor.[30]

In February 1935, eight months after graduating with honors in English, Epstein took the written and oral examinations for a license to be a teacher-in-training of high school English in the New York City public schools. Although she successfully passed both tests, Epstein was denied a license by the Board of Education's Board of Examiners because of "insufficient meritorious record and ineligibility."[31] The Examiners based their denial on a bylaw limiting licenses to candidates recommended by their colleges, stating that a hesitant endorsement of Epstein by Barnard's Dean Virginia Crocheron Gildersleeve, who declined to give her unqualified approval to Epstein, and a letter from another Barnard official were placed in Epstein's file at the Board of Education. The Examiners also claimed to have been informed by Barnard authorities that Epstein had taken part in several radical student demonstrations.[32] In addition, newspaper reports alleged that Gildersleeve informed the Examiners that Epstein's writings at Barnard were "intemperate," that Epstein had created disturbances at the college, and that Gildersleeve's reservations about Epstein were based on Epstein's "attitude."[33]

Supported by the American Civil Liberties Union, Epstein started what was to become a widely publicized and protracted court action against the Board's decision. Because her case is the first instance that has come to light of the rejection of a candidate for a position in New York's public school system based on so-called radical student activism, resulting in serious ramifications for many, it merits closer examination. When the standard form requesting an evaluation of Epstein was sent to Dean Gildersleeve's office by the Board of Examiners, it was filled out by Katharine S. Doty, assistant to the dean. On this form, question number eight asked: "To what extent can you endorse the application of this candidate for a teaching position . . . , basing your endorsement SOLELY upon his [sic] *character* and *personality*?" The choices ranged from "cannot endorse" to "endorse with hesitation or with reservations" to "endorse moderately" to "endorse with confidence" to "endorse with enthusiasm." To this question, Doty checked off "endorse with hesitation or with reservations." The next question asked to what extent the candidate could be endorsed, based "SOLELY on...*general scholarship*" and college work. Here Epstein was endorsed with confidence.[34]

Acting upon Gildersleeve's direction, Doty then wrote to the Examiners that she had neglected to include her usual accompanying memorandum on the blank sent her for Epstein, and wanted to give them some additional information. The letter began by characterizing Epstein as "an exceptionally able student," with "a rather brilliant and interesting mind and considerable literary ability." Doty then wrote that as editor-in-chief, Epstein "became passionately interested in Communism," under the influence of "young Columbia radicals." Charging her with using the college newspaper to further the cause of the radicals, Doty claimed this precipitated an altercation, as the great majority of students found Epstein's opinions and the manner in which she expressed them "very offensive," and asserted that her writing showed "very bad taste at times, as well as bad manners," mentioning that the editorial controversy ended with Epstein's resignation as editor. Doty then remarked on her antiwar activity, and in what was undoubtedly the most damning statement of all, informed the Examiners that Epstein had been a paid assistant on the editorial staff of the *Daily Worker*, the official newspaper of the American Communist party. Doty concluded with her observation that Epstein had always seemed a young woman of "pleasant manners and appearance, good voice, interesting mind."[35]

This letter prompted a Board of Examiners investigator to call upon Doty for further clarification, which Doty supplied. Acknowledging that Epstein had "top notch ability," and pleasing speech and appearance, Doty told the Examiners' representative that Epstein was elected to Phi Beta Kappa, despite the objection by some of the faculty because of her "bad manners." Commenting on Epstein's role as editor, Doty claimed that Gildersleeve felt Epstein was "riding ill-shod [*sic*]" over her staff and that some of the faculty, as well, found her "insufferable." She said Epstein ran antiwar and antifascist editorials "all the time," together with discussions of radical politics, adding that her columns were "filled up chock block with radical propaganda." Calling Epstein "ill-mannered" and "ill-bred" in her editorials, Doty averred that if the occasion arose, Epstein would "instinctively take the radical side of the fence. She would create a disturbance and arouse opposition among faculty and students." Then, adding fuel to the fire, she alleged that the antiwar group at Columbia, with which Epstein associated herself, was "synonymous with the Communist group."[36] Later, upset because of the press coverage,

Doty explained in a typed "Memo to the Dean" that it seemed impossible to avoid discussing the topic when the investigator insisted on justification of her criticisms, adding, in pen: "We'd better rate everybody 'perfect' in future!"[37] Both Doty's letter and her elaboration upon it had a most damaging effect on Epstein's quest to become a teacher, for they provided the Examiners with their excuses for denying her a license. The Examiners declared that Epstein had falsified her record by omitting to state that she had once been employed by the *Daily Worker* and that her "communistic" views and her advocacy of them disqualified her from being licensed. The Board further stated that Epstein had written articles in the *Barnard Bulletin* in which she espoused Communism and attacked the faculty.[38]

While the press was busy reporting her case, Epstein wrote Gildersleeve requesting that Barnard and its dean not condemn and repudiate her. She assured Gildersleeve that she had persistently avoided any utterance that might seem disrespectful toward her alma mater. Epstein pointed out that she had spent very happy years at Barnard, doing excellent academic work, and had many friends, especially among the faculty. She hoped that whatever the strain her "headstrong behavior" had caused the college and, likewise, whatever pain she suffered from the "petty persecutions" that had harried her as editor, that Barnard was "big enough and cared enough to let bygones be bygone."Although she admitted that some of her editorials were "reckless," nevertheless, she believed that "the passionate honesty which inspired it was recognized . . . I knew only that I cared tremendously about certain things: the wickedness of war; the bestiality of fascist militarism; and that I had only one way . . . of doing anything about them." Calling herself a "callow, hotheaded young person, with an occasionally reckless pen," Epstein added that she still did not believe she was ill-mannered, offensive, or subversive, as charged. She then rather plaintively asked Gildersleeve if she concurred with Doty's assessment of her and if Barnard had indeed officially renounced her.[39] Responding to this letter, Gildersleeve denied that Doty had any "special prejudice" against Epstein, and that the dean still maintained that Epstein was an "exceptionally able and interesting person," although she was somewhat unfair as an editor. However, she felt that "when dragged into the limelight with the blare of publicity," Epstein's past actions seemed "rather trivial."[40]

Apparently, to Gildersleeve the unfavorable publicity received by both herself and the college outweighed the seriousness of Epstein's being refused a license. Gildersleeve may have been disturbed by an editorial in the *New York Herald Tribune* supporting Gertrude Epstein that stated that the schools should not pass up the opportunity to have a "real live wire" who might animate students, just because the applicant "brimmed over with aggressive idealism." The newspaper observed that many people were "intemperate" in their salad days who might be "nicely mellowed" later. Exclusion of such young people from the teaching profession would be committing "a big sin" against students, because a pupil with "spunk enough to protest for peace is the sort who ought to be in colleges." The paper declared that the course followed by the Examiners was bound to have a "cowing effect" upon college students aspiring to teach, increasing teacher fear, "the bane of good teaching, particularly in these days when the need for aggressively progressive education to keep up with social change is necessary." The editorial directed itself to Gildersleeve personally, pointing out that in her long academic career she surely had seen enough intimidation of teachers and "the evil effect thereof on education" to know better than to bar the gates of the New York City public schools against a gifted student because that student as college editor had shown "more liberal spunk than most."[41]

Besides being concerned about such adverse publicity, the dean was distressed that she did not know how to answer the Board in future evaluation forms, even requesting Epstein's aid in solving her dilemma.[42] Epstein replied that her problem could be rectified by submitting a new statement to the commissioner of education, reminding the dean that she had been greatly hurt, not only by the license denial, but by the distortion of Doty's comments, which cast aspersions on her good name. On this letter to Gildersleeve, Doty penciled in that she did not really see why Barnard should do as Epstein asked.[43] In addition, they were apparently annoyed that the American Civil Liberties Union was handling the case. On a copy of an ACLU press release stating that "Dean Virginia Gildersleeve of Barnard had refused to give the girl an unqualified recommendation," Doty underlined the dean's name and typed a memo that read: "In view of the above release by the Communistic A.C.L.U., the enclosed articles may be of interest to you."[44]

At the same time, Dean Gildersleeve wrote William J. McGrath, chair of the Board of Examiners, asking how to avoid further problems with her evaluations.[45] McGrath sympathized with Gildersleeve for the "annoying" attempts to apply pressure on officials who submit "honest references," for which, he wrote, the Board honored her. Expressing his regret that reporters had used the statements, he then advised her that "the good of the school child" should continue to be her "lode star, as it is ours."

McGrath then declared that any college student who behaved in "so uncouth and unladylike a fashion as to cause you to believe that she is not fitted emotionally, temperamentally, or culturally to be a teacher" should be reported on adversely.[46] Gildersleeve then wrote Epstein about this letter and further questioned her about the evidence Epstein would be submitting in court.[47] Rather tersely, Epstein replied that while she was sorry Gildersleeve did not find it possible to give her an altogether new statement of character, she was nevertheless grateful for the dean's courtesy.[48]

Epstein's case was first heard in April 1936 in New York City, and although she lost that case because of a technicality, Epstein appears to have tried other tactics before appealing the ruling. Having exhausted her attempts to placate Barnard's dean or to obtain a reversal of her evaluation, Gertrude Epstein went ahead with her litigation. Her suit against the Board of Examiners, which had been filed by the New York Civil Liberties Committee of the American Civil Liberties Union in 1936, contested the validity of the bylaw requiring candidates for teacher-in-training licenses to have the endorsement of their colleges, claiming that this regulation illegally transferred to the colleges the selection of teachers. Her petition further charged that Epstein's political and social views, rather than her competence, were the reasons why the recommendation was withheld.[49] In their affidavit, the Examiners declared that Epstein had falsified her record by failing to state that she had once been employed by the *Daily Worker*. Epstein explained that because she believed college students ought to take an active interest in the social and economic problems of the day, she did temporary work in the newspaper's editorial office. As it was partly of a volunteer nature, which she considered "casual," she did not deem it the kind of employment information required on her application.[50]

Answering the Examiners' second reason for refusal of a license, that of her so-called Communist views, Epstein denied that she was a Communist or a member of the Communist party. To refute the Examiners' claim that she used the college newspaper to propound Communism, she submitted the front-page articles and editorials which appeared in the 35 issues published during her editorship. An analysis of this material indicates that 65 articles dealt with administration matters, activities, and talks by the dean and faculty; and 133 of the articles covered college activities unconnected with the antiwar movement. Only 11 articles covered the antiwar movement on the Barnard campus and another 27 reported on antiwar and antifascist activism, mostly at Columbia

University. Tabulation of Epstein's editorials shows that 12 of them were about the antiwar movement; 10 covered entirely local college matters; and the rest were about such disparate subjects as the college's Greek games, the mayoralty election, courses in the arts, book burning in Germany, a welcome to freshmen, the library, and the death of the king of Belgium. None of the articles or editorials attacked the faculty in any way, nor could they possibly be construed to advocate Communism.[51] Epstein also explained the circumstances which led to her resignation as editor-in-chief of the *Barnard Bulletin*. Katharine S. Doty had told the Board of Examiners that Epstein had used the columns of the publication to further the cause of radicalism, over the objections of the Undergraduate Association, the paper's sponsor, which, according to Doty, found Epstein's editorials offensive. Conceding that a Barnard poll showed that those who voted disapproved of her editorials by a vote of 158 to 47, Epstein stated that in this same poll, the students voted that the editor should have complete freedom in the expression of her own opinion in editorials, and that this vote was 157 to 38. Because the student government disregarded this vote and set up an editorial board of five to control the paper's policies, which Epstein believed constituted censorship of free speech, she resigned.[52]

Besides disputing the Examiners' claims, Epstein insisted that their investigation was biased; hostility toward her political opinions so beclouded their judgment that their determination was arbitrary, as well as an abuse of their powers.[53] Her lawyer concurred, stating that the Examiners made no real effort to ascertain Epstein's fitness as a teacher, never even undertaking an inquiry of the Barnard professors with whom Epstein had studied. Moreover, he alleged that Doty had no personal knowledge of Epstein, since Doty generally had very little contact with students.[54] To amend their failure to question the faculty or administration, Epstein submitted testimonials from Barnard faculty members, who attested to her academic distinction and courtesy. The chair of the English department stated that he was greatly impressed by Epstein's earnest desire to be of service to the community, and the dean of social affairs mentioned that although she and Epstein occasionally differed in opinion and that Epstein "clung with firmness to hers, she was never rude about them with me," adding that she would describe her personal relations with Epstein as "delightful."[55]

However, the first judge to hear her case ruled that Epstein should have gone initially to the state commission on education in Albany. She then took her case to Commissioner Frank P. Graves, who said he found no evidence to indicate the Examiners had abused their authority to determine the fitness of teacher applicants. Nor had he found that the Examiners acted with malice, and therefore he would not overrule them. Graves also upheld the Examiners' contention that Epstein was ineligible because she did not receive an endorsement from authorities of her college. Although Epstein argued that her graduation from Barnard was in itself an endorsement, Graves rejected this reasoning, deciding that if an applicant had a temperament or personality which was displeasing to the Examiners, or behaved in a manner they deemed inacceptable, the Examiners were within their rights to refuse a license.[56] Appealing this ruling again, Epstein was once more turned down in September 1938.[57] The four years she spent preparing to teach and the years expended in fighting the Examiners decision were for naught. Gertrude Epstein never did obtain a license to teach; instead, she became a medical writer.

The decisions rendered against Gertrude Epstein by educational authorities and the courts can be understood within the context of anti-Communist anxiety and fear of radicalism in the schools that was so prevalent during the 1930s. What is more difficult to comprehend is the role played by Virginia Crocheson Gildersleeve in preventing Epstein from teaching in the city's schools, for Gildersleeve's reputation was that of "a champion of young women with scholarly talents."[58] Although a conservative to the core, Gildersleeve professed tolerance and respect for left-wing students, especially the type she described as being very sincere, yet fanatical, uncompromising, and extremist and sometimes hard to fit into college life, stating that she "wouldn't be without them." She characterized a second kind of radical student as one who loved agitation and conflicts for their own sake, preferring martyrdom, "or perhaps just a row," to the attainment of her purported objective. Such a student, the dean determined, was "trying" to the rest of the community but "fortunately rare in women's colleges."[59] This delineation of a student radical cannot be taken as a description of Gertrude Epstein, since Epstein appears to have been straightforward rather than recalcitrant in her activism, and her refusal to accept being denied a teaching license hardly marks her as a martyr. Moreover, Epstein's antiwar beliefs were not that much in variance with Gildersleeve's, because during the antiwar strike of 1934, the dean was reported to have announced that anyone should be proud to take a cut from classes in order to attend the peace demonstration at Columbia.[60]

As for Epstein's columns during her stint as editor of Barnard's newspaper, her editorials are rather innocuous by present-day examples of student writing. Even in contrast to other college publications of the thirties, which often criticized specific college administrators or education in general, or attacked the sanctity of such hallowed campus traditions as college sports or sororities and fraternities, Epstein's editorials are almost reverent toward college icons.[61] And compared to the editorials in the municipal colleges' newspapers, Barnard's are quite tame. But as editor, Epstein was a visible and vocal target, and like so many other college editors who tended to lean to the left in their political views, she may have incurred the anger of faculty and administrators who were the protagonists in the move to impose censorship on the Barnard newspaper. This was a recurring struggle during the decade. In one academic year alone, that of 1931–32, eight editors were either dismissed from college or forced to resign their positions, including the editor of Columbia's student newspaper; and twelve others left under some duress.[62] Gildersleeve plainly did not want activism on the Barnard campus, as she told an assembly of students that while she hoped the college had some student activists, she requested that they "agitate" for their causes away from the school, adding that she would rather not ask anyone to leave the college, "for it is much more amusing to keep you all here."[63]

Dean Gildersleeve's hope for the existence of student activists coupled with her threat of expulsion is rather puzzling. One can only wonder whether she found some personal satisfaction in keeping Gertrude Epstein at Barnard, graduating her with honors, and then withholding the recommendation so necessary for a teaching license, fully realizing the implications of her refusal. If the dean was in such a dudgeon because Epstein's radical views were aired on Barnard's campus, surely once she had resigned as editor and confined her activism to the Columbia campus the dean's pique should have been assuaged. Aside from being engaged in Columbia's antiwar movement, Epstein appears to have devoted herself to the completion of her studies. She brought no adverse publicity to Barnard; nor did her name ever appear in any of the city's newspapers until she was denied a license by the Board of Examiners. Yet Gildersleeve seems to have gone out of her way to punish Epstein, in part for her political views, but quite likely because Epstein was Jewish.

Even during the Great Depression, when enrollments declined at Barnard, Gildersleeve was adamant about limiting the admission of Jewish women to the college.[64] While we do not know whether Epstein came from a German or Eastern European Jewish family, Gildersleeve made it her business to know such things about Jewish students, and made sharp distinctions between the two groups, denoting the latter as "a particularly crude and uneducated variety." Although she considered German Jews "charming and cultivated human beings," she referred to all other Jews as coming from a lower social level, comparing them unfavorably with most other Barnard students.[65] This anti-Semitism may well have contributed to her behavior toward Epstein, which was of an especially acrimonious and vengeful nature, although no mention was made of anti-Semitism by anyone during the Epstein affair. However embittered Epstein may have been toward Gildersleeve, she did not extend these feelings toward Barnard, for her daughter is a graduate of the college, and in 1984, Epstein was among those attending the fiftieth reunion of her class.

As Gertrude Epstein herself declared, the refusal to grant her a license served notice on the entire college world that entry into the New York City school system was forbidden to those who were active in unpopular causes, thus tending to "make cowards and hypocrites of students everywhere."[66] Because Epstein's fight to become a teacher was so highly publicized for so many years, the outcome of her case undoubtedly influenced many student activists. One such woman was Belle Aronoff, a member of the Young People's Socialist League and an antiwar activist while attending Hunter College, whose parents actually forbade her to continue her involvement while a student lest she endanger her chance at a teaching position. "I could not very well refuse," she related, "as my family was counting on me. I was part of a family plan. As the oldest, the plan was for me to help pay for my younger brothers' educations." Ruth Davidson was also enjoined by her family to cease her student activism at Brooklyn College, and did so because she felt she had no choice. Her family had sacrificed for her to train as a teacher, and she "simply couldn't go against them," adding that she merely changed her activism, participating in a "safe kind" of activism that could not be "tinged Red." Many of those interviewed mentioned friends or classmates who, fearing repercussions for their membership in left-wing organizations, decided to "soft-pedal" them or "just lie low until they had safe and secure jobs," as Rae Lieberman put it. Yet for as many who were deterred by the example of Gertrude Epstein, there remained many who were undaunted. Esther Rubin stood steadfast in her commitment to student activism despite following the Epstein case closely, as did Fanny Stein, who remembers being infuriated with the Board of Examiners, but was determined, nevertheless, to go on as "an active, card-carrying YCLer."

While we cannot measure how many student activists were affected by the discrimination shown Gertrude Epstein, it is even more difficult to estimate the percentage of women involved in student activism in New York City during the 1930s. Although there have been attempts to gauge the percentage of radical students active in the thirties, it is essential to understand that while students affiliated with Marxist movements exerted an influence far beyond their rather meager numbers, most student activists were definitely not radicals, but were liberals, with no formal connections to radical organizations. While Virginia Crocheron Gildersleeve was wrong to assert that most women students of the thirties were conservative, she was correct in her observation that there was always a "small but ardent" group of young radicals among the mass of students.[67] Because they were more articulate and conspicuous than most, radical students had a tremendous impact upon their peers, as when the entire slate of candidates endorsed by the American Student Union swept into office at Hunter College in 1936.[68]

As to students as a whole, even James Wechsler and Hal Draper, participants in the student movement of the thirties, admitted to a great disparity between those actively involved and those who were influenced by the activists. But as Draper has explained, surrounding the 1 percent who actually joined a student group were "concentric rings of influence, embracing different portions of the student body." Other students concurred with their programs, but could not take part in them for various reasons, such as a lack of time. Other circles of students existed, too, Draper asserts, who would support most campaigns on a particular issue, especially during the antiwar strikes. Even beyond the widest of these concentric circles were those students who, while never participating, were far from hostile to students' aims. Because the activists set the campus mood and tone, their ideas, rhetoric, devotion, and energy permeated the consciousness of the rest of the student body. Certainly the majority of students were devoted to their studies and to their personal lives, as well as to the pursuit of their degrees, but as Draper has argued, "even while doing so they could not help absorbing the climate of ideas which pervaded the *political* life of the campus as a part of the larger society."[69] And what is particularly significant is that the students of the thirties were quite well aware of the imprint activists made; Brooklyn College's yearbook noted in 1938 that while students were not united on many issues, "the totality of bombast" made a deep impression on all students as well as on the outer world.[70]

Former activists have expressed immense pride in the message they imparted to the world, believing they sparked social consciousness and awoke complacency as they furnished a critique of their society, along with providing many with a tolerance for people and ideas that were perhaps more radical than their own. Belle Aronoff assessed her participation as "very positive, even though we ultimately failed to promote pacifism," but reasoned that that cause "was doomed because of fascism. But we made people aware of Hitler's menace." "In retrospect," Fanny Stein recalled, "we students and the Left were the only ones who censured America for social injustices and for denying its citizens, black and white, young and old, their full civil rights," adding, "That's something I always enjoyed reminding my children when they were in college in the sixties."

Besides their contributions to the public in general, their undertakings endowed the women themselves with substantial benefits that they believe enhanced and enriched their lives. Through their activism they gained self-confidence, learned organizational and analytic skills, and were trained to question, to develop a critical attitude, and to respond to social problems.[71] Hunter College activist Sarah Ann Weingart noted most astutely that if a college student expected to serve humanity, she "might as well begin by working for her fellow students." She maintained that her extracurricular activities gave her a sense of reality that would help her fit into a world that demanded practical ability as well as book learning, for just as "education is a preparation for knowledge, so the extracurricular is a preparation for reality."[72]

Women activists did not disappear into oblivion; they were "not dead but simply obliterated" by becoming housewives, as journalist Murray Kempton has erroneously charged.[73] Many of the young women engaged in student activism became teachers in New York's public schools, where they applied the lessons learned from a student movement that has been called a training ground for trade unionists, and applied it to the city's teachers' unions.[74] Peace activists Estelle Greenberg and Evelyn Weiss served as Teachers Union representatives from their respective schools after obtaining teaching positions. Pearl Kagan, Myn Silverman, and Ida Mitnick were among the many former activists whose names appear on various programs sponsored by the city's teachers' unions. Still others participated in campaigns for improving school conditions, building new schools and developing curricula, or fighting to remove biased textbooks from the city's schools. Beyond educational concerns, former activists engaged in politics, usually of a liberal nature, although some continued as members of radical parties. Their student activism served as a matrix for a lifelong commitment to social and political activism. Esther Rubin exemplifies many of these former student activists who continued their activism as teachers. Rubin, who marched in the first student antiwar strike in 1934, has been marching ever since. She participated in each student peace demonstration held in New York City during the Depression decade; took part in rallies against fascism and against school retrenchment in New York City; and protested the verdict in the Julius and Ethel Rosenberg case, among others. "I went out with New York City teachers during their first strike, back in the sixties. I marched for civil rights down South and in Washington, and I've marched for women's rights," she recounted, and most recently, as a retired schoolteacher in her seventies, she paraded in an antinuclear demonstration. "And you'd be surprised," she exclaimed, "but I'm always meeting up with someone I paraded with back in my student days."

CHAPTER

5

EXAMINATIONS, ENUNCIATION,
AND ENDURANCE

*The Ordeal of Obtaining Licenses
and Appointments to Teach*

JUNE 20, 1935, the day she graduated from Hunter College, was one of the most important and memorable days in the life of Mildred Herman, the first in her immigrant family ever to attend college. Not even the student pickets outside Carnegie Hall, where Hunter's graduation exercises were held, nor the sporadic interruptions from the balcony (protesting the suspension of students for their antiwar activities), could diminish the joyous occasion for her. Some fifty years later, Herman recalled bursting into tears at the unexpected luxury of a bouquet of roses presented her by her family to commemorate the happy occasion. After the ceremony, all her relatives and neighbors called at her Bronx home, to pay their respects to her parents' daughter, "the teacher." The four years she spent at Hunter, preparing for a teaching career, had been a long and arduous ordeal. Schoolwork had to be interspersed with a series of part-time jobs and with assisting in the family luncheonette. Many sacrifices were made quite willingly, for the family looked forward to Herman's becoming a professional with a good steady income. But she faced many trying encounters with the formidable bureaucracy of the New York City Board of Education, and especially with its Board of Examiners, along with several years of frustration, before she would achieve this goal.

A young woman who had graduated from a training school or college had to undertake a number of steps before becoming a teacher in the New York City public schools. First, the teacher aspirant had to obtain New York State certification, a relatively simple process. However, the teaching certificate was valid in New York State, but not New York City, which had one of the most rigid procedures for licensing its teachers. Although all prospective teachers had held student teaching licenses while doing their student teaching in the city schools, they now had to apply for teacher-in-training licenses. The sole basis for granting such a license was the demonstration of the candidate's merit and fitness to perform the duties of a teacher, which was satisfied in a number of ways. The candidate had to prove she was a citizen of the United States and was at least eighteen years of age. The applicant also had to produce evidence of her moral character, as indicated in her personal life and in the performance of her duties. This was supplied by her training school through a personal evaluation by a dean, and was sent to the Board of Education, along with her academic record and reports of observations of her teaching by supervisors.

She then had to take a highly competitive and difficult written examination to demonstrate general intelligence and correct use of written language skills. If she was applying for a license to teach in the high schools or to teach special subjects, the exam would also test her knowledge of her subject matter or technical skills. An oral examination was required to demonstrate the quality and use of her voice, along with command and correct usage of the language. Part of this oral test was a personal interview, conducted by the Board of Examiners, to assess the applicant's personal appearance, bearing, and manners. Teaching and performance tests were used to ascertain teaching ability. The candidate was judged on the lesson presented, and supervisors were consulted to consider the candidate's capacity for school discipline, her ability to maintain order, to develop character in her students, and to secure the obedience and friendship of her pupils. She was also rated on her personal and social attributes, and on her power to win and hold the cooperation and respect of her teaching colleagues, her supervisors, and the community. The candidate was also required to submit to a meticulous physical examination. If she passed these tests, she was then placed on the eligible list to await an opening in the school system.[1]

The candidate first had to secure an appointment to take the rigorous and demanding written examination required for all people wishing to teach in the city schools. Not only did she have to know how to impart knowledge regarding the three Rs, or, in the case of obtaining a license for the high schools, the specialized subject matter; but she also had to demonstrate an understanding of the theory of education, child psychology, and classroom procedure, and even had to know enough about medicine to prevent the spread of contagious disease in the classroom. After the test, the candidate had to endure a long waiting period, usually six months or longer, before learning whether she had passed, and then had to bide her time until she was called before the Board of Examiners to undergo the oral part of the exam.[2]

As part of the interview test, the candidate was required to answer a questionnaire designed to determine her loyalty. She was asked whether she supported, both in and out of the classroom, the doctrine that political or economic changes are properly effected by orderly constitutional processes, not by violence; and was asked if she agreed that teachers should not use the classroom to disseminate propaganda or advocate such changes by violent means. Although the expression of loyalty had been part of the licensing system since the public school system was formed, it was first put into precise, written form in 1934. The applicant was also obliged to take two loyalty pledges, swearing to uphold both the state and federal constitutions. Compliance with these oaths was then recorded on all teacher personnel cards. The would-be teacher was also asked whether she had ever been defended in a civil or criminal action.[3] If she had been arrested as a student activist, this could bar her from obtaining a license, as it did one candidate apprehended for distributing literature on the Spanish Civil War.

Until the end of the 1930s, The Board of Examiners disclaimed any interest in the social or political views of prospective teachers, within the limits of its questionnaire on Americanism. However, it did receive reports from college officials detailing an applicant's character and loyalty. As the Examiners explained in the *New York Sun*, they took a lively interest in candidates branded radicals or troublemakers, although they insisted that there were no hard and fast rules to determine conduct undesirable in a teacher, and claimed that each case was considered on its own merits. Often they considered youthful radicalism to be part of an excusable maturation process; but other so-called radicals were deemed a potential threat to the school system and were denied licenses, despite the Examiners' contention that no one had been rejected for subversive views since the implementation of its loyalty questionnaire.[4] Although Gertrude Epstein argued that she was refused a license because of her radical sympathies, the Examiners claimed their refusal was due to her activities, which were "unseemly, ill-mannered, offensive, subversive of college discipline, and in general indicative of character and personality traits undesirable in a teacher."[5]

While Mildred Herman did not consider herself a student activist because she had no time for any form of extracurricular participation, she did walk out of classes during the antiwar strikes and signed countless petitions circulated on campus. She remembers being quite nervous, therefore, that the Examiners would ask about her involvement. "I was so paranoid I was afraid they might trick me into mentioning the wrong thing," she stated, especially about her membership in the Young People's Socialist League. To her great relief, their questions were merely perfunctory. It appears that the Examiners interrogated only those applicants whose radicalism was so noted in the evaluations provided by college officials. Fanny Stein, a prominent member of the Young Communist League, breezed through her interview in 1936, finding the Examiners "not probing at all. They never asked anything that would compromise my beliefs—or get me in trouble," she explained. As she had eschewed campus activism, the radical activities she engaged in within the YCL apparently went unnoticed by Hunter College officials. However, had she applied three years later and her membership in the YCL been revealed, she would have been excluded automatically from the city's school system. The Devany Law, passed in the spring of 1939, prohibited the hiring of anyone in a public position, including teachers, who advocated the overthrow of the government by force, which was interpreted by the Board of Education to mean members of the Communist party.[6]

As difficult as the written test was, and as fraught with anxiety as the loyalty segment could be for some applicants, the oral examination was what candidates dreaded most, prompting more requests over the years to the *New York Sun*'s "School Page" regarding clarification of the standards used by the Board of Examiners in speech tests than about any other aspect of the licensing process. A play written, acted, and presented by the Teachers Union Dramatic Group in 1936 illustrated how the speech examination was looked upon as the preeminent stumbling block for license applicants. In the play, a parody of *The Mikado*, the Board of Examiners fired a series of questions at a young woman appearing before them. They asked her whether she was a Communist, a Bolshevik, a Socialist; whether she belonged to a union; believed in inflation and deflation; or drank, smoked, danced, or lisped. After a brief conference, the bewildered candidate was informed that she had passed their test of her "cultural background." She was then handed a sheet and asked to read the sentences contained on it, "with expression." The Examiners' continual criticism of her reading finally provoked her to scream that they were "cuckoo," to which they responded by correcting her pronunciation of the word "cuckoo."[7]

The examination in oral English consisted of a general test and diagnostic tests framed to gauge mental qualities, aside from actual knowledge of facts, and to display various kinds of speech errors. An applicant for License Number One, which entitled the candidate to teach in the elementary schools, was required to sight-read; to read a poem or story of her choice, suitable for pupils in the lower grades; and to pronounce words from a list prepared by the Examiners. In addition, the Examiners interviewed the candidate to test her conversational speech. The examination for a license to teach the upper grades deviated only in that the Examiners selected the excerpt to be read, and the applicant was tested on her ability to summarize the passage and to explain its meaning and implications. To illustrate her contention that the Board always moved in "a mysterious way," a New York City teacher in the novel *Up the Down Staircase* related the problem her friend had with the Examiners during the Depression years. Her friend, a Millay scholar, was failed during her oral test for poor interpretation of a sonnet by Edna St. Vincent Millay. Her appeal was not granted, even after Millay herself wrote a letter to the Examiners explaining that this was exactly what she had meant in her poem.[8]

The candidate was judged on her appearance, neatness, "breeding," energy, and alertness.[9] Her voice was supposed to be audible, pleasant, and well modulated, without being nasal, high pitched, monotonous, strident, or noisy; and ought to inspire confidence, not fear. In other words, a teacher's voice had to be capable of being heard with pleasure, and certainly not with pain. Her speech was to be clearly articulated, grammatical, and free from vulgarisms and foreignisms. Any student whose speech was deemed defective, of poor quality, or having a foreign accent was screened by officials in the teacher-training programs. Sometimes her admission was contingent upon losing her accent.[10] Therefore, it does not seem likely that a license applicant would have reached the point where her speech would be called into question, yet the oral exam was a major component in the licensing test, and a source of great concern to both the Examiners and the candidates.

Always on the defensive about the oral examination, the Examiners insisted that no one was denied a license because of failure to pronounce a few words correctly. Those most commonly mispronounced, according to Dr. Margaret E. Lacey of the Board of Examiners, were: explicable, apparatus, data, sonorous, and leisure. But the Examiners averred that pronouncing "im-PO-tence" instead of "IM-potence" was not as bad as saying "lighten" for "lightening." The list of words to be pronounced consisted of many beginning with the letter "t" or ending in "ng," for many New Yorkers, especially the foreign born or those raised in an immigrant milieu, often substituted a "d" for the "t," or used a soft "g" in pronouncing words ending in "ng." The frequent inclusion of such words on the test was deliberate, because the Examiners believed that such mispronunciations should be a bar to teaching, not only because of the danger of imitation by pupils, but because it considered them cultural defects.[11]

Because educators have emphasized the "culturally symbolic importance of language," proper usage of mainstream English has been the core of the Americanization of immigrants and their children through their education in the public schools.[12] The daughters of immigrants were taught to imitate the speech and gestures of their Irish-American or Yankee teachers in order to be American, but for many, growing up in homes where only Yiddish was spoken, and living in predominantly Jewish neighborhoods, "the lessons didn't take," as Sylvia Schneider explained, especially under tension-producing circumstances such as the oral examination.[13] Irving Howe claims he was deterred from becoming a New York City high school teacher, as his father had hoped he would, because of the "legend" that candidates had to pronounce Long Island without a hard "g," which he believed was "clearly a trick for eliminating Jewish candidates." Convinced that the Examiners were on the alert for people with an "ng problem," Bessie Bernstein admitted that the speech test "scared me to death." However, she did not let it prevent her from successfully pursuing a career as a teacher.[14] The legend about Long Island can hardly have been only a legend, for teachers reported that Long Island was most definitely on their test; and the word lists on past oral exams, periodically published in the "School Page," contain Long Island, along with a great many other "ng" words.

If Howe is mistaken about the Long Island legend, he is correct about the oral examination often being used to keep Jewish candidates from teaching. Even though little overt anti-Semitism was evident in the hiring of teachers in New York's public school system because competitive examinations were the chief mode of selection, a more subtle version of anti-Semitism was manifested in the oral examination.[15] It was perceived as such by Jewish candidates who did not believe the list containing "ng" words was aimed at those with so-called New York accents, which would include applicants of other ethnic groups, but specifically those of Jewish background. Goldie Cohen and Sylvia Schneider pointed out that the oral exam had no mechanisms to screen out candidates with an Irish lilt to their speech, for they both recalled teaching with colleagues who spoke that way.

Perhaps some Jewish women, like Anna Chomsky and Jennie Pickman, were denied licenses for unsatisfactory pronunciation, without any prejudice on the part of the Examiners.[16] Yet others whose cases were reported on the "School Page" indicated that anti-Semitism was a factor in their failing the oral test. Anti-Semitism was not charged by Sarah Rader, a candidate for a high school teacher's license, when she protested the Examiners' refusal to license her on the basis of her supposedly unsatisfactory use of English. Citing Rader's graduation with honors from Hunter College and her Master's degree from Columbia University, Frank P. Graves, commissioner of education for New York State, called her record "enviable throughout," and in a rare instance of the Examiners' decision being overturned, ruled that Rader be licensed.[17] Nor was anti-Semitism suggested by Marion Rosenstein, who failed the oral because of the "ng" defect in her speech. Attempting to correct this shortcoming, she tried to enroll in a speech course at New York University, but was rejected by the professor of the course because he detected no problem, and sent a letter to this effect to the Examiners. Refusing to accept this as sufficient evidence of perfect speech, the Examiners advised Rosenstein to undergo an examination by the director of speech improvement in the public school system. After a severe test that showed not the slightest suspicion of a foreign accent nor any other speech defect, a statement attesting to this was given to the Examiners, who then ordered Rosenstein to take a new test. She passed this one and was then placed on the eligible list although, as Rosenstein explained, she had done nothing to correct the alleged defects that had been held against her in the earlier examination.[18]

The first time the Board of Examiners was charged formally with anti-Jewish bias occurred in 1931. This did not involve a teaching candidate, but was the case of a woman who had been a teacher and assistant principal of a junior high school in the city for twenty years. In the course of her career, Henrietta Miles had taken four tests: for License Number One, a reinstatement test, one for a promotion license in English, and the assistant principal's examination. Each one required an oral test and each one was passed successfully. Yet when Miles underwent the examinations to become a principal, despite having passed the written and interview segments of the test, she was recalled for a second oral test, which she failed on the basis of unsatisfactory oral English. Miles appealed the Examiners' decision to the New York State Department of Education, charging the Examiners with a distinct bias against Jewish candidates, claiming she was asked during her test whether she had been born in the United States, and where she got the name Miles. "The inference is plain," she stated, adding that one Examiner referred to an alleged type of error as "Yiddishism," which Miles found offensive, creating a "clearly defined issue," and produced ratings given by superiors who complimented her on her excellent use of English. However, the Examiners vigorously denied her allegations, claiming she failed because her speech was tinged with a foreign accent, thereby deviating from "standard English," which was attributable to her "foreign extraction and environment." They emphatically insisted that racial or religious prejudice was not involved, and Miles's appeal was turned down, imparting a very clear message to Jewish applicants that the oral examination could be used as a cloak to shield the Examiners' discrimination against prospective Jewish teachers.[19]

If a candidate was not weeded out by the oral examination, she was then obliged to pass a stringent physical examination to determine her physical fitness for teaching. Obvious physical defects such as limb deformities, facial disfigurations, and deafness automatically disqualified one from obtaining a license, nor were such people even permitted to enter the training schools. They were also discouraged from pursuing education courses in the colleges.[20] Clara Saks, who attended the Manhattan Training School, said that her sister had been barred from entrance there because she had a slight limp, having been born with one leg slightly shorter than the other. Even after enrollment, a student could be dropped if a disability occurred; this happened to an aspiring teacher and friend of Yetta Yuretsky, who lost three fingers in an accident during her final year at training school. Although her writing ability was not affected, the school found her disfigured hand offensive, even though it was covered by a glove, and, insisting that it would be both upsetting and distracting to pupils, forced her to quit the training program.

In addition to professional efficiency and lack of obvious deformities, the school system insisted its teachers meet the Board of Education's standards of physical presentability. Candidates could not be too short, too fat, or too thin, or possess other physical characteristics it deemed objectionable. Men had to be at least five feet tall and women, four feet, ten inches. Ruth Gold had hoped to teach high school chemistry, but a Hunter College dean told her that because she was only four feet, nine inches, she would never obtain such a position, but should, instead, teach kindergarten, where the height regulation was often waived. A too-youthful appearance could also be a detriment, and Etta Ginsburg was also prevented from teaching in the high schools because her appearance belied her age. "I always looked like a little kid," she explained, and indeed, in a photograph taken at the age of twenty-three, she resembled a twelve-year-old decked out in her mother's makeup and clothing. Her advisor claimed that the Examiners would be prejudiced by her appearance, which was closer to that of a student than a teacher; nor would they believe she could maintain discipline, so she, too, was slotted to teach kindergarten. Alleged obesity also barred many from teaching, as it did one woman who, at five feet, two inches and 165 pounds, was denied a license.[21] Another, who had been a substitute teacher for three years, applied for a regular license, which was denied because she was considered to be overweight. She appealed this decision, arguing that her weight never affected her attendance or performance, producing a commendation for exceptional service from her supervisor, but to no avail.[22]

Having passed the oral, written, and physical examinations, the applicant was then required to present a classroom demonstration, observed by a member of the Board of Examiners, and to submit her lesson plans to that member for scrutiny. Inspection of a class teaching report from a teacher's file shows that she was marked "very good" in reply to a query as to her teaching ability. The examiner's other comments were: "Easy and sympathetic manner, but firm in discipline—time well employed. Lesson varied. Class given ample opportunity to take part. Insisted upon good manners. Generous in praise." The applicant was also commended for her "excellent, dignified, well poised appearance."[23] Although allowances for nervousness were rather generous, as many reports in teachers' files attest, nevertheless, some did fail. Mildred Herman recalls that her anxiety was alleviated because she was observed by the assistant principal of the school where she had been a student teacher. Others interviewed said they were not watched by a Board of Examiners official, but an administrative official from the school in which the presentation was given, or by people from various departments of the Board of Education, and that the observation could last from about ten minutes to the course of the entire class.

A candidate could pass a difficult written examination, a trying oral and interview test, and a thorough physical exam, together with a searching classroom test, only to find that she had failed because of a biased letter or inconsistent report of a supervisor being placed in her file. In 1935, Laura Liebman was denied a license to teach high school English on the ground that her record was "insufficiently meritorious," despite the fact that tributes to her excellence as a teacher by her superiors were uniform in their high praise. Because Liebman was an active union member, the Examiners sought to keep her from the teaching ranks. Liebman had been the head teacher in a high school remedial reading project under the auspices of the Works Progress Administration, the New Deal agency that, among its numerous other functions, provided teachers for special education programs in schools throughout the country during the Great Depression. To avoid displacing employed teachers, the WPA supplemented, rather than replaced, the existing system of formal education by establishing such programs as remedial education, tutorial services, adult education, preschool education, and summer playgrounds.[24] Liebman served as president of the WPA Teachers Union, and belonged to the Unemployed Teachers Association.[25]

During an appearance before the Board of Examiners to appeal her failure to secure a license, she was asked if she had ever picketed, if she would picket again, and why. Liebman admitted to having done so in the past, and informed the Examiners that she would picket and demonstrate against war, against pay cuts, and for or against any other issue in which she was involved as a trade unionist. One of the Board members leaned forward and inquired archly, "Would you picket me?" This was followed by loud guffaws by his fellow Board members. Liebman said the Examiners told her quite flatly that there was no question about her ability as a teacher, but they were concerned about the extent that her union activities would encroach upon the proper execution of her teaching duties.[26] In a newspaper interview, one of the Examiners stated that the Board was not interested in the political views of candidates, but solely in their conduct and behavior in school, adding that Liebman's license was rejected because she had failed the class teaching test. She had actually received a passing grade in this test by the observer, but this grade was later overruled by the entire Board.[27]

To support their contention of insufficiently meritorious record, the Examiners alleged that Liebman distributed literature without the permission of her principal, and when reprimanded, asserted that she saw no reason for obtaining such permission. They also claimed that she disrupted faculty conferences in her efforts to promote the interests of unemployed teachers, and that she was an "agitator," and "not amenable to school regulations." They further accused her of taking part in a demonstration outside the offices of the Board of Education in which "denunciatory and scurrilous placards" were displayed, and at which Liebman made a "violent and inflammatory" address. Finally, they stated that she had joined some eighty-five summer playground program WPA teachers, who had left their pupils unattended in city parks while they demonstrated in a work stoppage protesting working conditions in 1935. Liebman was the leader of this demonstration, but had since proven to the Board of Education that the children were not unsupervised.[28] After receiving an extremely favorable testimonial to Liebman from the assistant superintendent in charge of remedial reading in the high schools, along with a barrage of telegrams and letters from labor groups and sympathizers in Liebman's behalf, the Examiners agreed to administer another test, and she was finally awarded a license.[29]

Another WPA teacher, Lillian F. Halpin, was also denied a license in 1938, after passing all the tests, because she too, had been part of the WPA protest. Supplied with an attorney from the Teachers Union, Halpin appealed the Examiners' ruling to the state commissioner on education, contesting her rating and alleging that the Examiners had concentrated solely on the fact that she had been a participant in the 1935 work stoppage. Commissioner Graves decided that because she had passed all the tests, the Examiners had erred in their determination, and ordered a license issued to Halpin.[30] Rose Olson was yet another woman victimized by the Board of Examiners because of her union activities. As chairman of the substitutes' committee of the Teachers Union, she frequently criticized the methods and conduct of the Examiners in relation to examination procedures and percentage of failures unrelated to pedagogic standards. Olson was rejected by the Examiners in an oral test for the senior high school English license because of what the Examiners claimed was a "foreign intonation, habitual use of poor English," and similar shortcomings. Her failure was in spite of the fact that she had passed an oral exam for the junior high school license only a short time previously.[31]

The same type of tests mandated for a teacher-in-training license were necessary for any teacher desiring promotion to an administrative position. Anyone aspiring to becoming department chair, assistant principal, or principal, or hoping to attain an even higher supervisory post was required to undergo oral, written, and physical examinations. Here a woman candidate would find herself under the double burden of gender and religious discrimination, for not only were few women to be found as principals in the city's schools, especially at the high school level, the definite purview of men, but in the mid-thirties, there were only five Jewish principals in New York City's fifty-five high schools.[32] In the late thirties, there was a clear preponderance of men in supervisory positions, although the number of women teachers from whom selections could have been made was six times as great as the number of men. In the higher positions, there was but one woman on the Board of Examiners, only one woman on the Board of Education, seven women among fifty-seven secondary school principals, seven women among thirty district superintendents, and twenty women among eighty-two junior high school principals. In other positions of high rank, the percentage of women ranged from 11 to 23 percent, with the lowest proportionate number on the Board of Superintendents. Women predominated only as elementary school principals, where 63 percent were women and 37 percent were men. While the elementary schools had but 1,401 men teachers as against 19,294 women teachers, of the principals in these schools, 102 were men and 343 were women.[33] Of the sixty-one women interviewed for this study, one woman left the classroom to work at curriculum development at the headquarters of the Board of Education; three chaired their departments in the high schools; three became assistant principals of elementary schools; and only one became an elementary school principal. While most admitted they had no desire for supervisory roles, preferring to remain as classroom teachers, several stated they did not believe it was worth having to take all the necessary courses and go through all the tests, as so few women were ever appointed.

Passing the series of tests required for a teaching license in New York City was by no means an easy matter, for only a small majority of candidates were successful. Even during the decade of the 1920s, when the need for teachers in the city schools exceeded the supply, most applicants failed to secure licenses. However, during the 1930s, the number of licenses granted dwindled from only 22 percent of all candidates for License Number One in 1930, to only 11 percent in 1932, to a mere 5 percent in 1934, which was the last time the test for elementary school teachers, once held twice yearly, was given until 1940. Judging from the written examinations printed in the *New York Sun*'s "School Pages," tests did not become more difficult than they already had been, but the wholesale slaughter of candidates occurred from the combination of a vast oversupply of qualified teachers, and the Board of Education's economy program necessitated by the Depression. Because of falling elementary school registers, and a drop in normal teacher turnover, as well as a class consolidation program that excessed over four hundred regularly appointed teachers, the Board of Examiners was charged with severely limiting the number of newly licensed teachers by failing all but a small, predetermined number. Thus, in 1930, they passed 1,423 applicants; but in 1934, only 194.[34]

If the candidate was one of those fortunate enough to be among the highest ranking on the tests, she was granted a license, and then placed on the eligible list to await an appointment. There was a series of lists maintained by the Board of Education: by the type of license and by the year the test was taken. The lists were arranged according to the scores the candidates received on their examinations. Moreover, the lists of licensees were promulgated on the basis of sex, despite the Board of Education's program of equal rights for men and women. This policy permitted married women teachers and made no distinctions between the salaries paid men and women. The practice of separate lists was begun by the Board in 1889 and condoned by it as necessary to maintain a balance between male and female teachers, so as to foster a better educational environment for its pupils. It further claimed that men teachers were needed to uphold discipline in the junior and senior high schools.[35]

Separate lists for men and women worked a definite hardship upon women candidates and resulted in unequal employment for women who were being discriminated against because men on later lists or with lower ratings were frequently given preference over women who had waited as long as ten years, in some cases, for a job. The ratio of sexes on the License Number One list was ten women to one man; yet the appointments were made in the ratio of four women to one man. In 1937, there still remained 250 women on the 1929 women's License Number One list; whereas all the men on that list had been appointed, many within one year. All the men on two later lists, March and July 1930, had been appointed, while none of the women on the same lists had received appointments by 1937. In yet other examples of the unfairness of separate lists, so many more men than women were appointed from the high school French lists that the examination in that subject was open only to men for six years; and in 1937, the German teacher-in-training examination was held for men only.[36]

The question of whether the Board of Education could legally promulgate lists on the basis of sex was taken before the New York Supreme Court in 1938 by Freda P. Lamar, who challenged the Board's right to leave her on a junior high school Spanish list while men with lower ratings had gained appointments. Her petition charged the Board with violating Article Five, Section Six of the New York State Constitution, which required that appointments be made in order of merit and fitness as established by competitive examinations. Denying Lamar's charge of sex discrimination, the Board contended that "a certain number of men as well as women are needed in the school system," and that the decision to appoint men or women to various school posts was little different from the decision that firemen shall be men or nurses women. Lamar's petition was no more successful than was the Monaco Single Eligible List Bill, both of which were defeated in the state capital in 1938.[37] The practice of issuing separate men's and women's eligible lists from the same examination and the barring of women from many tests was roundly condemned by the Teachers Union. In a letter to the Board of Examiners, in which he asked them to support the Monaco Bill, Charles J. Hendley, president of the union, asked for the elimination of a discriminatory system he called "odious" and unfair to both men and women.[38] Repeated efforts to do away with the separate lists that accorded unfair treatment to women by Johanna M. Lindlof, president of the Kindergarten–6B Teachers Association of New York City and the only member of the Board of Education to have been a schoolteacher, were routinely voted down by the Board. Separate lists remained in use in the city, with no direct action being taken, until World War II, when the shortage of men applying for teaching positions rendered the question moot.[39]

However, during the 1930s, the problem was compounded by the increasing number of men who sought the security of a public school teaching position with its steady income and pension rights, as opposed to the uncertainties of a business or professional career during the Depression. Whereas men had constituted only about 12 percent of the city's teaching staff in previous years, by the end of the Depression decade the proportion of men teachers reached an all-time high of just over 16 percent. A similar tendency for men to return to teaching occurred throughout the nation, as their percentage increased from 19 percent to 24.3 percent of the total teachers in the United States during the thirties.[40] In 1938, for the first time in two decades, more men than women applied for high school teaching licenses in New York City; and even in the elementary school lower grades, long regarded as women's almost exclusive field, men constituted 22 percent of the new appointees in 1936, which represented a 17 percent gain from the previous year.[41] Educators were gratified by the inroads men were making into the teaching profession, because it would supposedly "upgrade" the profession, and hoped their numbers would rise until the city's thirty-eight thousand teaching jobs were equally divided between men and women.

Women continued to predominate in the elementary schools, but not in the junior and senior high schools. Most men sought positions in these higher paying high schools, where women were at a distinct disadvantage because of the separate lists. Despite their recognized superiority, both academically and on the licensing scores, women would be passed over by far less qualified men for appointments. Men applicants for teaching licenses tended to come from the lower third of their college graduating classes, while the women came from the upper third, according to a survey conducted by the Board of Examiners. Their conclusions were based on a survey of the scholastic records of some four thousand candidates who applied for teacher-in-training licenses between 1933 and 1937. The study indicates that teaching as a profession was much more attractive to women than to men, despite the growing numbers of men entering the teaching ranks, since it was the first career choice for women, but became the choice for men who were experiencing difficulty in getting jobs elsewhere, as so frequently occurred during the Depression years. As a result, more men failed in the examinations than did women, but because of the separate eligible lists, those men with lower scores than women reaped an unfair share of the teaching appointments.[42]

Even with separate eligible lists for men and women, before 1928, all women on the lists received prompt teaching assignments. From that time on, the annual number of appointments decreased sharply until it stopped completely. Because of budgetary difficulties and the refusal of banks to continue to handle the city's loans unless the budget was reduced drastically, New York instituted a non-appointment policy in February 1932. With the exception of 250 high school appointments in October 1934, it was continued until February 1935, when the commissioner of the New York State Department of Education declared this policy illegal. New York City was almost unique among large cities in its hiring freeze, for despite similar financial difficulties, Newark, Chicago, Boston, and Philadelphia found it possible to continue making apppointments during the Depression. About 1,800 assignments were made in New York City in February 1935; and from September 1936 to September 1939, a total of only about 1,100 appointments were given. Further budget cuts in education resulted in a curtailment of new appointments for the rest of 1939, which meant that the chances for license holders to obtain positions were one in nine for teachers in the elementary and junior high schools; one in seven to teach in the kindergartens; and one in three to teach in the high schools.[43]

This non-appointment policy not only produced severe unemployment for teacher aspirants, but the backlog of lists could have meant the death knell of thousands of hard-won licenses, because ordinarily, the eligible lists lapsed after three years. However, because of persistent campaigns by various teacher organizations, list extensions were secured from the state legislature. For example, the 1934 License Number One list was to remain active until 1942, when it was projected that those on the list could expect appointments.[44] Of course, compulsory military service for men effectively reduced the number of men from both the ranks of the teaching staff and the eligible lists, so that appointments were attained much earlier. Extending the eligibile lists maintained the legal right to appointment for would-be teachers, as well as affording them a modicum of breathing space, and an opportunity to work for final appointments. However, repeated extensions of lists postponed the responsibility of the Board of Education to make appointments, and tended to undermine the morale of those awaiting the fulfillment of the Board's agreement to appoint.

An appointment as a teacher meant an assignment for a probationary term of three years, and if, in that period, service was satisfactory, tenure was then made permanent. A teacher then could not be removed, unless after a formal trial she was found guilty of immorality, conviction of a crime, or deceit in obtaining her license. If, however, her service was unsatisfactory within the probationary period, her license could be re-voked and the teacher dropped from service without the formality of a hearing. In actual practice, few teachers lost their licenses during the three-year period. During the school year of 1927–1928, 2,672 licenses were made permanent, and only five were discontinued. School officials considered the small number of licenses revoked to be a tribute to the efficiency of the Board of Examiners, who were responsible for culling out unsuitable candidates in their series of examinations.[45]

Teaching positions in the city's public school system were so highly prized that a licensing racket arose whereby teaching appointments were promised for a fee. Members of New York City political clubs took money from several women on the pretense that they could hasten their teaching appointments or get them placed on the eligible list. Although it was revealed that these unscrupulous politicians had no influence with the Board of Education, thousands of dollars were paid by scores of women desperate for teaching jobs early in the Depression.[46] Another form of extortion, disclosed by the Board of Education, was that of racketeers who extorted money from teachers, stating that unless payment was forthcoming, they would arrange to cancel these teachers' transfers from one borough to another, or to have the teachers placed in a less desirable school.[47] Rumors of similar fraudulent practices surfaced repeatedly during the Depression, but Board of Education investigations failed to expose further transactions.

While waiting for appointments during the 1930s, many teachers were completely unemployed, or did such work as department store selling, where their training was wasted. Others were able to benefit from the WPA projects in the schools. For some of those interviewed, their only employment came from such federally funded jobs as the summer playground program. Esther Kammen and Belle Aronoff were among those who served as tutors in the highly regarded WPA remedial reading and arithmetic projects. Evelyn Weiss taught history in an evening high school, and Shirley Siegel found a teaching position in a special program for the foreign born. Another project, underwritten by the City Emergency Work and Relief Administration, gave employment to about five hundred unappointed teachers. As one of them, Anne Kuntsler provided special coaching for children deemed slow learners in the city's schools. Thousands of teachers waiting for regular assignments worked as substitute teachers, most on a day-by-day basis. The most fortunate among them were those who obtained a permanent assignment for a term or longer to fill a vacancy created by sabbatical or maternity leave, or a leave of absence.

Substitutes covered the same work as the regularly appointed teacher, but on a per diem basis; they performed the same clerical work, yard duties, and extracurricular activities; and were subjected to the same observation and supervision as the appointed teacher. The use of substitutes represented a substantial savings to the city, not only in the lower salaries paid them; they received no vacation pay, no sick benefits, no pension credit, and acquired no tenure. Teachers in all but name and salary, their plight became the major union battle of the Depression, with the Teachers Union drafting legislation and fighting with the Board of Education to improve their condition.[48] The city's substitute teachers were not alone in their exploited situation, for in Boston, qualified teachers subbed for as long as ten years or more, which is about the same amount of time a New York substitute could wait for an appointment. However, in Boston, the substitutes were laid off every third year for a year, making them ineligible for tenure.[49] New York City's mayor Fiorello

H. LaGuardia complained that because eligible young teachers languished on the lists for so many years, the school system ran the risk of having teachers disappointed, embittered, and unenthusiastic when finally appointed.[50] Yet many of the economy measures which deprived teachers of well-deserved and long-awaited appointments were instituted by the mayor himself, and the substitute situation was not alleviated until the 1940s.

Having successfully negotiated the Board of Education's mine field of examinations, Mildred Herman was placed on an eligible list in 1936. Typifying countless other aspiring teachers, her name lingered on the list for years. From 1935 until late in 1937, when she was hired by the WPA for several months to tutor English in a high school, she was periodically unemployed, finding only occasional office or sales work. She was able to secure a few days' substitute work from time to time during 1938, which she recalled as being especially demoralizing, as she had to report daily to the Board of Education where she was shown a list of substitute positions and then had to approach the school to see if she could fill in for the period. In September 1939, her situation was relieved by her obtaining a permanent substitute position for a woman who was taking the mandatory one-and-a-half-year maternity leave. But it was not until September 1941, more than six years after her college graduation, that Mildred Herman received a permanent position to teach high school English.

CHAPTER

INSIDE THE SCHOOL

*The Shared Experiences
of New York City Teachers*

NEW YORK CITY'S PUBLIC SCHOOL system in the interwar years was not only the largest in the world, it was the most diverse, reflecting the heterogeneity of its population, with pupils from every socioeconomic stratum and every ethnicity. Many of its students were newly arrived immigrants from Southern and Eastern Europe, part of the great influx that had continued unabated until 1924, or were part of the first Puerto Rican migration to New York. During the 1930s, the children of refugees from fascism and Nazism were to be found in the city's schools. Most of these newcomers from all over the world spoke no English, yet they were placed in a school system that had finally become committed to muliculutral education, but had no bilingual education program. Sizable numbers of its pupils came from extremely impoverished, broken, or troubled homes, with their concomitant problems only intensified during the Great Depression. Other children enrolled in school suffered a wide range of physical or learning disabilities.

Yet the city was determined to educate all the children, as it repeatedly stated in its annual reports, entitled *All the Children*. This goal was to be accomplished by maintaining a variety of schools, besides the usual elementary, junior, and senior high schools. There were high schools for academically, musically, and artistically gifted students. There were numerous technical high schools, including one for the aviation trade, one for students pursuing jobs in the textile industry, and even one for future homemakers. There were special schools for disciplinary problems and for slow learners, as well as open-air classes for pupils with respiratory or cardiac problems. Moreover, these schools were located in areas as variegated as that of the five boroughs constituting the New York City school system, and encompassed such disparate locales as the congested Lower East Side, the rural setting of Staten Island, and newly developing neighborhoods like the Flatbush area of Brooklyn.

For all the diversity to be found among the experiences of the thousands of New York City teachers, there were certain conditions that were common to all, wherever and whomever they taught. Each teacher faced classrooms filled with students to whom she was charged with imparting the lessons prescribed by the Board of Education. This was to be done by utilizing the knowledge she had gained while training for teaching, in combination with the Board's approved teaching methods. In addition to her pupils, she would have to interact with their parents and the community, as well as with her colleagues. Each teacher was subjected to rating and supervision from school administrators, especially the school's principal, and was subject to the rules and regulations imposed by the Board of Education.

The teaching staff of New York City's schools during the 1920s and 1930s was not as diversified as that of the student population or the various programs offered by the Board of Education, for it was primarily female, and despite the growing numbers of young Jewish women coming into its ranks, still populated predominantly by women of Irish, German, and Anglo-Saxon Protestant backgrounds. A profile of the typical New York City teacher, provided in 1936 by a city newspaper, noted that the woman teacher, once the traditional "schoolmarm," had been a paragon of "forbiddingly angular rectitudes who carried her classroom didacticism too frequently into the parlor." But the new breed of teacher was now often attacked as a "radical, a mercenary trade unionist," who carried the modern woman's new freedom too frequently into the classroom.[1] The author further stated that the average New York teacher was a woman nearly forty years old, an age both older than the median age of teachers in the rest of the United States and decidedly older than the typical teacher of previous decades who, prior to 1920, usually taught for a period of only five years before leaving. Moreover, the average teacher in this teacher profile was both older and more experienced than the sixty-one former teachers interviewed for this study, most of whom were in their early twenties during the 1930s.[2]

Most New York City elementary school teachers earned more than $3,000 a year and high school teachers, $4,000 during the Depression years. However, these figures do not reflect the fact that during the thirties few people were hired in the city on a regular basis, and most teachers were usually hired as per diem substitutes at a far lower pay scale. The salaries quoted in the teacher profile are for those teachers serving for many years, and do not take into consideration the low starting salaries of $1,608 and $2,040 for lower and upper grade teachers. However, they do compare favorably with teacher salaries in the rest of the country, where the average urban teacher earned $1,900; the average rural teacher, $830; and half of all elementary school teachers were paid under $1,500 per year.[3]

Wherever the teacher was assigned, she faced a certain amount of uniformity in her setting, relating to both school building and to classroom. City schools, whether constructed in the nineteenth or twentieth centuries, were usually four to five stories high, with narrow courts, and insufficient windows. Schools were usually set right on the city's sidewalks, permitting little or no landscaping around the school, and allowing excessive and disruptive street noises into the classrooms. Most schools were situated on sites that usually did not provide adequate outdoor play areas. Despite the greatest school construction program in the city's history, which occurred during the 1920s, it was still necessary to keep in use many schools built in the previous century. Although the New Deal's Public Works Administration was responsible for the construction of fourteen new elementary schools, three junior high schools, seven senior high schools, and eleven additions to existing buildings between 1934 and 1938, lack of funds caused severe neglect of most school buildings, whether old or new.[4]

Whatever the school's condition, it was equipped within the main office with a time clock, which each teacher was required to punch before entering her classroom. Installed sometime during the 1920s, these clocks were a sore point for teachers, increasingly anxious during the interwar years to establish their standing as professionals. "They made us feel that we were nothing but factory hands," Miriam Minkoff asserted.[5] Inside the classroom, the teacher was confronted with nineteenth-century uniformity embedded in the design of classroom space. The classroom plan, standardized in the 1890s and utilized throughout the first half of the twentieth century, consisted of a classroom built around rows of permanent desks facing the teacher and the blackboard. The intent of this classroom organization was to enable the teacher to spot actual or potential disorder, and to provide a setting where students would work in an unvaried and methodical manner on their tasks, but it also discouraged student movement, small group work, or project activities. Each elementary classroom was outfitted with a portrait of George Washington, and every classroom in every school contained an American flag. Classroom photographs used by the Board of Education to illustrate its annual reports are almost identical to those of urban classrooms in other parts of the country during most of the first half of the twentieth century.

Many of the former teachers interviewed mentioned the poor lighting from the windows situated along one wall, which often failed to open properly. Elsie Winkler recalled that whenever it rained it was necessary to keep all the windows tightly shut, no matter the temperature. Former teachers attest to these classrooms lacking proper ventilation, being dusty, overheated, and improperly lighted. Adele Marie Shaw, a New York writer and teacher who depicted the "dark and dismal rooms" of the schools she observed in 1903, provided descriptions that parallel those given by teachers who taught in many of the older and more poorly maintained schools during the 1920s and 1930s.[6]

If the classroom setting was often unpleasant for both pupils and teacher, it usually followed that a total lack of comforts existed for teachers outside their classrooms, especially for those who taught in one of the city's older schools. Well into the 1930s, the Board of Education still maintained schools constructed during the nineteenth century. In the South Bronx, one school erected in 1871 was still in use during the thirties.[7] Luba Levitz taught in a school built in 1885 that had no electricity, only gas lighting, when she taught there in the late twenties. Her school also was without running water, a telephone system, and separate restrooms for the staff. During the twenties, city teachers complained that teacher restrooms were available only in the newer schools, and that they desperately needed more lavatories, lockers, and supply closets for their belongings and supplies. They expressed further dissatisfaction with the janitorial service and the way repairs tended to be made when school was in session, rather than during the summer.[8] The economies forced by the Depression meant that these older schools were never replaced, but fell into further disrepair, with teacher comfort a low priority to a school system grappling with stringent budget deficiencies. Throughout the decade, many schools had neither teacher lunchrooms nor restrooms. Some had no telephones; others had telephones that simply never worked.[9] Recalling the combined restroom-lunchroom in her school, Sylvia Rudzinsky described it as extremely small, furnished with "broken-down furniture," and so poorly lighted teachers were unable to grade papers there, adding that "we froze in winter and sweltered during the warmer months." The problem extended beyond the issue of teacher comfort for most teachers, principals, supervisors, and medical doctors agreed that the most serious deterrent to teachers' health was the lack of adequate restrooms, which caused fatigue and illness.[10]

However, some teachers were fortunate enough to be assigned to one of the city's newer buildings. Frances Klein portrayed the rest room at the school where she taught as "an oasis" because it was "so airy and cozy." Whether serving in a shining new building or an old decrepit one, most teachers tried to improve their surroundings, decorating the rest rooms with colorful prints and plants brought from home. As Leah Boroff explained, "If we had a comfortable room in which to relax, we returned to the classroom refreshed and invigorated." Some were quite inventive in their quest for a cheerful setting, like the teachers at one high school who converted the building's roof into a miniature health resort complete with steamer chairs where they corrected papers in the sunshine during fair weather.[11]

The physical setting was not the only dimension of the teacher's daily world imposed by the Board of Education. The teacher had no autonomy in determining how many pupils she would teach, which ones, or who would remain in her classroom and who would leave. Nor could she decide what subject or grade she would teach. She had no say in how long the teaching day would be, or of what duration a class period would be. She was allowed no input on texts used; on grading methods; on standardized tests; or on the format and content of report cards. Moreover, the Board of Education maintained that it was the teacher's responsibility to "provide motivation of purposeful activities, to foster pupil growth morally, mentally, physically, socially, to guide the pupil's educational, emotional and vocational choices," with the desired end product being "the socially efficient, patriotic citizen."[12] In reality, she found herself within a crowded setting, having to manage from twenty-five to forty or more children of approximately the same age who were involuntarily spending from one to five hours daily in a small space. In her continual exchange with individual students and groups, the teacher was expected to maintain control, to prescribe content, to capture student interest in the subject matter, to vary her levels of instruction according to student differences, and to show tangible evidence that her students had performed satisfactorily. This lack of autonomy differed from that experienced by women in the other semiprofessions who, while similarly constrained, nevertheless had more options regarding job dissatisfaction. Nurses could move from hospital to hospital, or from ward duty to private nursing, for example.[13] However, it was not always easy for a teacher to transfer to a different school, and shifting to a private school or relocating to another city usually were not viable choices.

Despite their having spent the better part of their lives actually observing teachers in the classroom, they found that once in their own classrooms, teachers soon found that their expectations differed from reality. Their training was seldom applicable to the classroom situation. They were surprised by the great demands on their time and energy, as well as by the abundance of clerical tasks. They found it harder than they had imagined to achieve discipline, and in general, teaching was far more difficult than they had ever expected. There were so many aspects of teaching that were not covered by teacher training, as one newly appointed teacher observed in her diary.[14] Reflecting on her first day in school as an elementary school teacher, she began in a state of euphoria, for her life's ambition had been realized. Intending to follow the set of notes she had taken religiously when in school, she soon found a more pragmatic approach was necessary. Many adjustments to previously held notions had to be made. She had never expected an overcrowded classroom without sufficient seating for her pupils. Nor had she anticipated a lack of communication between teacher and pupils; she realized that the children did not always understand her language. When she told the first row of students to hang their coats in the wardrobe, she had to explain who the first row was and had to show them the wardrobe. This new teacher had to learn to paraphrase her meanings into simpler forms, which she felt was "a come-down for a college grad," asking, "Why didn't they tell us these things at college?"[15]

A further impression of the actuality of teaching is provided by a science teacher who outlined a day in a New York City junior high school in 1938.[16] The former teachers interviewed for this study agree that, after making allowances for different grade levels and subjects, the depiction is quite accurate. The day began in the classroom at 8:20 A.M., before her homeroom students assembled. But the teacher arrived at school sometime earlier, as she was required to punch the time clock, and to be in the classroom at least twenty minutes before the arrival of her pupils. Constantly warned by administrators that lack of punctuality was considered a serious fault, all tardiness was duly noted on the teacher's permanent records, the Teacher Personnel Cards on file with the Board of Education.[17] Her time would be spent in seeing that all was in order, for educators took the old saying that "order is the first law of heaven" to be the first law of the classroom. The recurrent theme of Anne M. Limpus's helpful hints for the classroom teacher, which appeared in the "School Page" of the *New York Sun*, is "orderly" organization, through "orderly" arrangement of equipment and routine, which would bring about a smooth, "orderly" routine. The teacher was advised to begin the day by preparing her materials, which consisted of the roll book, with admission envelopes and discharge slips pasted inside the cover; twenty-week plans for all classes; a complete set of syllabi; inventoried textbooks; seating plans; fire drill cards; the daily plan book; paper, chalk, erasers, and other supplies ready; and charts and decorations in place. Closets were supposed to be in "order" and the teacher's desk "a model of orderliness."[18] The science teacher's first class consisted of forty-eight young people who had to seat themselves in the forty seats provided for them. Her first tasks were to collect Red Cross money, call for absence notes, interview a student cited for discipline by other teachers, take attendance, and fill out a truant slip. She also received a notice from the office which reminded her to total her monthly attendance sheet. Encouraged to aid students before school began, she assisted a pupil who came to her for help with her science homework. By nine o'clock, homeroom had ended, and she had to escort the class to the staircase.[19]

Four minutes later, her first class, all fifty of them, straggled in. Scarcely into a demonstration of air pressure, she was interrupted by a messenger from the office, requiring verification of a list. Seven minutes later came another notice from the office: "Do you wish to join the Junior High School Teachers Association? If so, sign your name and give the messenger a dollar." When the class ended and pupils were taken to the stairs, she had to clear the laboratory table, and get out other supplies for a different experiment. Another interruption demanded a report be sent to the office before 1:00 P.M. The next class was given a quiz. Because there were not enough seats for all the students, several had to stand at the side of the room lest two, seated in one seat, copy from one another. For the following class, she had to scurry about, trying to borrow a motion picture projector, for as another junior high school teacher explained, there was but one machine for use in history, hygiene, science, and geography classes. Getting the machine when the teacher wanted it required numerous consultations, compromises, and ultimatums. Because they were dignified members of "an honorable profession," she was proud to add that there was usually only one major fight each week. In the middle of the film, a messenger appeared with a note from the principal, complaining that her class was noisy on the stairway. Then the film showing was interrupted by a fire drill. Finally, the teacher was able to finish showing the movie, but without time for any discussion.[20]

At twelve o'clock, she was entitled to an hour for lunch. But first she had to rewind the film and return the projector, and then complete the attendance sheet, verify the list, and complete the report, which was due in one hour. When this teacher's next class began, she had to speak to her pupils about their conduct on the stairs, and then pass out Red Cross buttons. During the next period, she had to arrange for the entire class to take turns using the three microscopes assigned to her. This routine continued, with the occasional appearance of a messenger from the office bearing more notices or requests. At 2:30 her final class was dismissed. She then had to prepare for the Science Club, which she advised and which met for the next hour. After their dismissal, she began preparing the materials she would need for the next day's science experiments, and then attended an hour-long rehearsal for an assembly program. Teachers were encouraged to give freely of their time in behalf of pupils in after-school activities, as evidence of "the finer aspect" of their professional work, with no financial remuneration. By 4:18 she was en route to the subway, test papers under her arm.[21]

"Was this a typical day?" she asked. Her answer: "It was less strenuous than many other days." While she did not have a free period, she pointed out that she also did not have yard or lunchroom duty that day. Nor did she have to rush to an in-service course after school. No inventories of books or laboratory supplies were due, and she did not have to compute and enter the marks of thirteen classes that week. She also did not have any science notebooks or reports to examine; nor did she have to plan midterm exams or correct them. She did have trouble with several students who were considered behavior problems, but reasoned that it was to be expected because she really did not have time to understand and help them. This typical teaching day during the decade of the thirties differs very little from the depiction by Bel Kaufman in *Up the Down Staircase*, which described New York City teaching conditions two decades later, or that provided by Tracy Kidder, who spent one year with a New England classroom teacher during the 1980s. And Jessica Siegel's daily routine in a New York City high school during the 1987–88 academic year, as re-created by Samuel G. Freedman, is not that dissimilar from what transpired in city schools during the thirties.[22]

The junior high school teacher's typical day can be contrasted with what was purported to be typical school day experiences in New York

City, as provided by the Board of Education in its self-laudatory annual report for 1939–1940. This account featured a typical day at a New York City elementary school, a junior high school, and several senior high schools. Examination of the average school day in the life of "all the children" gave the impression that all the teachers were highly competent and devoted, and used the most progressive teaching methods in their lessons, which were eagerly and willingly absorbed by the students. The young people highlighted in this report all appeared to be model students, extremely bright and perfectly behaved. Every pupil and every teacher photographed in this, and indeed in all Board of Education publications, was white.[23] Moreover, they seemed to be highly motivated, which would belie the fact that most teachers believed the unmotivated student was their teaching problem of the first magnitude. All of the interviewees insisted that their most frequently recurring pedagogical problem was trying to make children want to learn.[24] This very slick public relations publication by the Board made no mention of overcrowded classes, lack of materials and supplies, slow learners, or disciplinary problems. Failing to take notice of the overabundance of clerical tasks with which each teacher labored, as well as the constant stream of interuptions to teaching, it left the reader with the supposition that all classrooms in New York City ran smoothly, without any problems manifested in the school system.[25]

Within the classroom, as well as within the system, teachers technically had no authority regarding the content of their instruction, for they were expected to follow the Board's syllabi and curricular bulletins first set forth in 1896, and altered occasionally through the years, which directed the teachers' attention to what should be taught and why.[26] Influenced by the pedagogical theories of John Dewey, who contended that the child, rather than the subject matter, should be the center of educational effort, as well as by the idea of the child-centered school, classroom teachers urged such modifications in the course of study and changes in their methods of instruction.[27] A decade later the "Activity Program," the first major change in the city's educational program, was undertaken. Based on the activity programs used by progressive school systems throughout the country, the program emphasized creative expression in art, music, and drama. It sought to develop self-control in children as opposed to control imposed by the authority of the teacher. Learning was to be largely experiential, within flexible time schedules. But the keystone of the program was to be the shift in the emphasis in teaching from the subject matter to the child.[28]

This divergence meant a transformation from teacher-centered to student-centered instruction. In an ideal teacher-centered classroom, teacher talk exceeds student talk during instruction. Student talk occurs frequently with the entire class, in a classroom arranged in the traditional manner, with the use of class time determined by the teacher. In short, as Larry Cuban has explained, it means that the teacher controls what is taught, when, and under what conditions within the classroom.[29] Student-centered instruction means students exercise a substantial degree of direction and responsibility for what is taught, how it is learned, and for any movement within the classroom. Cuban identifies the observable measures of this form of instruction as: equal amounts of student–teacher talk; small-group instruction rather than the whole class; student–teacher participation in the selection and organization of subject matter; student determination of the rules of behavior and penalties in the classroom; the availability of varied instructional materials; and classroom furniture that can be rearranged to facilitate small groups.[30]

Although the Board of Education's experiment with progressive education involved less than half the city's students and teachers, nevertheless, over 75,000 students and 2,200 teachers in 69 schools participated in the Activity Program from 1935 to 1941.[31] Yet the program was not really used in the high schools, according to Cuban, who asserts that since high school teachers essentially dispensed knowledge, their subject matter drove "methodology in the classroom. Skills are far more potent organizers of classroom tasks than subject matter." Moreover, external pressures such as college entrance requirements, vocational choices, and prescribed examinations such as the Regents' academic tests and College Board exams precluded instituting the student-centered classroom on the upper-school level. Cuban also believes that the program was absent from the high schools because the staffs were predominantly male, alleging that a child-centered program is more "attuned to women."[32]

Former high school teachers interviewed agree with Cuban's observations regarding the high schools, as do most of those who taught the lower grades. These women insist that it took an inordinate amount of patience as well as a "total re-thinking of one's educational beliefs" in affording some autonomy to the pupils, as Ruth Davidson explained. She added that it was "hard to imagine a man relinquishing power and letting the class have any say in anything." Yet the new program did manage to gain a foothold in at least one city high school, James Monroe High School, built during the thirties. Several former students and teachers have attested to the practice of progressive educational theories and the student-centered classroom in effect there. Kate Simon, who attended this high school, has written of its "unusually permissive curriculum," which required no math, and of its "indulgent English Department," which freed its students from ordinary curriculum rigidities.[33] Historians and social scientists are not in agreement about the extent to which progressive theories penetrated the classroom. In the Midwestern city they dubbed Middletown, Robert Lynd and Helen Merrell Lynd concluded that the attempt to instill progressive instruction was emasculated in favor of administrative efficiency, to the detriment of educational goals.[34]

Besides the move toward the child-centered school during the thirties, a small but distinguished coterie of progressive educational theorists closely allied with John Dewey at Teachers College, including George S. Counts, William H. Kilpatrick, Harold Rugg, and John L. Childs, believed education to be the fundamental method of social progress and reform. Presenting their public expressions in the journal *The Social Frontier*, they asserted that the key to meeting society's changing requirements was to provide teachers and students with a more profound understanding of the pressing issues of the day. Schools were to construct a new social order of greater equity and justice, teachers were to bring about societal change, and schools were to undermine the capitalist system by instilling leftist-liberal ideology in schoolchildren.[35] This reconstruction was "the road not taken," as David Tyack has termed it. It had little impact on urban education, for the call for such a revision, as in the case of more democratic education, demanded, for both teachers and children, considerable autonomy, which both groups commonly lacked. In times of economic hardship, an aura of distrust and intolerance for radical ideas prevailed among educational administrators and school boards, and with the insecurities wrought by the Depression, few classroom teachers could afford to put these theories into practice. New educational programs inevitably brought about even more red tape than had existed previously, along with more administrators and supervisors, more forms, more standardized testing, as well as new jargon. Changes in the hierarchical structure were not forthcoming and, essentially, the old order endured.[36]

Classroom teachers were conversant with pedagogical theories, as the interviewees insist, for they learned them in college and training school, through advanced courses, and through their own reading of educational journals and books. While educational theories did filter down to the classroom teacher, it was another matter to implement them. Even with the supposed support and encouragement of the Board of Education, it was often difficult to impossible to carry out these recommended practices in the classroom, especially during a period of economic retrenchment in funds allocated for education. Classes were usually too large; stationary classroom furniture was not replaced; and the cost of new texts and materials was beyond the budget. Teaching in Depression-era schools was like making "Bricks Without Straw," as an article in *New York Teacher* delineated, whereby an English teacher had no textbooks, a science teacher had to substitute the scientific method of procedure with teaching by "experimentless experiments," and a typewriting teacher taught without typewriters.[37] Despite these major impediments, the former teachers interviewed all insist that some variation, some bits and pieces of the program did permeate the classroom, usually at the teacher's discretion, by her tendency to select those student-centered practices she thought would benefit and not unsettle classroom routines.

In reality, teachers have always employed what has been termed the "hidden pedagogy," whereby teachers interpret the explicit regularities of instruction called for by textbooks and professionals, adapting those teaching methods that help them cope in a practical manner with the demands of an occupational structure over which they have little control. By constructing solutions in the shape of those expedient classroom routines and teaching methods that constitute their hidden pedagogy, teachers formulate survival mechanisms that crosscut the daily pressures of the classroom.[38] Once the classroom door closes, few principals and supervisors see what happens or can ascertain how much teachers use the syllabi, because their self-contained classrooms are "small universes of control with the teacher in command." Administrators refer to the "closed door" that teachers can put between themselves and administrative surveillance. Between the relative indivisibility of the teacher's tasks, and the unrationalized and largely intuitive nature of teaching technique, along with few settled matters regarding pedagogical methods and practices, control is restricted.[39] Teachers have never had much influence over school policy, curriculum, or texts, but, as Tracy Kidder has observed, they have always had a great deal of autonomy inside their classrooms, for the task of universal public education "is still usually conducted by a woman alone in a little room, presiding over a youthful distillate of a town or city." If the teacher is willing, she tries to "cultivate the minds of children both in good and desperate shape." Kidder further noted that some of these children have problems that the teacher has not been trained even to identify, so that she "feels her way. She has no choice."[40]

But most teachers were not alone in feeling their way, for their path was greatly facilitated by older and more proficient teachers, many of whom went out of their way to provide help and guidance for the newer ones, taking on the role of mentors. Each woman interviewed cited the importance of having a more experienced teacher serve as advisor, "showing us the ropes," as Sadie Goldman put it. New teachers relied on veteran teachers to aid them with classroom problems; to serve as confidantes; to explain the often Byzantine workings of the system and share their expertise in dealing with it. Former teachers were careful to explain that the role of mentor was not assumed out of any sense of sisterhood, since almost all teachers, especially on the elementary level, were female, as were most of the principals of these schools. Rather, experienced teachers provided counsel for newer ones from a solidarity born of their common status and workplace. Even when gender might have entered into it, as with higher administrators who invariably were male, it was more a case of the classroom teacher against "the powers-that-be . . . against the system . . . a feeling that we teachers were in this together," as described by Lily Gordon. Each of these teachers went on to serve as counselor and guide to other newly arrived teachers.[41]

According to the interviewees, mentors not only proved especially helpful in guiding new teachers in the ways of coping, with teaching methods and strategies for dealing with supervisors, administrators, pupils, parents, and the community; but they were also invaluable in assisting the newer teachers in the ins and outs of the extra professional work required.[42] The National Education Association estimated that while American teachers averaged nearly thirty hours per week of actual classroom teaching, in addition, elementary school teachers averaged nine hours per week in performing out-of-class work, and secondary school teachers expended an average of ten hours weekly in the same way. This extra professional work included keeping records, filling out reports, and grading papers. It also entailed fulfilling extracurricular assignments, providing voluntary service to student organizations, interviewing pupils, and holding conferences with parents, as well as interminable departmental, faculty, and committee meetings.[43]

By far the most time-consuming chore was clerical duty, which usually consisted of scoring tests and grading papers, along with the ever-escalating amounts of records and reports. During the late 1920s, most teachers throughout the country averaged only 4.9 hours weekly on paperwork—nearly one hour per school day for elementary school teachers and 5.4 hours weekly for high school teachers.[44] But as school routines became standardized, teachers were saddled with overwhelming and burdensome clerical details. Teaching in the largest and most bureau-cratic school system in the nation meant that New York City's teachers were inundated with forms, reports, censuses, surveys, grading, tests, and scores to a far greater degree than teachers elsewhere. The city's Board of Education noted in a 1930s annual report that teachers' clerical work had grown to an "amazing degree," because of the many new reports instituted during the decade, such as age reports, tedious health and record cards, roll books, and reports on numerous subjects, which frequently required extra work over weekends and into the late hours. One teacher asserted that she was doing three times as much clerical work in the thirties as she had done during the twenties, adding that her clerical work had also became much more detailed and complicated.[45]

Because of severe budgetary cuts during the Depression, the city's schools had a chronic shortage of secretarial and clerical workers, which further augmented teachers' tasks. In addition to their usual paperwork, they were now responsible for all attendance records, telephone calls to the homes of absentees, and for calling parents to discuss pupils' behavior, academic progress, truancy, and health problems.[46] Moreover, they were expected to be scrupulous in their record keeping, and were warned that accuracy was imperative, as they were considered the official records of the school system. Since they could be required as evidence in court, teachers had to be careful to date and to sign all reports.[47] Teachers also found themselves having to supervise the lunchrooms, late rooms, and school yards; distribute and mend books; hand-letter diplomas; and serve on the sanitary squad.[48]

Frequently they were called upon to cover the class of an absent teacher or to take an absentee's class into their own because the school was unwilling to spend the money to hire a substitute teacher.[49] Perma-nent substitutes, so prevalent in New York City's Depression-era schools because their salaries were so much lower than those of the tenured faculty, were often exploited and required to perform the despised cleri-cal work. Although resentful at having to type and run the mimeograph machine while serving as a permanent substitute, Charlotte Printz com-plied, but was so deeply humiliated when expected to scrub floors that after a futile protest to the principal, she felt she had no recourse but to quit her much-needed job. Enormously expanding pupil enrollment, to-gether with the greater emphasis educators placed on both individual pupil guidance and on the teacher's cooperation with pupils' homes, communities, and social agencies; as well as the growing demands for in-service professional study and for teacher participation in professional educational associations, all contributed to the tremendous increase in the professional load of classroom teachers.[50]

Yet the chief complaint among teachers, whether in New York City or anywhere else in the United States during both decades, was the constant interruption to their teaching that came from various sources, ranging from official requests for statistical data for the Board of Education to communications from principals seeking information on routine matters. Essay competitions and other contests outside the regular curriculum were frequent and time-consuming. There were also a spate of circulars detailing such matters as special drives for raising money, and special tributes, such as those for veterans of foreign wars or a notable the Board of Education wished to honor. There always seemed to be a day or week or even month earmarked for the commemoration of someone or something, replete with details for how the teacher was to engage pupil participation in "exalting the apple or the nation's founding fathers," as Rachel Berkowitz put it.[51] Principals were cited as the major offenders, although teachers also indicted the offices of the superintendents and especially the Board of Education, notorious for its last-minute requests, which usually entailed copious paperwork.[52] The average classroom lost thirty-five minutes per week because of these interruptions, which usually numbered about four per day, according to a survey of classroom distractions conducted in thirty-seven schools by the Teacher's Interest Committee of the Brooklyn Teachers Association in 1936.[53] Interference with classroom routine was not unique to New York's teachers, but existed as well in Middletown, where teachers were also irritated by the endless clutter of administrative reports.[54]

Along with the extra demands placed on teachers because of the Depression, New York City's teachers were also forced to take two pay reductions because of the city's budget crisis. In 1933 their salaries were reduced on a sliding scale, averaging 6.5 percent. The following year a further reduction, amounting to 10 percent of the salary budget, was imposed. Also, in 1934, teachers were required to accept a payless furlough of one month's work without pay. Their regular salary schedules were not restored until 1937.[55] Because of the budgetary cutbacks caused by the Depression, chronic shortages of materials and equipment were endemic in American school systems throughout the decade. There were not enough texts to go around, or they were severely damaged or out of date, and schools lacked funds to purchase magazines, maps, and dictionaries. The lack of supplies was felt most strongly in science, home economics, and the technical and fine arts.[56] But shortages were to be found in all classrooms. Faye Bronstein, a high school English teacher, remembered not being able to require that classwork be done in pen and ink because the school could not provide them and many of her students could not afford to buy these materials. Teachers dipped into their own pockets to provide such necessities as paper, thumb tacks, crayons, and paste.[57]

A dearth of supplies was but one manifestation of the devastating effect of the Depression on public education. The elimination of teaching positions and of such programs as evening and summer schools, athletic centers, and music instruction coincided with an extremely high increase in high school attendance.[58] The amended Compulsory Education Law of 1936 raised the age at which children could leave school to join the work force from fourteen to sixteen. This requirement, along with parents' growing conviction that a high school diploma would enable their children to obtain a better job, kept students in school longer.[59] However, what was undoubtedly the strongest factor in this rise in high school attendance can be attributed to the scarcity of jobs available to young people during the economic turmoil.[60]

For the classroom teachers, the economic crisis made its greatest impact on their increased professional load, as measured by pupil–teacher ratio, class size, length of the school term, and the number of hours required for instruction and for out-of-class activities. However, it does not indicate the total professional load, for there were other factors adding to the teacher's load, including: the length of class periods, the number of those periods for which preparation differed from that of any other period, the nature of the subject taught, and the degree of responsibility for out-of-class activities, irrespective of the amount of time required.

The most radical and most prevalent problem for the teacher was the enormously increased daily pupil load, the result of efforts to keep school expenditures low. While the average elementary class in the United States had 34 pupils, New York City classrooms were far more crowded. In 1934, 72 percent of New York City's classes had more than 35 pupils; 42 percent of its classes had more than 40 pupils; and 13 percent had more than 45 pupils. A small percentage of classes actually had more than 50 pupils enrolled.[61] One New York teacher had taught four classes averaging 25 pupils and supervised a homeroom of 25 in 1925. In 1933, she had to teach five classes averaging 34, and had at least 35 pupils in her homeroom. This increase of 80 more students per day meant adjusting to the unalterable physical conditions of a schoolroom designed for 25. Somehow she had to devise a way to place 36 children, and provide ufficient light, fresh air, blackboard space, and elbow room for all. For his English teacher, the problem of aisles loomed as large in her life as he problem of teaching correct grammar.[62]

As the exigencies of the Depression expanded the task of public education, this added burden, as well, fell on the shoulders of the classroom eacher. Because of the Depression many high school students attended chool who were neither academically nor temperamentally suited for the classroom. These students, designated by the Board of Education as "maladjusted," further added to the classroom teachers' problems, which ran he gamut from trying to motivate them scholastically, to having to provide special tutoring, to dealing with discipline problems.[63] However, it vas not only the older child who was classified as maladjusted. The ill effects of the Depression were to be found in the psyches of children of ll ages. Children, as well as adults, experienced what a physician has ermed "epidemic demoralization" to describe "the sense of despair and uncertainty which descends on those who must live by the charity of others," for, with parents unemployed and constantly worried about paying their bills, many children had lost the sense of security that is the essential need of every child.[64]

Prior to the Depression, teaching in New York City high schools had been relatively "simple and tranquil" in comparison to the experience of many high school teachers during the thirties. During the 1920s, most students attended school because they wanted to be there; therefore high school teachers tended to teach only the most capable who were headed for a definite goal, and who fit into the curriculum or left. No attempt was made then to differentiate and adapt teaching methods to meet individual differences, and teachers had sufficient time and energy to concentrate on their classroom teaching. In the 1930s, sweeping changes in the outside world were reflected in their larger, more heterogeneous student body, for the economic strains of the Depression caused emotional disturbances, maladjustments, and guidance problems with pupils. In addition, the center of teaching shifted from subject matter to a consideration of the nature and needs of the human elements involved in real education. Teachers also had an expanded and more varied curriculum to over. All these changes led to the increase in the number and complexity of teachers' responsibilities. Describing the differences in teaching between the two decades, an elementary school teacher stated that it had been easier in the past. The three Rs were the foundation of the curriculum. All lessons were based on the syllabi, and information was obtained from texts. Much stress was placed on drill and review and subject matter, with memorization emphasized, and frequent testing. The class, rather than the child, was the unit of instruction, and discipline was strict. By the 1930s, teaching was supposed to be based on the child's needs, and one lesson was supposed to dovetail into another. While this ideal was not always realized, teachers were under contraints to make every attempt to meet it. They were always on the alert for new materials and new methods, spending endless time searching for them.[65]

Even if a teacher did hold sway behind the closed doors of her class-room, employing whatever teaching methods worked best for her, every New York City teacher, regardless of where or whom she taught, or whatever the duration of her service, was subjected to supervision and rating by administrative superiors. This was done through the mechanism of the teacher rating sheet which, for most of the 1920s and 1930s, consisted of a long list of specific items upon which principals had to give judgments semiannually.[66] In addition to noting latenesses and ab-sences, a partial list of categories for ratings included the teacher's "per-sonal tidiness," her use of voice and English, her accuracy in keeping records, her ability to cooperate with other teachers, her "power to inter-est," and her skills in presentation, questioning, drill, and classroom control.[67] Although the majority of teachers reported that relations with administrators and supervisory officers were on the whole cooperative, democratic in spirit, and harmonious, ratings of the personal traits of teachers were a source of bitter disputes between teachers and supervi-sors, and the most frequent cause of appeals. Associate Superintendent Jacob Greenberg admitted the impossibility of adequately rating a teacher's personality, finding no relation between a "delightful personality and success in teaching."[68] If teacher ratings were a necessary evil in a large school system, teachers believed they should be reduced to the most basic terms, a mere "satisfactory" or "unsatisfactory" notation with an accompanying explanation in the case of the latter.[69]

Supervisors joined with classroom teachers in urging simplification of the rating system. In 1936, the Teachers Union charged that the rating system had "degenerated to a system of discipline and regimentation that promotes servile obedience and conformity rather than teacher initia-tive." It suggested greater cooperation between supervisor and teacher in an organized effort to improve teaching standards. Following a two-year study of the twin problems of rating and "creative supervision" by school authorities, the Board of Education abandoned the old system of rating teachers for excellence in specific items. In September 1938 it introduced a new one in which teachers were rated as either "satisfactory" or "unsatisfactory," and in which detailed explanations were permitted only in the event of an "unsatisfactory" rating.[70]

Although the Board of Education's stated purpose in supervising its teachers was to improve classroom instruction, supervisors were also required to judge the teacher's performance. However, these two intentions proved dissonant whenever a supervisor entered the classroom. Teachers who participated in a National Education Association symposium on supervision and the classroom teacher admitted that they had no marked disinclination toward supervision, but urged that it be helpful and constructive, which it often was not. They claimed that too many supervisors offered destructive criticism only, calling for mutual appreciation of problems and duties, with respect for each other's viewpoints.[71] Ida Levinson believed that while many supervisors "enjoyed wielding their power over teachers," most simply had been out of contact with actual classroom conditions for so long that they failed to understand the teacher's perspective. Too often, Rose Jacobi stated, supervisors left teachers humiliated and discouraged, feeling that there was nothing worthwhile in their teaching. Those being supervised were most grateful for a modicum of encouragement from school authorities. It was not the teaching load that fatigued one teacher, but the prevailing atmosphere of restraint. "Teaching becomes a burden when work is not appreciated and when we are treated as inferiors by administrators," she explained.[72]

Supervision and rating in New York City's schools was administrated and carried out by the school principal who, as the chief officer of the school, exercised a great deal of power over the life of a teacher. Besides being the one who decided what classes and school assignments a teacher should get, the principal could harass the teacher by unfriendly supervision or by hindering promotions. The principal could cause a teacher to be transferred to a less desirable school, often a distance from the teacher's home. But the principal's greatest power lay in rating the teacher's classroom performance. Because an unsatisfactory rating could ultimately result in a teacher's dismissal, the principal became the most important reason for teacher conformity.[73]

Teachers, administrators, and union officials were all cognizant of how the rating system produced compliance from the teaching staff. Dr. Abraham Lefkowitz, the first legislative representative of the Teachers Union and a retired principal, charged that principals regarded themselves "as bosses, the schools as their enterprise," and the rating system "not as a source of inspiration, but as a club or six-shooter pointed at the head too often of the most inspiring and stimulating teachers."[74] A

111

Brooklyn high school teacher concurred, stating that colleagues' fear of the principal caused them to cater to him to avoid his enmity. This culminated in teachers so timid that they had "no opinion of their own."[75] The prevailing philosophy among teachers was that heads of schools tended to be tyrannical, thereby necessitating a certain degree of conformity on the teacher's part in order to get on better with principals. Describing how supervisory practices affected the freedom of New York City's teachers, District Superintendent of High Schools John L. Tildsley observed that discipline or even the threat of discipline was not needed when teachers generally realized that nonconformity injured them and that "conventional ideals and implicit obedience are the means to professional advancement."[76]

Considering their immigrant backgrounds and political beliefs, many of the young women who became teachers during the interwar years did not conform to "conventional ideals," nor would they subscribe to "implicit obedience." Yet in an equally important aspect, they served as a novelty in urban education by representing a new and unique contingent in the ethnic makeup of city teachers. Having Jewish teachers must have had some effect on their pupils, especially the Jewish ones. But their impact is difficult to measure. Parents' evaluation of their children's teachers sheds very little light, for all parents' appraisals are usually based on what their children's experience was during schooling and how their children felt about teachers. This can often be too subjective. There was a segment of the population who believed the schools were doing what it wanted them to do: the schools were preparing children for entrance into institutions of higher learning or for jobs in a market where they could expect fair competition, thus insuring a high degree of satisfaction with the teaching staff. Certainly, perceptions of the effect these Jewish teachers had on the children of other ethnic groups, such as the African-American community, calls for an in-depth study of its own. However, one can speculate about how Jewish parents felt about the Jewish teachers who taught their children. Since many of these Jewish parents were of the immigrant or second generation, they undoubtedly placed a great deal of importance on the role of education, and held teachers in high regard. A sizable number of their children were doing well at school, aiming either for civil service jobs or for further education. For many, their children's academic and vocational success, the close rapport established between the young Jewish teachers and their pupils, along with the close relations many of the parents had achieved with these teachers would all contribute to a very positive assessment of these teachers' impact.[77]

Nor is it very practical to ask students to assess their teachers, for it was always the favorite teacher, the one who inspired and encouraged, who was remembered, along with the least-liked teacher, the one with the disagreeable personality, or the one who taught the subject that gave one so much trouble. Usually, when asked to evaluate a teacher, most adults and children tend to focus on the qualities of a teacher's personality, rather than on her merits specifically as a teacher.[78] As a general rule, those who did well in school had favorable impressions of their teachers, while those who were less successful had negative memories. Sometimes former students have shown their appreciation for teachers by remaining in touch through the years or through tributes and testimonials to former teachers. Several of the women interviewed produced letters and cards from their former pupils, thanking them for their inspiration and encouragement. Thirty-six years after they left Lillian H. Rosenberg's classroom, a group of her former pupils gathered to honor her, stating that she "made things come alive" in her classroom. One of the organizers of this reunion stated that Rosenberg inspired her to become a teacher.[79] A number of others have been fêted by their students and presented with such tokens of esteem as the small gold ruler worn on Myn Silverman's bracelet, and the crystal apple proudly displayed by Fanny Stein.

Writers who attended city schools during the interwar years sometimes provide assessments worth considering, such as Kate Simon, who wrote of her "indulgent" teachers who loved all their "promising children with a springtime faith." Or Irving Howe, who has written of public schools "that really were schools," and "devoted teachers whose faces lived in memory longer than their names," who worked hard trying to drive "some knowledge, even a few ideas into our heads." Howe has recalled that it was the high schools that gave New York "a good part of whatever morale it managed to keep during the Depression years," and that "there was pleasure in the work of learning." He believes there was an air of "intellectual openness and eagerness in school, a feeling that students were being led, gently or roughly, into experiences somehow good for us, though it was only natural that as young human beasts we should resist them." Alfred Kazin provides a dissenting opinion, allowing that while teachers were to be respected "like gods," nevertheless, all week he "lived for the blessed sound of the dismissal gong at three o'clock on Friday."[80]

113

The primary mode for assessing the results of teachers' instruction employed by educational administrators was that of testing. Citywide tests at various grade levels which were conducted with increasing frequency during the twenties and thirties indicated that the achievement levels of city children as a whole were consistently above national norms. However, there is no reason to believe that these tests are any more conclusive evidence of achievement or lack of it than is most such testing of schoolchildren, especially when there is the attempt to compare different schools or school districts. Taking all factors into consideration, such tests can be interpreted in such a variety of ways, usually to support whatever contention it is that the tester wishes to prove.[81]

Although most revisionist historians of public education in the United States are critical of almost all its aspects throughout its history, others believe the Depression years were special. They subscribe to the belief, held by almost all of the former teachers interviewed, that despite all the hardships brought by hard times during the thirties, the period was the golden age of New York City's public schools. Selma Berrol, who acknowledged the "pool of extremely well-qualified teachers," has also termed the decade the city's "Golden Age" of education. Echoing this sentiment is historian Sol Cohen, who has written, "As any adult New Yorker who has been a student or teacher in the city public school knows, the city's teachers . . . look back to the 1930's as their Golden Age." To Diane Ravitch, great advances were made in public school education in the interwar years, which she attributes to the incorporation of the principles of social work and psychology into the school system, through the combined efforts of the Board of Education and the Progressive Education Association. She also believes the Depression was responsible for much in the way of improvement, such as the large-scale federal assistance that provided new schools and additional personnel. Ravitch cites "the atmosphere of experimentation, stimulated by the activity program," which excited the admiration of other educators, and notes that in this period, the city's elite high schools were recognized as the best in the nation. And she praises its teachers who were of "unusual caliber," and who in better times might have become college professors.[82]

Whether the 1930s was a golden age for New York City teachers, students, or education in general may be impossible to determine. Whether the young Jewish women who entered its public school system in ever-increasing numbers during the interwar years were better teachers than their predecessors or those who followed them cannot be measured either. Most likely, numbered among their ranks was the entire spectrum of teachers, from the good and the bad to the merely indifferent. Whatever their general impact on the classroom, their growing presence brought a new dimension to the classroom, based solely on their ethnicity. For, as Deborah Dash Moore has observed: "Immigrants and their children learned a version of American life under the tutelage of teachers named Jones, O'Reilly, Smith, and Kennedy; the second generation and their children would also know teachers named Golden, Kaplan, and Kaminsky."[83]

CHAPTER

7

A VERY LONG DAY

Teachers' Duties after the Dismissal Bell

"BEING A TEACHER CERTAINLY was not a case of just going to school at nine o'clock in the morning and leaving at three in the afternoon," explained Bessie Bernstein, who taught in New York City's public schools from 1928 until her retirement in 1960. "Nor was it a case of merely hearing the day's lesson and assigning the next day's," she added, "but it involved hours and hours of extra work, all of it done outside the school and outside school hours." She was referring to the time teachers had to expend in completing work that could not be finished during school hours, as well as preparation time, professional study, and membership in teachers' organizations, unions, and community groups. "We did not live and breathe teaching," according to Pearl Kagan, another former teacher, for these were young women who were intent upon their private concerns. "However, teaching did seem to be in our thoughts most of the time. I don't know of another profession where you had to be so involved outside the workplace." One could always spot a teacher's home, Kagan alleged, "because there was always a place, usually the dining-room table, just strewn with papers waiting to be corrected." Undoubtedly, most teachers laughed sardonically at the "practical" suggestions for teachers, obviously prepared by some unknown administrators. Teachers were admonished not to carry their work around with them, but to "Lock your cares in your desk when the day's work is done."[1]

With the continual erosion of teachers' free periods over the years because of the increased demand of clerical work, and such extra tasks as lunchroom and yard duties, large percentages of teachers had no time to devote to class preparation or the correction of students' work during the school day. Thus, they found themselves joining their pupils in doing homework during their evenings and weekends.[2] One teacher estimated that it took 525 minutes to read 175 themes, checking for spelling, sentence construction, punctuation, the ability to follow the assignment adequately, and originality. An English teacher complained that the work load was so heavy she could not do her job well. With so many papers to correct, she could only assign compositions every two weeks, rather than weekly.[3] Besides having to do homework, teachers were encouraged and often required to have close contact with parents. Sometimes this could be accomplished by after-school visits held in the school, but frequently, especially when there were problems with the students, visits had to be made to the students' homes during evenings or weekends.[4] In addition, teachers felt it important to remain abreast of the times in their reading of subject matter and educational material. To keep in sympathetic touch with students' minds, an English teacher believed she ought to read the books they delighted in, as well as the books on education and psychology she considered necessary professionally. To keep from "senile decay and to retain remnants of faculty to appreciate the aesthetic," she needed to wedge in reading worthwhile new books and the occasional classic, leaving her without much time for repairing her clothes, meeting with friends, attending theaters or museums, and so forth.[5]

Further inroads on a teacher's time were caused by the periodic broadening of the objectives of education which implied additional services for pupils. The health of the city's schoolchildren became an added imperative for schoolteachers during the 1920s after a study revealed malnutrition among the city's schoolchildren. Thus, the schools embarked on a health campaign through which the curriculum was to teach nutrition and first aid.[6] The food education segment of the program included dispensing low-cost milk to elementary schoolchildren, as well as the establishment of a free lunch program for the needy in all the city's schools. By 1925, the program had expanded so that free and nutritious lunches were served in twenty-eight elementary schools in the poorer sections of the city.[7] In conjunction with assuming a considerable share of the responsibility for the health of their pupils, teachers now had the supplementary paperwork necessary for the collection of milk money and from the complicated health records, which rarely could be completed during school hours.[8]

Although the public schools' food and health programs, combined with the rise in the standard of living during the 1920s, helped bring about marked improvement in the physical condition of the city's children, a serious relapse occurred with the onset of the Great Depression. During the early thirties, the city's health department reported an increase in malnutrition among schoolchildren, from about 13 percent in 1929 to more than 20 percent by 1932.[9] In response to this threat to their students' well-being caused by the economic emergency, New York's teachers contributed 1 percent, then 3 percent, and finally 5 percent of their salaries to the School Relief Fund to assist pupils and their families.[10] Along with providing rations of milk to children at intervals during the school day, the fund distributed eyeglasses, shoes, clothing, carfare, and incidentals, and maintained a hot lunch program that provided what was often the only nourishing meal a child received.[11] With a total personal contribution by teachers estimated to have been between 5.5 and 6 million dollars, the fund served lunches to more than 62,000 children. In the Bronx alone, one out of six schoolchildren was a recipient of the lunch program.[12] Because their pupils' health was of paramount importance to them, teachers were willing to put aside their strong antipathy to extra administrative work and to the stacks of paperwork engendered by such projects. Moreover, they not only did the necessary clerical work, along with contributing money both privately and through the fund; they also gave freely of their personal time when students' health might be at risk. For example, during a holiday week, teachers reported to the schools, taking turns helping to serve breakfast and lunch, to make certain that the thousands of children being fed at the schools would not be deprived of meals.[13]

As one of twenty-five teachers selected by the superintendent of schools for special commendation, Martha Aaron was one of those who volunteered for lunchroom duty during school holidays. During the school term, she supervised the free lunch service, where she could be found coaxing and cajoling children to eat some of the more unfamiliar items on the menu. Believing that her responsibility did not end with "the mental nourishment of the classroom," she was cited for tactfully inviting undernourished children to early breakfasts in her classroom and for taking small groups out for refreshments in the afternoon. It was reported that no child in her class went without food, shoes, or clothing because she often gave money to her pupils' families, paid their bills, and acted as advisor in their difficulties.[14]

During the interwar years, New York City teachers had to assume many of the functions of understaffed and underbudgeted social agencies. Most teachers were unhappy, as one teacher stated, in having to act as "policemen, psychologists, doctors, and clerks."[15] Yet it was in these roles that they perhaps played their finest part, for most teachers seemed to have given of themselves and their own depleted funds with genuine and heartfelt generosity. Of the twenty-five teachers selected for recognition by the school system during the thirties, almost every biography provided by the Board of Education mentioned the time and money these teachers expended to help feed and clothe children from underprivileged homes. Moreover, they provided the services of social agencies in guiding and advising both children and their families. Their generosity and selflessness appear to have been representative of a large segment of the teaching population during the Depression decade, according to interviewees, who cited many examples of teachers extending help to the needy. The "School Pages" of the *New York Sun* and the publications of the two teachers' unions also contain many such examples of charitable work done by teachers during the thirties, as do the testimonials produced for those teachers who lost their jobs during the McCarthy era.[16]

The city's teachers appeared to have heeded the request of Superintendent of Schools Harold G. Campbell, who, in a 1934 address, urged teachers to change their attitude from "Live and let live," to "Live and help live."[17] Paying further tribute to the city's teachers, the Board of Education recognized that they made "one of the finest contributions in the history of the school system" in the many things they did, "aside from giving monetary assistance, to help the youngsters take an objective view of the economic misfortunes of their parents and make normal adjustment to their circumstances." The Board added that teachers "proved their integrity and devotion to their profession during these trying years."[18] In several instances, teachers went above and beyond these measures, going so far as to obtain custody of extremely needy children so they could be raised in the teachers' homes. Minna Wiseman arranged for a motherless child whose father was being sent to prison to live with her while the child's father was incarcerated; and Rose Litvinoff adopted an orphaned pupil, rather than see her sent to an institution.[19]

A considerable amount of time was given, as well, to advising and guiding students in their extracurricular pursuits. Since the 1920s, the schools had placed great emphasis on the extracurricular activities of young people. Equal opportunity for student participation in school organizations was meant to express and uphold educators' commitment to "equalization of opportunity," providing a "natural matrix" for democratic ideals and objectives.[20] Because extracurricular activities play a vital role in modern educational objectives, teachers have borne their share of the burden with no reduction of teaching hours or other duties. Among the nation's high school teachers alone, approximately 76 percent participated in the guidance and direction of extracurricular activities.[21] The National Education Association found that extracurricular work of a voluntary nature accounted for the greatest amount of school time expended by teachers outside the classroom, except for clerical work, during the 1930s.[22] In New York City, all its public schools, whether on the elementary, junior, or senior high school level, presented assemblies for the student body at least once a week. Weekly assemblies at a Brooklyn high school during one term included talks by personnel directors from businesses, drama, music, and a presentation by the Red Cross. The school band and choral group took part in most of the programs, all of which were organized and overseen by the teaching staff.[23] "Beyond the Classroom," a 1930 Board of Education survey of junior and senior high school extracurricular activities, listed nearly two hundred different activities in these schools, without mentioning the proliferation of such groups within the elementary schools. Among those included in their study were student government organizations, debating clubs, athletic groups, dramatic societies, orchestras, honor societies, language and science clubs, and student newspapers and magazines that more than ten thousand teachers supervised and advised.[24]

To show that the teachers in the New York City public schools did far more for their pupils than merely teach the syllabi of their respective grades, Superintendent of Schools Campbell devoted the contents of his 1938–39 annual report to the city's teachers. Professional biographies of twenty-five men and women selected by Campbell as "typical of the teaching staff" were presented in his report.[25] The "typical" services described range from individual coaching of slow pupils after regular school hours to advising a wide array of pupil interest clubs and organizations to social services for boys and girls from poverty-stricken homes. One teacher worked after school hours providing special instruction to youths enrolled in an art club. Another teacher conducted a club whose members visited museums, newspaper offices, and the planetarium. A third, a biology teacher for blind children, organized a science club and arranged for these pupils to compete in city science fairs. Virtually all twenty-five teachers cited as model teachers in the report were engaged in some form of extracurricular activity over and above the regular duties of the classroom.[26] Moreover, each of the women interviewed was involved in extracurricular activities in varying degrees during most of her teaching career. These women adamantly dispute the contention of sociologists like Dan Lortie that few married women teachers, or even most married or single teachers in their twenties, spent much time outside the classroom on school activities.[27] They insist that they devoted a considerable amount of time and energy participating in extracurricular activities throughout their professional years.

Besides supplementing the regular instructional program, by sharing common interests through extracurricular activities, teachers and pupils often forged close bonds. In but one of many such examples, Ruth Davidson's love of the theater prompted her involvement in obtaining Broadway tickets at greatly reduced prices for her high school pupils. "I really came to know my pupils, and they, me, when we spent time together attending plays and later, discussing them," she explained, adding that these young people kept in touch with her in later years, recommending plays and sometimes inviting her along.[28] The extracurricular activities also served as an instrument for dispelling those stereotypes that served to keep teachers and students apart. After playing Ping-Pong or acting in a comedy skit in a faculty-student assembly with a young teacher scarcely out of college, students had difficulty seeing the teacher as an ogre or as a straitlaced old maid. Through the close personal ties which resulted from their participation in extracurricular activities, teacher–pupil relations "underwent subtle transformations," as one sociologist has noted, for with the influx of second-generation Jewish teachers into the school system during the interwar years, the ethnic antagonisms experienced by the second generation during their school years in the city were dissipated.[29] In New York City, where four-fifths of all high school students took part in some club or activity, those most likely to participate were women, and those most active were Jewish. These female Jewish students now had teachers who were young Jewish women with whom they could establish a rapport.[30] This rapport was most often reached through the time the two groups spent in extracurricular activities of a mutual interest.

Rapprochement with students, both Jewish and non-Jewish, frequently extended beyond the schools and into the teachers' own homes. Rachel Kalman recalled that as a young, unmarried teacher she coached a high school debating team whose members often visited the apartment she shared with her mother and aunt. "They knew we were always glad to have them. My mother loved cooking for them, so they brought us their appetites, their company, and their problems," she said, explaining that they obviously felt they could "relate to me because I was only a few years older." Ida Rubinstein, who lived "within a stone's throw from the school where I taught," had pupils "popping in and out of my home." Ostensibly visiting her for extra help in their schoolwork, they also looked to her for extra help with their personal problems, she stated, adding that she became their "mother confessor." Other teachers held parties at their homes or took their pupils on Saturday morning excursions or held "open houses" in their homes for boys and girls who wished to borrow a book or to drop in to talk over their individual problems. One teacher held Saturday evening discussion groups at her home, open to her high school pupils and to former pupils. These gatherings were so popular with young people that they attended regardless of the weather, discussing such topics as current affairs, race relations, books, plays, movies, and jobs, always concluding the evenings with music and refreshments.[31]

Cordial relations between teachers and pupils from all ethnic backgrounds helped to establish empathy between teachers and parents, as well. During the 1920s, a barrier existed between parents and teachers, as they rarely came into contact unless a major problem occurred. However, during the thirties, the schools attempted to foster close relations between the two groups through the formation of parent-teacher associations, by encouraging parents to visit classes, and through frequent meetings between faculty and parents.[32] The spirit of congeniality that existed between Jewish students and Jewish parents through their involvement in extracurricular activities also helped pave the way for closer relations beyond the long-standing affinity between Jewish parents and teachers in general.[33]

Equally demanding of teachers' time outside the school was an "alertness program" of professional courses the Board of Education mandated for teachers who "needed stimulation to avoid falling into a rut." In-service training, a requirement most other professions did not have, was intended to keep the teacher up to date in methods and subject matter. In a rapidly changing world, the Board asserted, teachers could not afford to stand still, but had to learn new facts, theories, and methods, and needed to keep alert, interested, and modern, as well as to grow and develop while busy teaching others. Courses in health education, safety, lip reading, and problems of delinquency would make them more effective teachers. Art, music, literature, history, and nature study courses would give them a broader cultural background. Instruction in puppetry, drama, and construction would furnish them with new and useful skills. Courses in educational theories and methods would result in improved classroom techniques. Beginning in September 1930, every teacher not at maximum salary was required to attend thirty hours of lectures during the year as evidence of professional alertness. Extension courses, each counting as two semester hours, were offered by the Kindergarten-6B Teachers Association, the Bronx Boro-Wide Teachers Association, the city municipal colleges, Teachers College, and New York University. They were to meet the requirements for annual salary increments and for the two-hundred-dollar salary differential for teachers having thirty semester hours of work beyond the baccalaureate.[34]

Soon an extensive range of courses was offered, most of a professional nature, such as laboratory techniques for biology teachers, techniques in remedial reading, methods of presenting current economic problems, classroom discipline through personality adjustment, and using visual aids in the classroom. Others offered little that could be applied in the classroom, such as a Theater Goers Alertness Course where teachers attended current Broadway productions and later met to discuss them. Aware that some courses were of rather dubious value, the Board of Education undertook closer regulation of the in-service requirements, and emphasized courses dealing with specific problems in city schools. By 1940, teachers could take nearly one hundred diverse courses dealing with practical issues directly related to the city school system.[35]

This alertness program was roundly criticized by both the Teachers Union and by teachers. The latter were so irate at the initial charge imposed for these courses that the Board of Education rescinded all fees. The Teachers Union condemned the alertness program, especially the requirement that teachers take courses as a condition for salary increment, for it insisted that only satisfactory ratings should be a qualification for teachers' salaries. It further argued that such limitations on salary and tenure rights set a dangerous precedent for further restrictions, all part of a general attack on teacher standards.[36] Many teachers resented the impositions placed upon them by the Board of Education. They were annoyed that only one correspondence course could be submitted in a fifteen-year period. Study groups, travel, and reading innumerable books, from which they professed to get much more stimulation, were not acceptable to the Board as being either educational or broadening. For many teachers, attending approved courses meant two to three hours of travel to hear a one-hour lecture in a crowded hall. Teachers complained that most lecture centers were inaccessible and that they were too tired to make long trips. They also mentioned that attendance cut into time previously allotted to teachers' organization meetings.[37]

Despite their objections, thousands of teachers unaffected by the law, those already at maximum salary, took courses voluntarily. In one year, over ten thousand teachers took over fourteen thousand courses. Twenty-five percent studied for alertness credit, and 75 percent took courses because of their own interest. Many other teachers wanted instruction in the technique of the new activity program installed in the city's schools, because the majority of them had been trained in the use of more formal methods. Thousands of teachers were enrolled in the extension courses, attending hundreds of lectures on the objectives, methods, and use of new materials, which the Board insisted would lead to fundamental changes in the basic concepts and methods of education.[38]

Besides taking in-service courses, women teachers enrolled in a multitude of courses at the various colleges and universities in New York City, often for higher degrees that would lead to promotions, and just as often for no benefit other than their own intellectual interest. "After a day of talking with no one but seven-year-olds, I needed some mental exercise," Rebecca Tisch explained. Others took courses during the summers, looking for new devices for teaching, and trying to incorporate what they learned into their daily lessons. During the thirties, New York University held a popular summertime course, Leisure-Time Activities for Teachers, where teachers learned such arts and crafts as jewelry-making, carving, knitting, producing motion pictures, and photography. One hygiene teacher took a course in leather-working to get practice for training her scout troop in this activity. A good many who attended were preparing to take charge of student clubs, and the majority in the class stated they were learning new activities more for classroom work than for their personal pleasure.[39]

The focus of teachers' professional interests outside the school was the teachers' associations formed by the educational staffs of school systems throughout the country. These organizations, representing a great variety of types, functions, bases of membership, and political theories, proliferated in New York City, numbering over one hundred in the midthirties. Completely independent of the school system, with membership open to all, their primary concern was to develop better methods of teaching and to raise the professional standards of teachers, as well as to improve their economic position by seeking legislation on salaries, pensions, and tenure. Most were interested in changing curricula, and they also attempted to influence city authorities to construct better school buildings, and to improve conditions for both teachers and pupils.[40]

In New York City, associations were organized in three different ways. One was according to salary schedules, like the Kindergarten-6B Teachers Association, which had been formed in order to protect salaries. Another organizational method was division along geographical boundaries, with each borough having its own association, like the Brooklyn Teachers Association. The other main classification was according to subject matter. For example, the High School Teachers of English Association had been organized so that teachers could study their discipline's particular problems. Yet other groups were based on special needs or services; others were divided between the sexes, like the Interboro Association of Women Teachers, which had led the fight for equal pay for equal work in the decade before World War I.[41] Some were umbrella organizations, like the Teachers Council, a federation that served to coordinate activities; or the New York Society for the Study of Experimental Education, concerned with pedagogical problems such as testing or the curriculum.[42]

The largest and most powerful of all teachers' associations was the Brooklyn Teachers Association, formed in 1874, whose membership ranged from teacher-clerks to teachers to assistant superintendents, and numbered over nine thousand during the twenties and over eight thousand during the thirties. Though it was concerned with all matters affecting the conduct of education in the schools, the association actively protested having teachers serve as volunteers in after-school, weekend, and holiday playgrounds during the 1920s, as it was convinced the city could and should pay special teachers for that work. Nevertheless, because its members were drawn from every salary and service rank, it believed that, rather than get involved with issues over which its members might disagree, it would eschew "aggressive campaigns" involving disputed questions of policy. However, the BTA would protect those rights and privileges once they were secured. Combining both professional and pedagogical interests, the Brooklyn Teachers Association also presented its own radio broadcasts and maintained an extension department of education courses, most of which could be counted as credit to meet alertness requirements. The BTA offered its members low-rate medical and insurance plans, which were apparently an inducement for many to join, according to Rose Litvinoff, Clara Saks, and others among the former teachers interviewed. Although the BTA was preoccupied during the thirties with tenure, sabbatical leaves, salaries, and pensions, a good deal of its activities centered around lectures, excursions, and entertainments.[43]

Teachers' associations were also divided along religious lines, with Catholics, Jews, and Protestants having separate groups in New York City. Studying teachers' organizations in New York and Chicago during the 1930s, William W. Wattenberg concluded that, unlike the situation in Chicago with its religious antagonism among teachers, New York's groups attempted to maintain amicable relations. Each group invited the leaders of the other groups to participate in its affairs. While it was undeniable that religious prejudice existed among teachers, Wattenberg insisted that on the surface the effect upon professional organizations seemed insignificant. One of these groups, the Jewish Teachers Association, was established to aid Jewish children, collecting funds for their organizations, dealing with educational problems peculiar to Jewish students, and educating its members as to events among Jews in the world, without offering religious instruction. The organization's social activities seemed its most important component to Wattenberg, as well as to the interviewees, several of whom said they belonged to this group because, as Anita Levy admitted, "it was a good place to meet men and they had excellent dances." Still other associations were engaged in raising and dispensing funds for the aid of needy teachers or pupils. Another, the American League Against War and Fascism, was formed to combat militarism or fascism in the schools and to assist teachers in academic freedom cases.[44]

Addressing problems brought about by the hiring freeze of the Depression years, two teachers' groups were formed to safeguard the interests of those who wished to enter the teaching force. The New York Association of Unappointed Teachers admitted only those who actually held teaching licenses and who had yet to receive a regular appointment. The Unemployed Teachers Association encompassed everyone who wished to teach and who had not received regular employment. Both groups had been active in extending the life of the lists of eligible teachers whose eligibility might have been destroyed by expiration of the lists. Both groups engaged in legal action to force the Board of Education to appoint teachers to regular positions. Through mass meetings and demonstrations, they protested abuses in the hiring of substitutes, and attempted to obtain work relief projects for the employment of members. They also objected to one teacher's holding two or more teaching positions because they wanted to free evening and vacation school jobs for members. Their campaign to make it illegal to hold multiple positions resulted in passage of the Dual Job Law in the spring of 1939. This legislation opened up hundreds of teaching positions, although by this time both groups had disbanded to join the teachers' unions.[45]

Among the most active teachers' organizations were those formed to protect the interests of teachers on the given salary schedule, such as the High School Teachers Association, with a membership of five thousand; and the Kindergarten-6B Association, which was the largest salary schedule group, having eight thousand members during the thirties. Both groups were involved in salary, pension, tenure, and sabbatical matters, as well as in civic affairs; their interest in purely pedagogical problems was very slight. Because a higher salary was desperately needed to offset the ever-rising cost of living for city teachers, it was the focus of these organizations for many years, beginning in the period from 1914 to 1920, when the cost of living practically doubled while salaries remained unchanged. Their repeated efforts during the twenties resulted in some relief in 1920, but no significant raises were received until 1928.[46] Before they received a major salary increase, so many teachers had to supplement their teaching incomes with after-school occupations that the teachers' organizations were shocked to note the number and variety of jobs to which teachers had to resort in order to augment their salaries, work carried on under the most taxing nervous and physical strain.[47]

The women interviewed say that this problem was greatly increased with the Depression, for many of them were teaching only on a per diem basis, and frequently family members were unemployed. Moreover, because most of those interviewed were young teachers, none of them received a maximum salary, and without additional income, they would have been in dire straits during the thirties. The majority of teachers in the city's evening and vacation schools also taught in the regular day schools during the twenties and well before passage of the Dual Job Law. Holding two full-time teaching positions meant they were not fresh and full of energy, but were tired and suffering from the effects of overwork. Some teachers said they spent as much as 1,500 hours per year on necessary work outside their teaching duties. The extra jobs they took included clerical work; camp counseling; sales work; teaching such subjects as singing, musical instruments, and English to foreigners; and proofreading.[48]

When the Depression hit, the Board of Education eliminated as many positions as possible and filled vacancies with substitutes at per diem rates far lower than those of tenured teachers, while also increasing classroom size. In January 1933, despite assurances of no pay reductions from Fiorello H. LaGuardia during his mayoralty campaign, salaries were reduced on a sliding scale, averaging 6.5 percent. The following year saw the salary budget slashed by another 10 percent. Although those teachers hired prior to 1929 were relatively well off during the Depression because they had fixed incomes at a time when prices were falling sharply, new teachers were teaching at the lowest possible salary, or were paid on a per diem basis.[49] Knowing the intricate financial history of her profession, and realizing that each increase was won through hard battles, one city teacher stated that she would fight "bitterly and unendingly" against any attempt to lower her income. To aid these teachers, and to restore the salary increases won after such a long and hard struggle, professional organizations enlisted their members in a pay raise campaign, which lasted until salaries were reinstated in July 1937.[50]

Because teachers were so visibly active in their campaign for higher salaries, which was waged to a great degree in the media, the popular assumption was that their primary concern was for matters that directly affected their economic welfare. The public insisted that they were interested only in salaries and pensions, calling them selfish and unconcerned with improving school conditions.[51] However, William W. Wattenberg, who attended scores of meetings of New York City teachers' organizations, found that in 1934, sessions covering such issues as the prevention of delinquency, academic freedom, current political problems, the Teachers Union's legislative program, and new teaching techniques were attended in large numbers. Judging by the attendance, he concluded that the matters of greatest general professional interest were not directly concerned with salaries and pensions.[52]

Some of the professional and salary schedule groups were able to draw a large proportion of their membership into active service, although the larger professional associations made almost no demands on their members, many of whom joined simply to take advantage of their benefits or social programs. Although most teachers belonged to at least one organization, meetings often were poorly attended. In theory, teachers could join any or as many as they wished, and some actually belonged to nine or more. Of the women interviewed, all belonged to at least one, and the majority belonged to both a borough-wide and a salary schedule organization. Secondary school teachers also belonged to an organization dealing with a specific subject matter, and they seemed to be the most actively involved. Like Ida Mitnick, most teachers cited lack of time for the low attendance at many meetings. According to Mitnick, marking papers, doing clerical work, and taking alertness courses left teachers little time for activity in these organizations. Still, many must have found time, because all the officers of these organizations were teachers. With the interviewees, age appears to be the main factor for their lack of involvement in professional organizations. Most of the officers and membership were older teachers, who often made their younger colleagues feel uncomfortable at meetings. These women insist they were treated with a certain condescension at best, and often with downright hostility, if they proposed anything the older and far more conservative leadership felt was tinged with radicalism. "They were very anxious for us to serve on committees and were all over us at meetings to sign up," Dora Fein related, "but if we ran into them in school or at a conference somewhere, they would look right through us." Ethel Cohen told of a similar occurrence, adding that association members took every opportunity to discount the younger teachers' lack of experience. Many said they just kept away from the organizations, attending only when there was an especially interesting lecture, but avoiding most meetings and what they deemed to be the least attractive social events. Ethel Cohen, Dora Fein, and several others said they did not really become active in professional organizations until after they had been teaching for over twenty years.[53]

While the membership of most professional organizations tended to be composed of male and female teachers over the age of forty, the leadership was predominantly male, although the teaching force in New York City was overwhelmingly female. By the 1930s, the Brooklyn Teachers Association had only one woman president in its sixty years of existence, although its committee chairs were evenly divided between men and women. The Bronx Boro-Wide Teachers Association had but one woman president in its ten years as an organization, yet Pauline Michel Papke, a Teachers Union activist, headed the High School Teachers Eligibles Association for most of its existence during the thirties.[54] Most groups chose supervisory officers who were invariably male to act as leaders.

Annual reports for the Brooklyn Teachers Association during the twenties indicate an equal division among male and female officers, although none of the women was Jewish. One Jewish woman did chair a committee though, and two more were among the board of trustees. There was one teacher association composed entirely of women who taught beauty culture in the industrial and continuation schools. Moreover, in 1939, its president was a Jewish woman who taught at a Brooklyn vocational high school. Jewish women as leaders of the professional organizations appear to have been something of a rarity, again probably because most of them were very young teachers during the interwar years, and not assertive enough or interested enough to make a bid for a leadership position or respected enough to be elected.[55]

If younger teachers were not very involved in the affairs of local teacher organizations, New York's teachers in general were sometimes criticized by out-of-town educators for intellectual inertia because they participated very little in the proceedings of the National Education Association or similar national organizations. Defending the city's teaching staff against this charge, District Superintendent John L. Tildsley insisted the schools were "seething with experimentation." There were constant faculty conferences, teachers attended voluntary university courses in great numbers, hundreds had authored books, and a good percentage traveled to foreign lands and read professional periodicals. Moreover, he added, legions of city teachers were engaged in community work for various professional or cultural associations. The names of New York's teachers were usually absent from the programs of national organizations, not because of provincialism or lack of intellectual curiosity, Tildsley explained, but because the many universities and professional organizations located in the city were enough to satisfy the needs of any teacher.[56]

Teachers were well represented in national or sectional general education and subject associations, according to District Superintendent Tildsley. He reported that sizable numbers also belonged to local teachers' associations, as well as local subject associations. Because there was a meeting of some educational association in New York City every day of the week, its teachers had little reason to travel. However, the Board of Education's journal indicates that permission was frequently granted for women teachers to travel to such professional meetings as a National Education Association annual convention in Detroit, and a meeting of the Society for the Promotion of Engineering Education in Cambridge, as well to such local conferences as one for American Instructors of the Deaf at Columbia University.[57]

Moreover, city teachers were involved in a wide variety of other professional concerns, from university study, reading general education and subject periodicals, to giving cultural and professional talks, as well as publishing professional and cultural books and articles. Scholarly research and authorship produced studies in fields ranging from educational theory to politics to Chaucer. Publication of a book of professional or cultural value could be offered for any two increments, within a period of three years after publication. The response to a 1938 questionnaire sent to city teachers listed 916 published and 131 unpublished books, as well as 130 theses for degrees written by New York City teachers. One woman reported having written or edited twelve books. Of the women interviewed, Mae Cogen wrote a pamphlet about the history of Brooklyn; Evelyn Weiss wrote several articles on applying the activity program to the teaching of social studies; several had published storybooks for young children; and others had written various articles for magazines for classroom teachers. Most attended professional meetings of some sort at some time, usually those held in New York City, and all took advanced courses in local universities. Several of those especially active in the teachers unions gave presentations at union meetings and conferences; and Belle Aronoff, Esther Rubin, and Betty Perlman contributed articles to its publications.[58]

Besides being involved in professional associations and scholarly pursuits, many teachers belonged to faculty clubs that were established to take care of teacher welfare and teacher interests of a more personal nature than those encompassed by the larger organizations. Some of these groups went beyond such local concerns, like the Faculty Club at one high school, which not only was involved in raising money for student and refugee relief, but also issued many political statements, such as its condemnation of Nazi outrages and its advocation of a trade embargo on Germany. Teachers also formed organizations for the benefit of the community. One such group was the Neighborhood Teachers Association, which engaged in work among foreign-born women in New York City, visiting homes, teaching English, and conducting study groups.[59] Sarah T. Stieglitz wrote in the "School Page" of the *New York Sun* about some of the civic activities carried out by her teachers' club, which was involved in improving neighborhood recreation and sanitation conditions, along with raising funds for needy children. "All this takes time and energy," she explained, "but we give of that freely and joyfully as a supplement to that which we aim to achieve in the classroom—healthier and happy citizens."[60]

Indeed, time and energy were expended, not only of necessity, but frequently with a willing heart by the city's teachers. Those who disparaged teachers by claiming they were overpaid because their hours were supposedly short appear to have been ignorant of exactly what teachers did. For public school teachers in New York City, and especially the conscientious and dedicated ones, their work day was an extremely long one that never seemed to end with the dismissal bell, but continued long into the night. Teachers advised students, met with parents, provided social services, graded papers, prepared lessons, and attended courses or association meetings. Sometimes their day never ended, for they often lay awake at night, as Rebecca Tisch recalled, "worrying about how to obtain some much-needed supplies, or even worse, how to help an impoverished or troubled child."

CHAPTER

 8

PROFESSION OR PROCESSION?

Schoolteaching and Motherhood

"TEACHING," ALLEGED AN American educator during the interwar years, "is not a profession, but a procession," referring to the high rate of turnover among women teachers.[1] Ever since the nineteenth century, when schoolteaching in the United States became a feminine occupation, the rationale for paying women teachers low salaries and for deterring their entry into supervisory positions has been that teaching was not a profession, but merely part of a procession in women's lives that concluded with matrimony and motherhood. Allegations of frequent teacher turnover, charges that teacher-mothers had higher absentee rates, and assumptions that married women had insufficient time for teaching and family, to the detriment of both, caused school boards to bar married women from teaching. Even in those cities that permitted married women to teach, repeated efforts to displace them occurred during the Great Depression. New York City, however, was an unusual arena, because it was not only the largest school district in the United States, but it also had one of the most liberal policies regarding teacher-mothers during the interwar years, permitting married women and even mothers to continue to teach. Examination of the records of New York City teachers who took maternity leaves and then returned to the classroom proves that when married women were afforded the opportunity to combine teaching and motherhood, they demonstrated that teaching was not a procession, but a lifelong commitment to their chosen profession.

The practice of barring married people from teaching has a long history in the United States. The first such ban occurred in 1690 in Hingham, Massachusetts, although it was directed at a man, rather than a woman. The selectmen in that community refused to hire a married man on the economic ground that support of a family would necessitate a higher salary; they were directed to hire a schoolmaster "as cheap as they can . . . provided they shall hire a single man and not a man that have a family."[2] By the early nineteenth century, with the development of common schools, public school teaching had become almost completely feminized because unmarried women provided an expedient source of inexpensive labor, since school boards throughout the country were still unwilling to pay schoolteachers salaries that would enable men to support their families. During all of the nineteenth century, married women were not permitted to teach, a proscription in effect in more than 70 percent of the nation's schools well into the 1930s. As late as the 1950s, women were not allowed to teach after marriage in many major cities, including Boston.[3]

No state was on record as passing legislation bearing directly upon the employment of married women teachers; local school boards had the power to terminate the employment of married women on their teaching staffs.[4] The exclusion of married women teachers was first challenged in New York City in 1903 after the automatic dismissal of Mary L. Grendon upon her marriage, but was not ruled upon because she had delayed in bringing her action to court. The next year, Kate M. Murphy, who had been a public school teacher for eleven years, sought reinstatement from the dismissal that ensued upon her marriage. The court ruled that marriage was not a cause provided by law for which a teacher could be dismissed, and ordered her reinstatement.[5]

In 1915, the New York City Board of Education established its formal policy regarding married teachers, which it stated in Section 67 of its bylaws: "Any woman member who marries while in service and any student who marries while at teacher training school shall report that fact immediately, with the name of her husband, to the Superintendent of Schools, who shall record the name and report to the Board of Education. Failure shall be deemed neglect of duty and an act of insubordination."[6] Married names were entered on every permanent teacher's record on file. However, men were not required to report marriages, and their marriages were never recorded.

The issue of whether absence for childbirth should deprive a married woman teacher of the right to be reinstated was settled once and for all in New York City in 1915, when Bridget Peixotto, who had had a child during the three months she was away from her classroom, was refused the right to return to teaching on charges of neglect of duty through absence caused by childbirth. She then took her case to the courts, which ruled that married women teachers had the legal right to the benefit of a leave of absence necessary in the case of childbirth, and that such leave could not be construed as neglect of duty. The Board of Education was further enjoined from filling a position vacated by a teacher on maternity leave with a new appointee, but had to employ a substitute, keeping the position open for the teacher until the expiration of her leave. Because of the Peixotto case, the Board of Education formalized maternity leaves in 1915. As soon as a woman became aware of pregnancy, she was obligated to apply for and immediately accept a two-year leave of absence. Failure to do so was deemed neglect of duty and an act of insubordination.[7]

Permission for married women to continue teaching meant that couples who could not afford to marry at a young age on the man's income alone could now do so based on two incomes. However, in most of the United States, the marriage rate for young women teachers between the ages of twenty and twenty-nine was quite low because of educational require-ments, hopes and ambitions for social status, and because many school boards still required resignation upon marriage. The general marriage rate dropped precipitously after the onset of the Great Depression, reach-ing the lowest point in the recorded history of marriage in the United States in 1932. By early 1933, the tide had turned for the general popula-tion, but not for most American teachers, whose rate of marriage de-clined even further during this period.[8] There was a general tendency to postpone marriage during the 1930s; nevertheless, marriage rates among Jewish women continued to rise.[9] Of the sixty-one Jewish women inter-viewed, all but one married. Moreover, twenty-five of the women in this group married at either the age of twenty-two or twenty-three; and forty-nine of them married between the ages of eighteen and twenty-five. The majority were married during the thirties, and none said she felt she had to postpone marriage because of the economic climate. Yetta Yuretsky joked that Jewish mothers advised their sons to marry teachers so that they could always count on "a good, steady income."

The decades that followed New York City's acceptance of married women teachers coincided with far-reaching changes in the makeup of America's work force. The most important of these was the increased proportion of working wives in the United States, a trend that began in the twenties, when married women made up 12 percent of the work force, and continued even during the thirties, when they comprised 15 percent of all workers.[10] Among the female workers classified as professionals during this period, two-thirds were teachers.[11] These trends combined to produce escalating numbers of married teachers throughout the nation, and especially in the New York City public school system. This was accomplished despite a small drop in the proportion of female teachers after 1930, when they had constituted four-fifths of all teachers, thus stemming the century-old tide toward feminization of the teaching force.[12]

Although American communities continued to refuse to hire married teachers, in 1931 one in every six elementary school teachers was a married woman. Yet only 20 to 30 percent of cities of ten thousand people or more employed married teachers.[13] In spite of prohibitions against married teachers, their proportions went from 17.9 percent in 1930 to 24.6 percent in 1940. In large cities like Los Angeles and New York, which had no restrictions on married teachers, they made up approximately 50 percent of the women teachers.[14] This growth is even more spectacular when one considers the matrix of hostility toward working wives, and especially married teachers, during the Depression years.

Yet even in this decade of ever-heightening public disfavor toward married teachers, the women interviewed remained steadfast in their belief that teaching was their vocation. They strongly believed that women had every right to careers, as well. Although job security for teachers on leave from the classroom to care for children had been for them an inducement to become teachers, they nevertheless insisted that the principal attraction of teaching was their ability to become a member of a highly prestigious profession, for which many believed they had a calling. Teaching meant so much to them and to their families that they never considered it a mere stopgap occupation. "I always planned on a career in teaching, whether married or single," insisted Miriam Minkoff. "Can you imagine what it meant to my immigrant parents, that their daughter had a teaching certificate?" Hannah Austerman asked. Several others cited the enormous sacrifices made by their families so that they could obtain their educations. Most of the former teachers also stated that they did not undergo the great difficulties they experienced before receiving their positions, only to relinquish teaching to become housewives. "I invested too much of my family's resources, and of myself and all my dreams, not to mention money into the pension plan, for me to abandon teaching," Anne Kuntsler explained.

Aware of their unconventionality, they readily admit masking their commitment to their profession when dealing with those who did not view working wives and mothers with approval. During the twenties, they used the "pin money" argument, explaining to critics that they were helping raise their standard of living by providing luxuries not possible on a single salary. In the following decade they tended to emphasize the necessity of their earning money, even in cases where this was not entirely true, tending to use necessity as a rationale because it was socially acceptable. Although these women never joined any feminist organization during the interwar years, nor was feminism part of their vocabulary at that time, nevertheless they profess to have been "living examples of feminism," according to Belle Aronoff. She, along with most of the other informants, maintains that their acting on their certainty that not only did women have the right to work if they so wished, but that they also had the right to consider their work a profession to which they were dedicated, defined them as feminists. Yet they failed to see that by using the pretexts of working for pin money or for economic need when not applicable, they undermined feminism and weakened the force of their beliefs.

The increased employment of married women during the interwar years, especially in the white-collar sector, produced a proliferation of articles in educational journals and popular magazines that dealt with the desirability of working wives. The subject of married women as teachers also generated heated debates in the media. Opponents of women teachers invariably placed women in a no-win situation, for they were damned if they were married and damned if they remained single. As a 1932 radio address put it, the teacher who remained single was penalized by being called an old maid schoolteacher, and the teacher who married either was condemned for daring to continue in her profession, or was penalized by being removed from her job.[15]

Critics called young unmarried teachers "the bane of many school systems," and based their objections on allegations that teaching was not a profession for these women, but was a stopgap until matrimony and motherhood. Older teachers who were unmarried were branded as embittered, frustrated neurotics, whose ostensible incompleteness of experience led to a sourly cynical philosophy of life. Unmarried teachers were also faulted on eugenic grounds because, as some educators and eugenicists insisted, they were above average in heredity and ought to bear children.[16] If the teacher was married, she was charged with neglect of home and familial responsibilities; critics insisted on the incompatibility of housekeeping and schoolteaching. Because she was too tired from dual roles, which were impossible to carry out equally well, her home was messy, and her husband, "poor fellow!" was shabby. Her dirty, unkempt children, given to lying and fighting, wound up in the crowded juvenile halls with the other offspring of working mothers; or else she was too preoccupied with household and child cares to be an effective teacher.[17]

Still others attacked married teachers as being less amenable to supervision by school authorities because, coming from two-income families, they were supposedly more independent than their male or unmarried female colleagues.[18] They further argued that married teachers were not willing to assume their full share of responsibility, and had no desire to keep abreast of their profession. Critics also stated that there was more tendency for single women to continue their professional studies than for married women. These arguments were disproved by most studies conducted by educators; one study found that married women actually spent more time on their work than single women. Furthermore, married teachers provided better service on extracurricular assignments, complained less about increases in their teaching loads, and spent more time in school with children. The study also found that married women teachers seemed more interested in out-of-school activities and were more often leaders in teachers' clubs and community organizations than unmarried women.[19]

Repeated arguments that women teachers, and especially married ones, were absent from school more often than men, inspired a myriad of studies to support this allegation, few of which were conclusive. Most indicated that while women were away from classrooms more than the general average, the differences were slight. Overall, in the United States, unmarried women averaged five absences per year; married women, six and one half per year. In another such study, statistics showed that married women in some large cities had fewer absences.[20] In 1938, the Board of Education's chief medical examiner, Dr. Emil Altman, whom the New York City teachers' unions had often accused of overt hostility toward married teachers, produced his own study of city teachers to support his contention that there were too many married women in the system. Altman noted that of the 37,000 public school teachers during the interwar years, 30,000 were women, 15,000 of whom were married. After studying their official records over a fourteen-year period, he charged that married women stayed away from school for longer periods than did both unmarried women and men teachers.[21] Examination of approximately five hundred of these same attendance cards, covering a twenty-year period, was conducted for this study, comparing the absentee rates for equal numbers of men and married women teachers. Findings indicate that male teachers averaged less than two absent days yearly, and

137

married females averaged less than four absences a year, concurring with the figures provided by Altman.[22]

Altman also mentioned the frequency of women absent because of family illness, referring to the Board of Education's policy permitting teachers to take unpaid leaves to care for sick family members. Inspection in the Board's journal of both the names of those granted such leaves and of such absences noted on personnel cards indicates that unmarried as well as married women were granted such leaves, although all leaves of this nature averaged only about forty during each year. Moreover, there is no record of one male teacher who either applied for or was given such leave, which demonstrates the primacy of women, whether married or single, as the principal caregivers for ailing family members.

However, Altman made further inferences about married women teachers, which certainly could not have been derived from the teachers' personnel cards. He stated that they did not regard their jobs with the same enthusiasm as unmarried teachers, took less interest in their pupils, and that for many, teaching was merely a means of getting "pin money." He further added that married women did not make the best teachers because they disrupted the continuation of service by taking maternity leaves, which meant that their places were filled by substitutes. Altman concluded his report with the specious statement that teaching and motherhood could not be combined successfully because marital problems brought on by "divided allegiance" caused scores of women to become unhappy, distraught, and nervous, which ultimately led to their going "to pieces."[23]

Supporters of married women teachers argued that if all-around competency was not the sole test for the employment and retention of teachers, the profession would be reserved as a haven for "spinsters and immature girls exclusively," for the exclusion of married women was "a Victorian and latter-day Fascist conception of women's place in the world." They pointed out that the woman who wanted to teach after marriage was probably one who felt an unusual aptitude and regard for her profession. Moreover, as the United Parents Association believed, marriage and motherhood provided a more sympathetic understanding of children, whereby the teacher-mother would be able to bring fresh insight into the psychology of other people's children, and by studying her own children, could better understand the child's nature.[24] Professors of education at American universities and teachers' colleges agreed, stating that marriage rendered more valuable educational service from women. In addition, most studies of the relative efficiency of single and married women teachers usually found that the two groups were about the same.[25]

While most challenges to the right of married women to work during the twenties were based on moral scruples or views about women's place in the home, economic arguments occasionally surfaced as well. Those opposed to married teachers insisted that it was not fair to give a job to a woman who had a husband to support her, and who was working only to provide extra luxuries. Other detractors claimed that because the married teacher had extra income available, she underbid single women, forcing salaries to a lower level, thus cheapening the profession.[26] However, during the 1930s, economic objections acquired additional force. Hostility toward married women teachers intensified because of the the uncertainties of the Depression, the enforced economies practiced by school systems, and rampant, nationwide unemployment. Writing about the teaching profession in her study of working women during the thirties, Lois Scharf observed that when the Depression "compounded the social pressure against working wives generally, the status of married women teachers deteriorated further," adding that: "Nowhere was proposed and actual discrimination against working wives more pronounced."[27]

Attesting to the widespread prejudice and discrimination against married women teachers throughout the United States, the National Education Association reported that women teachers were discriminated against more than other female wage earners. As one teacher complained: "When a woman teacher marries, her contract is cancelled, but when a man teacher marries, his salary is increased."[28] Any married woman drawing a salary from tax sources during the Depression years was in an insecure position, as taxpayers demanded that married women be dismissed to provide jobs for unemployed men. Yet the average woman teacher supported dependents, often as many as married men, as was revealed by interviews with former New York City teachers. During the thirties, they often had spouses out of work, and their salaries were the only family income. More than one-half of the interviewees said they could not have managed during those years without the benefit of two incomes because they were the sole support of unemployed family members, many of whom actually lived in their homes, and almost two-thirds of these women contributed to the support of aging parents. But besides their being paid by public funds, the high visibility of teachers in their communities placed them in a most vulnerable position. Moreover, teaching wives were perceived as, and actually were, middle-class women challenging middle-class social values, for as Scharf noted: "They were not just economic competitors for jobs at a time of economic distress but also social threats to treasured institutions and behavioral patterns."[29]

139

Yet women's right to work was under attack during the Depression years. In a nationwide move to oust married teachers, proposals were made to forbid two incomes from public coffers. If a teacher's husband was also on a public payroll, it was expected that the wife would resign her position to open up jobs for the unemployed. Even Eleanor Roosevelt let herself be taken in as she argued against a "family bureaucracy" in the civil service, suggesting that income be the basis of awarding civil service positions. Roosevelt insisted that income should determine the number of positions in a family, thus rejecting a woman's essential right to earn her own livelihood in her own chosen manner.[30] In 1939, New York City's Mayor Fiorello H. LaGuardia instituted a similar drive against dual jobholders. Although he insisted he had no intention of dismissing married teachers, only married couples who held several jobs between them, the drive seemed to be directed against married women whose husbands held jobs in public service. Because most men earned more than women (male high school teachers earned higher salaries than female elementary school teachers, for example), when married couples had to choose between the two salaries, simple economics dictated that the woman should resign her position. Although this attempt to legislate married women out of teaching met with strong opposition from Johanna M. Lindlof, the only woman Board of Education member, and from both teachers' unions, these critics were unable to defeat what the Teachers Guild termed a "totalitarian measure to control family incomes."[31]

After passage of LaGuardia's Dual Job Law in 1939, he further harrassed married teachers by forbidding husbands and wives to teach in the same school. Finding more than one hundred such combinations in the city, he ordered one member of any married couple teaching within the same school to be transferred.[32] Fanny Stein, Elsie Winkler, and Rose Litvinoff were members of such pairs, and were quite resentful of this measure. However, most of the others interviewed had mixed sentiments because such arrangements often affected teacher morale. Several cited situations in which one spouse was a teacher and another a supervisor which often led to unpleasant complications. Sadie Goldman recalled an incident involving a husband and wife who taught in the same high school department. When the husband was being criticized by a superior the wife forgot "her professional role. She rushed to her husband's defense . . . and received a severe administrative reprimand."

Many critics were not content with merely disqualifying married women teachers, but sought to reverse the feminization of the American public school teaching staff by arguing that women in general were inferior teachers. Calling women teachers "a millstone about the neck of those struggling to give teaching the dignity, stability and recognition it deserves," one principal claimed that the majority of the nation's teaching personnel were made up of young, unmarried women who looked forward only to the briefest kind of stay within their ranks, and to whom teaching success was merely an incidental, not an ultimate goal.[33] Other critics, who assumed that marriage expectancy was the constant, active, and time-consuming interest of all unmarried women, charged them with wasting most of their time in social frivolities.[34] Young single teachers were presumed to be rather remote from problems involving the improvement of classroom proceedings because their connection with the school was seen only as an unavoidable stage in their contemplated and much-desired matrimony.[35]

Those who took this stance usually turned to the high incidences of teacher turnover to bolster their arguments. Critics and supporters alike noted that the average length of service of women teachers in the United States was only six years.[36] As Dr. Alice V. Keliher of the Progressive Education Association warned, the denial of the right of marriage to teachers would mean closing the teaching profession to thousands of capable women. It would mean that they could enter only as a temporary occupation, knowing that when they married, they had to leave. She asserted that married teachers were superior because they were making a better, more normal adjustment to life. Teaching, she maintained, should attract the finest type of persons, and this would not be possible if women knew they could not make it their profession. As a temporary stepping-stone to marriage, it would entail a "terrific turnover."[37] Yet supporters and detractors alike seldom acknowledged that permitting married women teachers, and instituting maternity leave, invariably produced stable teaching staffs, as was the case in New York City.

The mandatory leave of absence without pay was reduced to eighteen months in 1937, and women could request an extension of this time, if they so wished. In case of economic need, which had to be thoroughly investigated to determine the extent of the applicant's financial situation, a woman could request to return after only one year, or if pregnancy was terminated due to miscarriage.[38] Some cities actually attempted to restrict the number of children teachers might have. In Buffalo, during the thirties, women teachers were allowed only two maternity leaves. When the New York City Board of Education tried to impose a similar limit, it was vigorously attacked and prevented, not by liberals, but by Catholics opposed to birth control.[39]

With the institution of liberal maternity leave, bearing a child for New York's female teachers no longer meant that the woman had to withdraw from the teaching force. New York City's teachers filed for maternity leave in continually escalating numbers. Not many women applied for leave during the first ten years that the policy was enforced; the *Journal of the New York City Board of Education* listed every applicant, and the date that leave was granted. A significant change can be seen beginning in 1926, when 33 women applied. This undoubtedly reflects the entry of a large group of young women into the teaching staff during this period when jobs were so plentiful. By 1929, the Board reported that approximately 500 maternity leaves had been granted each year, with a total of 962 women absent from school on their two-year leaves. In 1935, the total number of women out on maternity leave had increased to about 1,200. However, even though the number of teachers who availed themselves of maternity leave grew each year, the figures provided by the Board in its journal are greatly inflated because they include all women employed in every capacity by the Board of Education, not just the teaching staff.[40] Although the birthrate among the Board's employees reached its lowest point in 1932, after that it continued to rise, even with a Great Depression in force. Maternity leaves continued to be taken by more and more women, and 1937, the year that coincided with the reduction in the required leave, was the peak year for maternity leaves during the thirties.[41]

During the Depression, some women often found the mandatory unpaid maternity leave a definite financial hardship, so they resorted to various ploys to circumvent the policy. Some attempted to conceal their pregnancy and remained in the classroom; others took sick leave, or applied for various other types of leaves of shorter duration. Recognizing these women's dilemma, the Teachers Union recommended that women be allowed to continue to teach as long as their health permitted, for a period of five months, instead of having to apply for leave immediately upon learning of their pregnancy; and also urged that if a woman so wished, she be admitted back to the classroom after only a year.[42] However, the Board remained adamant about women leaving at once, and circulated frequent reminders to the staff of this policy. They also required teachers to sign statements that they were fully aware of the law and all its ramifications.[43] Throughout the thirties, circumvention continued, despite the Board's punishments, which consisted of reprimands, docking of pay, forced extensions of leaves, fines as high as $300, and threats to bar future violators from ever teaching in the city's schools.[44]

The majority of the city's teachers adhered to the law and availed themselves of maternity leave. The Board of Education's journal published the names and dates of all such leaves granted, recording over 3,000 from 1920 to 1940. The teacher personnel cards of more than one-third of these women were studied to determine whether they actually returned to the classroom after their leaves had expired.[45] During the interwar period, 89.4 percent of a total of 1,212 women continued in their classrooms until retirement, with the vast majority retiring sometime during the 1960s, after having taught for 30 years. A mere 9.7 percent resigned from service, for reasons unspecified on the cards; only 4 of the more than 1,000 were fired; and 8 women died before reaching retirement.[46] These figures attest to teaching being a profession, rather than a brief interlude prior to matrimony and motherhood for these women. These findings are echoed in the data provided by the Jewish teachers who were interviewed. Only 3 of the 61 in this group had no children, and the majority retired during the sixties.

The ethnic breakdown of the women applying for maternity leave is as follows: 20.2 percent were Irish; 50.9 percent were Jewish; 25.6 percent had names that were either Anglo-Saxon, of ethnicity other than Irish, Jewish, or Italian, or could not be determined; and only 3.2 percent were Italian. No significant differences in commitment to their careers were found among these ethnic groups, for the percentage of those teaching until retirement does not differ appreciably among the four groups studied.

Moreover, there appear to be no striking differences in the number of children teachers in each group bore, as the majority had one or two.[47] Among the Irish teachers, 42.4 percent had one child, and 33.5 percent had two children. However, judging from the ages indicated on teacher personnel cards, the majority of Irish-American teachers tended to marry at a later age than the other groups, and had their first child while in their thirties. During the interwar years, the Jewish birthrate in the United States is estimated to have fallen by almost 40 percent, a trend underscored by New York's Jewish teachers, who seldom had more than two children; 45.4 percent had one child, and 44.2 percent had two children.[48] The percentages for Italian teachers are similar: 38.5 percent had one child, and 46.1 percent had two children. The fourth undetermined category is almost the same, as 46.6 percent had one child, and 37.6 percent had two. Although American Jews have been considered the most successful of American major ethnic groups with regard to family planning and birth spacing, most New York City teachers of all groups appear also to have practiced birth control and to have succeeded in family limitation.[49]

In addition to maternity leave, New York City teachers also had the option of taking unpaid child-care leaves of absence. However, few women chose to do so, preferring to return to their classrooms after their mandatory leaves. Of the women whose personnel cards were studied, only one woman applied for such leave during the 1920s. During the next decade, only fourteen of the more than one thousand studied took child-care leave. The Board of Education reported that no leaves of absence to care for a child after maternity were applied for between 1933 and 1937. However, it stated that over two hundred such leaves were granted in the last two years of the decade; but again it must be noted that this number included both nonteaching employees and teachers.[50]

"How do they manage it and how does it work?" Virginia MacMakin Collier, an advocate of working wives, asked in 1926, about how women combine marriage with careers.[51] One might also ask how teacher-mothers were able to manage their careers when they had very young children, for child-care arrangements were one of the most difficult problems for mothers who worked outside the home. Although some private nursery schools already existed during the early decades of the twentieth century, they were few and far between. Moreover, they tended to have a somewhat unsavory reputation. New York City, which passed laws in the years immediately following World War I requiring licensing and regular inspection of day nurseries, provided for little enforcement of these laws.[52] In 1938, as part of a national program, the federal government funded nursery school education which, in New York City, was administered by the Board of Education. Another program, the Nursery School Project, initially carried on by the New York State Education Department and then transferred to the Board of Education in 1938, maintained a total of 15 centers which enrolled 650 children between the ages of two and four years, nine months. Yet they did not begin to meet the need for nursery school services. In the Bronx alone, there were but two: one small one, under the auspices of a local Catholic church; and another run by the Works Progress Administration. For school-age children during the Depression years, many of the public schools remained open as play centers five days a week between the hours of three and five P.M., providing supervised activities for neighborhood children aged five through eighteen.[53]

The lack of adequate day nurseries was often cited as the primary difficulty facing married teachers, resulting in their dropping into and out of the profession in order to bear children.[54] Yet the scarcity of child-care facilities did not deter New York City's teachers from becoming mothers, and most left the classroom only for the mandatory maternity leave. Their ability to continue teaching while having pre-school-age children at home was facilitated then, as always, by other women. For as Belle Aronoff said: "Any woman who carries out the combination of work and motherhood, does it by climbing up on the shoulders of another woman." This was certainly the case for all of the fifty-nine former teacher-mothers interviewed for this study.

However, these Jewish teacher-mothers from New York City differed from the professional women, most of them teachers, who were studied by Collier during the 1920s. Collier found that only 8 percent of the women in her study depended upon another member of their family for child-care assistance, since almost half of them employed servants. Nor did Jewish teachers resemble most wage-earning women who, in the absence of relatives, tended to arrange for substitute care for their pre-school children from friends or neighbors who did not work outside the home.[55] Family members provided child-care service for all but one of the former teachers interviewed, and few of these women ever employed any servants. Ruth Gold, the only woman whose child was looked after by a housekeeper, had no living relations. Her career was "of such great importance to me, I was determined that motherhood would not keep me from it. Fortunately, my husband's business always did well, even during the Depression . . . so we were able to afford help, and a wonderful woman looked after my home and child for twenty years," Gold related. For the rest of the informants, family members not only looked after their small children, but did so cheerfully, according to several of these caregivers. They were following patterns established in the previous immigrant generation when such arrangements were often necessary. Although the most frequent caregiver was the child's grandmother, other female relatives, ranging from sisters to sisters-in-law, aunts, or cousins, also contributed their services. Like most other Jewish women of their generation, they interacted most often with their own kin, and had a wide variety of kinds of assistance that they exchanged with relatives, much of which involved child care.[56]

Familial caregiving benefited from Jewish family living arrangements; families tended to live either together or in close proximity. The key motif expressed in Jewish family patterns was an effort to preserve the solidarity of the family. This cohesiveness was not unique among Jewish families, but was prevalent among the first two generations of most

145

immigrant groups, persisting until the post–World War II exodus to suburbia.[57] During the interwar years, it was almost unheard-of for unmarried Jewish people of any age to live apart from parents or family members. In the rare instances when this did occur, the single person residing away from parents was considered morally suspect. Every one of the former teachers interviewed resided with her parents or some family member until marriage. After marriage she either continued living with parents or in-laws, or remained in the same neighborhood with one set of parents. Moreover, the interviewees insist that widowed parents rarely lived alone, residing with a child, either married or single, or at the very least in the same neighborhood; this second generation still adhered to the age-old obligation of Jews to take care of elderly parents.[58] Two-thirds of these women lived with or near family members, most often parents or in-laws, for most of the first twenty years of their married lives. Usually they shared the same apartment; sometimes they had separate apartments in the same two-family or multiple apartment dwelling. In a number of instances, family members who provided child care resided down the street, or around the corner, or within easy walking distance.

During the Great Depression families often had to double up, which may have stretched kinship relations and caused friction from overcrowding and loss of privacy. But privacy was less important than hospitality to this generation, as it had been for their immigrant parents, who had generously opened their doors to relatives and friends in need of homes, whether their stay was to be temporary or permanent.[59] When Yetta Yuretsky's brother-in-law lost his job, he and his family moved in with hers. This afforded her the opportunity to continue teaching, "because I now had my own sister to watch my child. My sister was already housebound with a little one, and insisted on watching mine as well. Who could be better than my own sister?"[60]

These women not only preferred having family members tend their children because of the convenience, but they also deemed familial care to be best. They subscribed, as well, to the belief that while it was to be expected that older children were placed in the care of classroom teachers, the very young should not be placed with "strangers," as it was put. A certain stigma was attached to sending a child to nursery school whether private or public. Ida Rubinstein, forced by a series of circumstances into enrolling her three-year-old in a nursery maintained by the Board of Education, recalled feeling disgraced for having done this. "The shame lasted far beyond the four months he attended," she said. "I knew

hese schools were for underprivileged working women and I was embar-
rassed to be lumped with them," Rubinstein explained, adding that she
was also humiliated that "strangers had to care for my son." Besides the
pain she suffered from her presumed loss of middle-class status, she also
"felt less than adequate. I wanted to be Supermom."

This syndrome is not a new phenomenon, arising from recent feminist
movements, but has long been a part of the lives of wives and mothers
working outside the home; even at the turn of the century, investigators
noted the orderly appearance of most married workers' homes.[61] While
New York's teacher-mothers were not subjected to the same sort of
community surveillance and regulation as their small-town and rural sisters during the interwar years, and while they insist that friends and
family were supportive of their desire for motherhood and careers, they
also felt it incumbent upon themselves to maintain extremely high standards of competence as housewives and as mothers. "It was vital that no
one be given the opportunity to even suggest that perhaps I was slacking,
that maybe it was too much for me," Charlotte Printz stated. "My windows had to shine like everyone else's," she proclaimed. Sylvia Schneider
mentioned that, like clergymen's children, schoolteachers' children were
closely scrutinized. If their behavior was imperfect, it became a reflec-
tion upon their mothers' teaching competency. "My child's appearance
had to be just so," Rose Jacobi said, "for we were supposed to not only
keep up standards, but to set them." "Clearly," as one historian has
observed, status attached to competent housewifery (or motherhood) "was
not diminished in value for women who worked outside the home. They
needed to meet community and personal standards of excellence in their
domestic role. This testifies to the centrality of that role for feminine
identity."[62]

Because they had complete and satisfactory arrangements for caring
for their children, teacher-mothers believed they were able to combine
both motherhood and careers successfully, without deleterious effect on
either, but with each enhancing the other. They believed their classroom
performance benefited by their being mothers as well as teachers, agree-
ing with the professional women studied during the twenties who said
that in their work they actually drew on the experience of being wives
and mothers.[63] The organization and self-discipline needed to negotiate
homemaking, motherhood, and career served to set a positive example
for their children, according to the interviewees. "After seeing me correct
papers or draft lesson plans night after night, my children never put up a
fuss about their homework," Dora Fein explained. Because a teacher

147

"commanded great respect in our neighborhood," Sadie Goldman's son "felt special . . . that it was an honor to have a mother who was a teacher." Several said that one of the best aspects of being a teacher, according to their children, was that they were able to spend so much time with each other on long holidays and during the summer. Finally, the interviewees pointed to the fact that, as teacher-mothers they inspired their own children to follow in their footsteps, for one-fourth of their offspring went on to become teachers themselves.

While these women confessed to occasional problems stemming from their efforts to combine marriage, motherhood, and career, they tended to minimize these problems. All of the interviewees insisted that their professional lives did not impinge upon their personal lives, and were adamant that their private lives had no detrimental effect upon their performance in the classroom. Moreover, according to the informants they were successful in all their endeavors: they were accomplished teachers, had happy marriages, and all their children turned out well. If this is an unusually idyllic picture, it is one that is dictated by the limitations of employing the methodology of oral history. The interviewer is hampered not only by the vagaries and frailties of human recall, but by the ever-present tendency to idealize the past, often providing evidence more of vanity than veracity. While there is a paucity of documentation to support their claims, it is certainly true that these women all taught, with the obvious approval of the Board of Education, until retirement. Their personnel cards do not indicate any reprimands by their superiors, and ratings other than "satisfactory" are rarely to be found on any of their cards. Moreover, there is a remarkable absence of divorce among this group, for only four of the sixty women who married were divorced, and three of these women divorced rather late in life. As for their children, an interviewer has to take into consideration parents' natural tendencies to brag about offspring. However, many of the interviews conducted for this study were arranged by the daughters of the former teachers; their pride in their mothers' accomplishments was quite palpable.

While a complete and satisfactory arrangement for caring for their children was the paramount component in enabling teacher-mothers to pursue careers, other requisites were essential, as well. Those interviewed concurred with a study of white-collar and professional wives whose subjects also stipulated the following factors as a requirement for the successful integration of marriage and careers: husbands' active cooperation; health to stand the strain of conflicting interests; adequate household assistance; and training and work experience before marriage.[64]

Many of the interviewees scoffed at the notion that schoolteachers have abbreviated hours, pointing to their long days and nights of professional work. Faye Bronstein often envied a friend who worked at a bank, stating that her friend was the one with short hours, who never had papers to correct at night, and "could put all thoughts of her work away when she left the bank, unlike teachers whose work was always in their mind." But all concurred that along with child-care and housekeeping arrangements, their husbands' cooperation and encouragement was vital in their pursuit of motherhood and career. Several, like Fanny Stein, who termed their marriages "collaborations," had husbands who were in the public school system, as well, and these women said that both viewed their family life and their careers as collaborative efforts.

In addition to their dual roles as mothers and teachers, many of New York City's Jewish teachers added another one, that of activist. Many of the interviewees participated in professional and community organizations, teachers' unions, and political groups. In addition, many of the same names appeared as both applicants for maternity leave and as officeholders for various groups. One such woman was Mildred Flacks, who entered the city's teaching staff in 1932, and had a child during the latter part of the decade. During the thirties and forties, she was not only a union activist, but was one of the most involved participants in a series of organizations that worked for improvements in the Bedford-Stuyvesant area of Brooklyn where she taught.[65] Among the most prominent women who managed motherhood, career, and activism was Rebecca Coolman Simonson, who received her permanent teaching license in 1921, married in 1923, and took a two-year maternity leave from 1927 to 1929, during which time her son was born. She joined the Teachers Union shortly after she began teaching, and when the Teachers Guild was formed, she switched her allegiance to this union. During the thirties, Simonson served as chair of the Classroom Teachers Committee and vice president for elementary schools, and in 1941 became the Guild's president, in which capacity she served for twelve years. She was also a member of the Board of Examiners, a vice president of the American Federation of Teachers, a delegate to the United States Commission of the United Nations Educational, Scientific and Cultural Organization, and participated in numerous White House conferences on youth, yet did not retire from her sixth grade Bronx classroom until 1955.[66]

Combining activism with motherhood and teaching was not uncommon among the young Jewish women in New York City's teaching staff. But it was unusual for women to have the opportunity to be activists in

149

conjunction with their roles as mothers and teachers during the interwar years. These teacher-mothers demonstrated that women were capable of secure marriages, well-run homes, of arranging for excellent child care, and serving as effective and conscientious teachers, in addition to working for the betterment of their profession, their community, and society. Undaunted in their commitment and dedication to their chosen vocations, they not only defied determined efforts to remove them from their classrooms during the Depression, but continued teaching, even during the decade of the "feminine mystique." By remaining in the classroom until retirement, while also being wives and mothers, they refuted the charge that teaching for women is a procession, rather than a profession.

CHAPTER

 9

ANTI-UNIONISM, ANTI-SEMITISM, AND ANTI-COMMUNISM IN NEW YORK CITY SCHOOLS

INEXTRICABLY CONNECTED to the strands of anti-Unionism, anti-Semitism, and anti-Communism that prevailed in New York City during the Depression years were the Jewish women who taught in its public schools. As these strands became intertwined during the late 1940s and early 1950s, when the school system embarked on its own version of McCarthyism, these women became hopelessly snarled and entangled. The New York City Board of Education, incited by the anti-Red hysteria that overtook the United States, sought to rid its schools of teachers it suspected were members of the Communist Party. All of the teachers it fired during these years were Jewish, and all were members of the Teachers Union.[1] These Jewish women, many of whom exemplify the Jewish women who entered the teaching staff of New York City's schools during the interwar years, were denied the profession for which they had prepared so hard and to which they were so devoted.

Like the majority of those interviewed for this study, many of the Jewish women who became teachers in the years between the wars were the daughters of unionists. Therefore, they readily joined the Teachers Union, Local 5 of the American Federation of Teachers. Those among them not from union backgrounds also joined because they subscribed to the growing belief that unions were the best way to secure better working conditions. As New York City's public schools grew, administrators sought to expand the schools' capacity, differentiate offerings, socialize new immigrants, formalize control over the teaching staff, streamline operations, and keep down costs. In response to the centralization and bureaucratization of urban education, teachers formed their first union in 1916. Union objectives were to provide legal protection of teachers' interests, protect them from oppressive supervision, increase the efficiency of the schools by promoting good teaching and good working conditions, provide for systematic study of school problems by teachers, promote the participation of teachers in school administration, and cooperate with parents' associations and other educational groups.[2]

The TU had three major concerns during the twenties. The first of these centered on reform issues such as health and physical facilities, and experimental schools. The second dealt with bread-and-butter issues, like salaries and the relationship of the union's legislative program to that of organized labor in New York State. The third issue was academic freedom. Insisting that education should be divorced from religion, the union called attention to incursions of church into the state. It opposed religious groups like the Newman and Menorah clubs meeting in the schools and argued against released time for religious instruction.[3] By the thirties, its program included relief of overcrowding, provision for child welfare and teacher welfare, solution of teacher unemployment, democratization of the schools, support of progressive education, and federal and state aid to schools. It launched a campaign in reaction to the city's efforts to stop multiple job holding by single individuals, get married women out of teaching, and require all teachers to be city residents, arguing there should be no such restrictions. Some of the interviewees, however, concurred with Celia Lewis Zitron, a TU activist, who believed that the overriding issue during the thirties was fascism: the fight against it at home and the campaign for collective sanctions to stop aggression in order to prevent a second world war. Almost each issue of the union's publication during the 1930s deals with the effects of fascism on education, providing teaching materials and programs to counterattack inroads of religious and racial bigotry among pupils.[4]

Broadly reformist and not particularly radical, the Teachers Union was committed to the amelioration of poor social and economic conditions through gradual reforms. Change would be brought about not through mass action or coercion, but through persuasion. Unionists preferred letter-writing, lobbying, and personal diplomacy to mass picketing and strikes. They were interested in protecting the school curriculum from political interference, especially from right-wing and patriotic groups, concentrating on keeping the Daughters of the American Revolution and the American Legion from playing a part in the social studies curriculum. Most social studies texts of the 1930s frequently failed to confront the controversies of the era, but accepted the changing times and new world leadership with little criticism. Social studies were the only part of the curriculum to come under attack by the union, as its members had great faith in the ability of social studies, when taught correctly, to create an atmosphere agreeable to social change.[5]

The union's leaders were liberal and pro-labor, many of them raised in the pro-union social environment of the Lower East Side, the sons and daughters of unionists, primarily in the textile trades; and much of its militant leadership came from Socialist party ranks. Activist Rebecca Coolman Simonson, who later became president of the Teachers Guild, was born into a family of trade unionists and Socialists. "At that time," she explained, "socialists were unionists and there was no debate about that."[6] The initial leadership of the Teachers Union was not representative of the diverse elements of the teacher population of the city. Although the union attempted to include non-Jews among its leaders, most of its officials tended to be Jewish male high school teachers, with one Jewish woman among its early groups of officers. The degree of male leadership is significant, for the vast majority of city public school teachers were women teaching in the elementary schools.[7]

Despite predominantly male leadership of the Teachers Union during the twenties and early thirties, the activism of women, like that of their counterparts in Chicago, Boston, and Minneapolis, is noteworthy.[8] Moreover, the large number of Jewish women, a minority among the city's female teachers, is quite remarkable. In 1925, Jewish women composed 50 percent of the union's executive board. They also comprise the majority of names listed on membership applications. The minutes of meetings held in 1929, 1932, and 1933, containing the only membership lists still in existence, indicate twice as many women as men in attendance, and most of these names appear to have been Jewish.[9]

Various pamphlets and papers list considerable numbers of Jewish women as members or chairs of committees, and serving as delegates to the American Federation of Teachers conventions. They also acted as union representatives to city schools during this period. All of those covering the elementary schools were women, mostly Jewish; and a sizable number of the representatives to high schools were Jewish women as well.[10] By the mid-thirties, the union's leadership changed as more women, especially Jewish women, began to play a major role in its affairs, assuming prominent roles now that the stability and status of the union was assured.[11] Those former teachers interviewed attest to their commitment to teacher unionism, as all but two belonged to unions during the twenties and thirties. Coming from trade union backgrounds themselves, "How could I not join? I was raised among unionists," Shirley Horowitz explained. Furthermore, more than half of these women were activists during this period, and another eight became more involved in later years.

During the thirties, the union's membership grew and also changed. By 1932, the teaching staff was clearly divided into two groups: those regular teachers who were appointed before 1929 and the substitutes or per diems. When the Teachers Union admitted unemployed and substitute teachers in 1935, its membership grew from 1,200 to 3,500 in less than one year, and by 1938, it boasted 6,500 members.[12] However, the union concentrated on protecting salaries, pensions, and the rights of regular teachers, despite its increasing ranks of unemployed and substitute teachers. Many of these unemployed or exploited substitutes joined one of several opposing factions springing up within the union, arguing that the first priority should be the plight of the underemployed and unemployed.[13] Even young Jewish women who had been campus activists were exasperated by "the perpetual debates about whether we should write Roosevelt another letter about Spain or demand trade embargos," as Esther Rubin stated. "What we needed," she explained, "was something done about the plight of the per diems, which most of us were, and less about the Spanish Loyalists." At the same time, a highly organized Communist minority began a strong challenge for control, dividing union forces into bitter factions, culminating in a split when the non-Communists formed the Teachers Guild in 1935.[14]

With two teachers' unions in New York City, membership continued to grow as teachers joined to deal with the many economic and professional issues of the Depression years. Teachers began responding to calls for mass demonstrations in the city and mass delegations to Albany. Even those unwilling to join began to turn to the unions for information, advice, and for help in grievance cases.[15] Yet at no time during the thirties did either union enroll a majority of the teaching staff, for to be a union member, a teacher had to be willing to take some risks. Unions were not popular with educational officials, including most principals, and petty harassments were not uncommon. Union members were sometimes singled out for extra duties, and were often passed over for promotions.[16] Those too vocal or too visible often found themselves punished.

Helen Weinstein's efforts to organize a parade for a union cause was written up in a city newspaper. After reading coverage of the event, the superintendent of schools had her transferred to a distant and inconvenient school because she had aroused "the ire of people against their employers." When told that parading was an American institution, he replied, "Not for teachers."[17]

Although the unions underwent considerable growth during the thirties, and although they were sincerely committed to nonsectarian policies, both unions were heavily Jewish in composition, while the school administration and teaching staff were predominantly Irish Catholic. Administrators viewed the unions as an ethnic power play, as much as a conflict of issues and principles. Non-Jewish teachers failed to join in numbers commensurate with the hegemony they enjoyed in the school system. Although neither the Teachers Union nor the Teachers Guild publicized their Jewish membership, because they were trying to attract all segments of the teaching staff, the unions were perceived as Jewish unions, and few Irish-American teachers joined during this period of religious antagonism between the two groups. Moreover, the Jewish composition of the unions made them targets of the anti-Semitism that prevailed in Depression-era New York City. Evidence of this anti-Semitism directed against union membership abounds in the files of both the Teachers Union and the Teachers Guild, which contain hate mail, much of it anonymous letters addressed to Jewish union officers.[18] The unions also failed to recruit Irish-American teachers, undoubtedly more conservative than their Jewish colleagues, because union leaders were often radicals.

Some teachers, both male and female, were reluctant to join the unions because they perceived a dichotomy between professionalism and unionism. Upwardly mobile and identifying with the middle class, these teachers viewed themselves as professionals (although their status was actually that of semiprofessionals) and unions as decidedly working class.[19] Others joined, yet were not quite comfortable as unionists. Celia Lewis Zitron captured the ambivalence that some union members felt when she noted that: "Even among teachers sympathetic to labor, the conviction that membership in a union meant a loss of professional status was deeply ingrained."[20] Yet these teachers, upwardly mobile new professionals who came from union backgrounds, still perceived themselves "to some degree as workers in juxtaposition to employers; they still saw themselves as the exploited."[21] This group of teachers who were still conscious of themselves as workers was in perfect synchronization with union leadership. In interviews, former teachers who were also union members would refer to themselves in one sentence as "professionals," and in another as "trade unionists," or "members of the working class." Replicated repeatedly on the pages of the *New York Teacher* and the *Guild Teacher* was the same dichotomy, as these union publications wrote of teachers as professionals in one column, and on the same page termed them workers or trade unionists. The teacher-unionists interviewed saw no contradiction. Nor did Jurgen Herbst in his study of teachers and professionalization when he posited that teachers did not view unionization as "a rebellion against the idea of professionalization in teaching, but a demand that they be accorded...professional recognition and opportunities."[22]

However, during the interwar years, most teachers, whether unionists or nonmembers, were victims of their own prejudices and did not always face reality. The majority hid their powerlessness behind their professionalism and refused to take collective action to improve their wages and better their working conditions. They formed endless associations and discussed a variety of questions, but they never came to grips with the question of who really controlled the schools. Yet they were realistic enough to realize that with so many unemployed, the 1930s was hardly a decade to channel discontent into militancy. Nor could strikes be considered viable, "because there were thousands of teachers who would have jumped at the chance for a job," as Frances Levy stated. Moreover, a certain complacency went along with being employed as a teacher during the Depression. As Fanny Stein, who had a permanent job throughout the decade, explained, "We were pretty lucky and we knew it. When you looked at coal miners or mill workers, you realized your problems could not compare."

Those who did join made an important decision, however natural if one was from a trade union family, for membership meant responsibility for paying dues, attending meetings, and serving on committees or as school organizers, and represented some degree of commitment and vulnerability. But despite all the problems, union leaders and members continued to believe that unionism was the best way to protect teacher rights and promote educational reform. Their concern with salaries and pensions was seen not solely as bread-and-butter trade unionism, but as an effort to bring the material position of teachers into line with their professional status in society. Because they were the sons and daughters of Jewish socialists, or had grown up in the labor movement themselves, they used the organizational form with which they were most familiar. Through education and experience, they added attitudes about professionalism, reconciling the disparities in the two concepts. Unionism became an expedient means for carrying out both the material and professional reforms that they believed would improve the quality of the teaching staff and raise the status of the educational enterprise in general.

But outspoken support of teachers' unions caused innumerable conflicts during the thirties. Supervisors often punished teachers for their union membership by giving them unsatisfactory ratings. Careful reading of the "School Page" of the *New York Sun* and the *Journal of the Board of Education* indicates that these women protested their adverse ratings. As a matter of fact, the only published accounts of teachers appealing these ratings to the Board of Education were those of union members, perhaps because they had union backing in their cases. Often the principals were extremely petty and vindictive in dealing with these union members. Mildred Schoenbaum was rated "unsatisfactory" and her dismissal recommended because she used the school mimeograph machine to prepare invitations to a Teachers Union tea.[23] Blanche Horowitz was transferred after having posted a union notice on the school bulletin board. In 1939, Helen Weinstein was the only teacher to receive permanent tenure in the face of an adverse service rating. Her principal rated her "unsatisfactory" in self-control, use of voice, ability to cooperate with other teachers, and control of her class, despite over two years of satisfactory service. When she charged the principal with being biased against union members and using the rating system as a reprisal, the principal admitted that he wanted every member of the Teachers Union "out of my school." The Board of Education then ruled that his rating was prejudiced and granted her tenure, along with a transfer to another school.[24]

Most teachers believed that it was almost impossible for the individual teacher to secure redress from the Board of Education on an appeal against a principal's rating.[25] A former counsel for the Teachers Union alleged that principals who gave adverse ratings or transfers as punitive measures did so with the assurance that the legal structure available to the teacher is "calculated to discourage and stifle protest," adding that all presumptions favored the supervisors. During the appeals process, the teacher was exposed to "merciless quizzing," and was cross-examined as if she were a culprit. Without benefit of counsel, the teacher was rarely a match for experienced, domineering prosecutors who pounced on her confusion, exploiting her inexperience as a means to establish that the principal was always right.[26] According to the former teachers interviewed, most would have been reluctant to seek a rating reversal during the Depression years, when teaching positions were at a premium. As

Belle Aronoff explained, "It was hard enough getting appointed. One would have been crazy to jeopardize the security this job afforded." The feeling of futility was probably reinforced by the publicity given to Board procedures by teachers' organizations and by the teachers' unions, and was especially underscored by the disclosure in the press of the odds against winning appeals, which were twenty-nine to one. In 1936 alone, of the thirty appeals that were initiated by teachers against local school authorities, twenty-nine were lost.[27]

As for the political beliefs of the city's teachers, while a number of Communist party members did teach in the city's schools, according to most accounts, including several of those interviewed, they apparently constituted only a very small portion of the teaching staff. Ten of the interviewees were members of the Communist party at one time, including Fanny Stein, who remained a member until 1956. A sizable proportion of the sixty-one former teachers interviewed said that they were Socialists, but most claimed to have been "Roosevelt Democrats." The results of a questionnaire for city teachers sponsored by the John Dewey Society for the Study of Education in 1936 showed that the general tendency of teachers was "leftish" with "pale pink" rather than "red" coloring. The study found that while there was a predominance of teachers holding socialist convictions, only a small group actually voted for the Socialist party. This study also noted that while the great majority of teachers saw the need for far-reaching economic and social reforms, their dissent from the status quo was of a gradualist rather than a revolutionary approach. Furthermore, the questionnaire also indicated that the radical group was the better informed on social issues and public problems.[28]

City teachers felt they could express their support of high income taxes, and their belief that labor was pitifully underpaid. However, they were not free to support pacifism or total disarmament.[29] Opposition to military training in the schools brought them into conflict with groups which sponsored junior military organizations holding training in the city's schools. The president of one of these groups instructed students enrolled in its program to report any teachers who "expound foreign-inspired, un-American philosophy" to the authorities for disciplinary action.[30] Criticism of the government was dangerous as well, and most teachers felt they could not criticize the president or the federal government. Evelyn Weiss was censured by her principal because she asked her high school civics class to debate whether President Roosevelt had too much or too little power. She was warned not to "plant any seeds of doubt in her pupils' minds." Hannah Austerman was berated several times by school officials for remarks that students reported she had made in her classroom. She recalled being reprimanded for stating that a number of congressmen were racists, and for stating that the United States had "a long history of inflicting injustices upon many of its citizens."

As Superintendent of Schools Harold G. Campbell warned, "There is no room in the public schools for any teacher . . . who does not give allegiance to the fundamental principles of the Constitution," or for any who taught children "subversive" doctrines. He insisted it was the duty of teachers to teach "the right attitude toward American history and American traditions."[31] Another New York City school administrator was quite forthright about the consequences of criticizing the government, insisting that the teacher's attitude toward patriotism "must be taken into account" in determining promotions, adding, "We cannot concede that 'intellectual freedom' is synonymous with . . . the right to sneer at our institutions."[32] Nor could teachers safely protest police harassment of Communist demonstrations or suggest that children absent themselves from school to march in May Day parades.[33] Speaking to the Catholic Teachers Association of New York in 1938, Monsignor Fulton J. Sheen advocated that any teacher who cooperated with the "agents of Stalin" by sending children to participate in the May Day parade ought to be declared ineligible to teach.[34] "One had to be so careful about May Day," explained Fanny Stein. "Of course I always marched in the parade, but I never had the nerve to say so. I just took a sick day," she added, and said she tried, as subtly as possible, to encourage her pupils to do the same.

In New York City, Red-baiting and teacher-baiting of this sort went hand in hand in the interwar period. Sadie Ginsberg had the somewhat dubious honor of being the first city teacher to be dismissed for membership in the Communist party, in 1919.[35] Two years later the Lusk Laws were passed, requiring all public school teachers to be loyal and obedient to the governments of both New York State and the United States, and forbade teaching of the violent or unlawful overthrow of government. Shortly after passage of these laws, Sarah Hyams was severely reprimanded because as a member of the Left Wing Section of the Socialist party, she was deemed to hold political views that made her "unfit" to teach; and in 1921, Rachel R. Ragozin was dismissed for membership in this group. In 1934, after the repeal of the Lusk Laws, the Ives Law was promulgated, forcing all teachers to take a loyalty oath.[36] During the thirties, an atmosphere of fear and uncertainty regarding the economic situation prevailed among all teachers. Added to this was the aura of insecurity and trepidation brought about by the dread of being labeled a subversive, whether the teacher belonged to a radical political party or was nonpolitical. One teacher admitted to being "pusillanimous" about airing her views during the Depression years, stating, "I'll play it safe. I have to hold my job." Another said she feared that by expressing her own opinions she would place her job in peril. "One knows enough to walk softly," she admitted.[37]

Attacks on teachers' loyalty came not only from legislators and politicians, but from the popular press, from self-styled patriotic watchdog organizations, from school administrators, and from pupils and parents. New York's Mayor Fiorello H. LaGuardia warned teachers of foreign languages that they were limited to the teaching of language and literature, and were not to "get any propaganda" into their teaching, because "Our form of government is the best that the human mind has been able to devise." Superintendent of Schools Campbell reminded teachers that they should lose no opportunity to inculcate devotion to American ideals, pointing out that history classes offered exceptional opportunities in this respect.[38] Throughout the thirties, the Hearst-owned press waged a protracted campaign against so-called "radicals" in the public schools.[39] Another publication that was not only vehemently anti-Communist but anti-Semitic as well, was the *Educational Signpost,* published by an anti-Communist organization, the Educational Discussion Group, which later became the American Education Association. This organization attacked any sign of Communism in the schools, along with progressive education. It attacked the American Student Union and its activities, and suggested that loyal teachers denounce their radical colleagues to their superiors.[40]

Pupils were also encouraged to monitor teachers and to report to their parents any remark that could be construed as pro-Communist or anti-government, so that parents could then complain to school administrators. In one of the city's high schools, a student jumped up in a history class in the midst of a lesson on the Soviet Union based on the department syllabus and called out: "All these things on the black-board are lies. You're a semi-Red . . . I reported you to the Friday night meeting," referring to a group called the Sentinels. The Teachers Union reported cases of anonymous letters sent to the Board and complaints to principals about teachers' loyalty.[41] In 1936, one parent wrote to a school authority that a young woman taught "matters that are calculated to train the young mind in directions opposed to the system of Government under which we live," also alleging that she instructed her history class in matters "diametrically opposed to the truth." Specifically, the parent claimed that the teacher had praised the Soviet government, and said both the Spanish-American War and World War I were caused by William Randolph Hearst and "other capitalists." Fortunately for this teacher, her principal defended her, stressing that she led students in patriotic songs during assemblies; but she was warned to be "careful and accurate and American with respect to the proper teaching of History."[42] Several interviewees, especially those who taught history or civics, experienced such accusations, some of which were quite ludicrous, as was the case with Hannah Austerman, who had a parent complain when she told her pupils that both Washington and Jefferson had been slaveowners. "It sounds comical and sometimes these complaints were nothing more than crank letters," she stated. Nevertheless, the teacher was constrained to defend herself. Too many of these reports not only added volumes to a teacher's permanent file, but tended to incur the annoyance of the principal and other supervisors.[43]

Because of this constant chipping away at teachers' liberty, the Teachers Union established a Committee on Academic Freedom whose task was to deal with individual cases brought to its attention. Since the union was not powerful, it could not set down broad principles of academic freedom and expect them to be respected by administrators. What it did do was to concentrate its energies on the individual cases at hand, enlisting the support of civic groups, other teacher organizations, and sympathetic administrators on behalf of the accused individuals, thereby mitigating teachers' fears somewhat. The Committee on Academic Freedom also was active in disseminating lesson plans and other presentations to combat intolerance and anti-Semitism.[44]

Anti-Semitism was inextricably linked with anti-radicalism, especially during the thirties, when this coupling plagued Jewish teachers. Deep-rooted antagonisms, exacerbated by powerful events abroad and Depression-induced insecurities at home, produced ethnic conflict that marked New York City life during the decade.[45] Teachers were assailed, both in print and over the airwaves, by the demagogic Catholic priest Father Charles E. Coughlin, who combined his teacher-bashing and Red-baiting with anti-Semitism. The November 6, 1939, issue of his national publication *Social Justice* was headed "Are Reds in Control of New York Schools?" The magazine listed the officers, executive board, "prominent members," and "leading radicals" among the members of the New York City Teachers Union. Next to each name was a designation: "Jew," "Jewess," "Gentile," and "Undetermined."[46]

Anti-Semitism also found its way into the city's schools, often fueled by such organizations as the American Education Association and the Teachers Alliance, according to Board of Education member Johanna M. Lindlof.[47] In one school, stickers were found reading "Gentile Teachers Organize or Lose Your Jobs to the Jews . . . Join the Gentile Defense Front." In another, stickers with the worst types of caricatures of Jews, bearing the slogan "Don't Buy from Jews!" were found pasted on stairways. In yet another, a leaflet with the heading "Teachers Union Mostly Jews," and subheaded "Communism is Jewish," was distributed. And in a further instance, a mother objected to her daughter's teacher "because she was Jewish."[48]

Often anti-Semitism was to be found as well, among Jewish teachers' colleagues. Besides reflecting the intolerance to be found within their ethnic groups, the problem was intensified by the feelings of displacement experienced by many teachers of Irish and German backgrounds who had entered the school system, once considered their bailiwick, prior to 1920. Jewish women were now competing for scarce and highly prized teaching positions, thereby causing considerable ethnic resentment.[49] Frequently the increased Jewish–Gentile contact among teachers produced ethnic strains and spurred separatism, rather than friendship; the two groups even maintained quasi-segregated restrooms.[50] "It was particularly painful when teachers made a point of reading the *Signpost* in the teachers' room," recalled Mildred Herman, stating that by doing so the teacher who read this anti-Semitic publication conveyed "the message, loud and clear, that she didn't like Jews." Although a number of the interviewees attested to strained relations between the two groups of teachers, many others insist they never encountered the slightest bit of hostility, veiled or otherwise, from other teachers. Elsie Winkler insisted that whatever strains might have existed could be attributed to the differences in age, since most of the gentile teachers were considerably older than their Jewish colleagues.

Nevertheless, the presence of anti-Semitism was an intrinsic part of life for these women. Although they thoroughly despised anti-Semitism in all its manifestations, its presence neither surprised nor shocked them. As Belle Aronoff emphasized, "We grew up on stories of the pogroms in the old country, and it always surrounded us here in America. It was a fact of life." Many of the interviewees adopted the Marxist belief that anti-Semitism would be obliterated once the economic and social orders were changed. Others viewed the problem as one of ignorance, certain it would vanish once people were taught that anti-Semitism was "illogical and un-American," as Lily Gordon explained. "Many of us tackled it head-on, in the classroom, forever teaching tolerance. We also used union publications to get our message across," she stated. Most of the interviewees claimed that they encountered all sorts of prejudice on a frequent basis, and confronted it, whether it was another teacher or a supervisor. Failure to respond to ethnic or racial slurs was considered a serious lack of character. Gordon recalled entering the teachers' lounge with another Jewish teacher, overhearing two colleagues engaged in anti-Semitic remarks as a third Jewish teacher sat in silence. According to Gordon, "First we reprimanded the two anti-Semites. Then we took the Jewish teacher aside and gave her a dressing-down for allowing such filth." Anti-Semitism may have been "a fact of life," as alleged, one that saddened and disturbed these young women greatly, but they reacted to it with anger and with a fierce determination to root it out wherever and whenever possible.

Yet anti-Semitism caused many Jewish teachers to become sensitive to the invidious effects of bigotry of all kinds. Because there were Communist party members or sympathizers among city teachers, their concern for oppressed minorities paralleled the party's commitment toward African Americans. Party members exerted a profound effect on African Americans during the Depression era, and as Mark Naison has noted in his study of the Communist party in Harlem during the 1930s, "the most significant presence came in the schools themselves, where white Communist schoolteachers maintained close working relationships with black teachers, parents, and community leaders," not only in Harlem, but in Bedford-Stuyvesant, another African-American neighborhood in New York City, as well.[51]

These Jewish teachers were deeply affected by the horrible conditions in Harlem and the deplorable state of its schools. The first day twenty-three-year-old Alice Citron entered P.S. 184 in Harlem in 1931, three years after being graduated from Hunter College, determined her life as a teacher in the years that followed. She remembered that her sensibilities were assaulted by the "agony of life in Harlem," by the abandoned tenements, and the children, with "no joy in their eyes," who looked like they had never eaten. Although she had come from an impoverished family herself, what she witnessed in Harlem was a different poverty, unlike her own poverty, for there seemed to be no hope for the residents of Harlem. The school itself was an old, shabby, neglected building, with "nothing to induce children to learn."[52] It was understaffed, "a place of chaos," with "teachers going in and out of the place like a transient hotel." Assigned to a room with broken blackboards, a class of over forty children with "the most horrendous personal problems," Citron made up her mind "to be the best teacher that I could humanly be and to fight for the children."[53] Four years after Citron first entered a Harlem school, a twenty-seven-year-old graduate of the Maxwell Training School finally received a permanent appointment to P.S. 170, also in Harlem, after years of serving as a substitute. This teacher, whose case did not receive as much publicity as some of the other Communist teachers later dismissed from service, will be called Dorothy Rose here.[54] In a letter to a New York City assistant superintendent of schools, Rose wrote of her shock at finding double and triple sessions, overcrowded classes, broken-down school plants, and lack of recreational facilities, all of which she insisted were responsibile for the riots that had taken place in Harlem that summer. Therefore, as a teacher in an underprivileged area, she felt she had a professional responsibility "to attempt to alleviate and change this situation."[55]

Both teachers, ahead of their time by several decades, supported the African-American quest for cultural recognition, contending that the African-American experience ought to be acknowledged and celebrated, and that the children they taught were entitled to learn about the contributions of their people. Rose and Citron spearheaded a drive to remove biased textbooks from the schools, especially those that debased minorities.[56] In her letter to an assistant superintendent, Rose wrote that such textbooks helped further the tensions that erupted into riots in 1935, adding that these books omitted the participation of African Americans in American history, and showed "outright bias and prejudice," thus giving African-American children "the impression that they are inferior."[57]

Deciding that African-American children "must know they are people," these two teachers also joined forces with other teachers to establish Negro History Week as part of the school program. After a summer at the University of Mexico studying African-American history and culture, Citron revised her school's history curriculum, using a booklet she wrote on African-American culture and successes, and during every history period she taught, she included African-American history. She wrote plays for her classes, dramatizing themes from their history, took them on field trips, compiled bibliographies on African-American history for other teachers, and displayed pictures of notable African Americans in her school. Often books and materials for these projects had to come out of her own personal funds.[58]

Because they believed that the Board of Education treated minority children like stepchildren, these women embarked on a campaign to improve conditions for ghetto children. Citron's battles with the school system began even before she had secured a position, for she served as secretary of the Unemployed Teachers Association and was a leader in its frequent controversies with the Board. While still a probationary teacher, she headed the Communist party's teacher branches in Harlem, where she organized and led a drive to upgrade conditions in Harlem schools. This was tackled through a whirlwind of activities that continued throughout her career. She prepared studies, reports, and surveys; sent articles to the press; established a community-wide association to fight for better schools; and spoke to church groups and civic organizations.[59] In conjunction with these efforts was Citron's participation in the Teachers Union. A frequent contributor to *New York Teacher* and to the union's annual education conferences, she usually addressed issues relating to African-American children.[60]

Never one to shrink from controversy or confrontation, this remarkable and energetic woman's presence in the Harlem community was deemed highly provocative by the Board of Education. Because she publicly agreed with a Harlem clergyman who had accused the Board of neglecting local schools and discriminating against its children during a 1933 meeting of the Harlem Parents Association, she was criticized for failing to protest his indictment. The New York City Board of Superintendents stated that it was the duty of every teacher to defend the school system against "unfounded, wild, and reckless statements," adding that her denunciation of the Board, as well as her exhortations to the audience to take part in mass action, constituted "acts of disloyalty to the education system," which "may not be subjected to attacks by one of its employees."[61] The Board retaliated by giving Citron an unsatisfactory rating, by depriving her of her annual increment, and by denying her a permanent license. Bolstered by an aroused and indignant community, Citron sued the Board, which was then forced by the courts to reverse its decision. However, Citron was more fortunate than her husband, Isadore Begun, who was one of three teachers fired in reprisal for protesting school conditions, and never reinstated.[62] Undaunted by the Board, Citron continued agitating on behalf of the children of Harlem. One of her principal and most successful strategies was to engage the community in pressing for improvements. Because she considered the schools to be an integral part of the community, Citron attempted to bring the community into the schools. By involving the people of Harlem with its schools and activities, she believed she could inspire the community and demonstrate that it was possible to implement change.[63]

More than a teacher, Citron was regarded as a friend who fought for the community and worked tirelessly for the children of Harlem. She raised money to send them to summer camps, and personally financed the needs of many of its most deprived children. The president of her school's Parent-Teacher Association noted that Citron "even comes to homes to help slow children. And she puts her hands in her own pockets to help buy shoes and get dental care for needy children." Another parent claimed that Citron was "everything to our neighborhood, to the community as a whole, to the Negro people. . . . At any time when anything came up, we could go to her." Tributes from supervisors, colleagues, parents, social workers, community leaders, and former students filled volumes of her scrapbooks, yet on February 8, 1951, she was removed as a teacher for refusing to answer questions about membership in the Communist party.[64]

Anti-radicalism and anti-Semitism during the thirties led to the harassment of many teachers, but more lost their jobs during the second Red scare of the late forties and early fifties, despite acknowledgments that they were outstanding teachers. Dorothy Rose, who had also labored both inside and outside the classroom for the children of Harlem, was also fired in 1951. Like Citron's, her teaching record was impeccable; and she, too, was active in the PTA, helped send schoolchildren to summer camps, and worked to establish neighborhood nursery schools. One parent was so touched by Dorothy Rose's personal interest in her child that she named her next child Dorothy, in Rose's honor.[65] Another Jewish teacher who had fought Jim Crow in the Brooklyn neighborhood of Bedford-Stuyvesant was also dismissed from service. Mildred Flacks, who had been teaching since 1932, and was considered a model of the best in modern teaching, had been highly visible in her activism on behalf of schoolchildren and the community, and was a noted union activist, like Citron and Rose. Flacks served in various capacities on many school and community committees, including the Council of Bedford-Stuyvesant–Williamsburg, a grass roots movement she helped found in 1943 which was responsible for getting three new schools built in the area by 1951.[66]

In all cases, the Jewish teachers caught in the net of McCarthyism were Teachers Union activists like Citron, Rose, and Flacks, who had exceptional teaching reputations, and who gave freely of their time to help and guide schoolchildren.[67] Dorothy Bloch, who taught in what was euphemistically termed "the more difficult" vocational high schools, was commended for her volunteer activities, which included acting as faculty advisor to the school magazine, and was praised for approaching parents and children "in an endeavor to understand their difficulties at home and in the community," yet was fired as an alleged Communist.[68] Minna Finkelstein, another dismissed Jewish teacher, had been commended as eager to volunteer her services for the school and to use her own funds to take pupils on field trips, and was well known for her cooperation with parents on projects to develop better understanding between the community and the school.[69]

One of the most prominent of the Jewish women whose teaching careers were terminated because of alleged membership in the Communist party was Celia Lewis Zitron, an especially innovative language teacher who had introduced the study of Hebrew in the city's high schools. For twenty-six of her twenty-seven years of teaching, she was a leading member of the Teachers Union, which she considered the most effective organization for improving conditions for teachers and students. In her capacity as chair of its Academic Freedom Committee, she defended a number of teachers who had been victimized by tyrannical supervisors, and led many campaigns to combat anti-Semitism and to maintain academic freedom in the city's schools. In frequent articles in the Teachers Union publication, and in speeches at many of its conferences, her views on the rights and responsibilities of teachers as citizens in a democracy were made public.[70] Taking on the Rapp-Coudert investigations, the Hearst press, anti-Semites, and the American Education Association, in 1940 she warned teachers to be on their guard, because these groups all sought to discredit teachers as disloyal and subversive.[71]

However, these activist teachers, who were later seen by the general public as Red menaces who threatened the very fabric of society, were not perceived as such by those who knew them best. Parents, fellow teachers, and residents of the communities in which these women taught all rallied to uphold their right to remain in the classroom when they were brought up on charges of belonging to an organization that advocated the violent overthrow of the established government. Statements of support were issued to city newspapers, and the Teachers Union printed testimonials in pamphlets that were used to raise money for legal fees. A tribute held to honor Alice Citron, and to demand that she be allowed to remain in Harlem, was so jammed with her admirers that most were forced to stand.[72] Encouraging as this support was, it had no impact on the Board, which never rescinded the dismissals. The late 1940s and early 1950s were characterized by a fear that has withstood the test of time, and has left great scars among the city's Jewish teachers, many of whom indeed were or had been Communists. Quite a few of the women interviewed insisted on anonymity, decades later, rather than "rake up those old coals," as Fanny Stein put it. Her husband, also a Communist, opted for early retirement lest he be called before the Board to answer questions, a dread shared by all radical teachers. "We lived on tenter-hooks, worried that someone else would name us, even if we were never called," Stein added. This postwar Red hunt not only caused deep-rooted apprehension, but resulted in at least one tragedy.

The unfortunate teacher was Minnie Gutride, a forty-year-old woman who had been teaching since 1931. She was called out of her classroom two days before the Christmas holidays in 1948. Questioned by an assis-tant superintendent, who was accompanied by an official stenographer, Gutride was asked whether she had attended Communist meetings eight years previously, and then was threatened with possible charges of insub-ordination, along with vague references to court action. After her interro-gation, she went to the Teachers Union for help. Rose Russell, the union's legal representative, immediately wired school officials, protesting Gutride's brutal treatment, and met with officials the next day, further condemning their action. That same day, New York City's Hearst-owned newspaper, *The Journal-American,* published an account of Gutride's being accused of being Communist, adding that her late husband, who had died during the Spanish Civil War, had been "a charter member" of the party, an allegation with no foundation. Since her husband was born in 1911, he could scarcely have been a charter member of a group founded during his childhood.[73] Overcome with despondency, Gutride killed her-self. She was found dead two days later, amid presents and toys she had bought for the children in her class.[74]

Although Minnie Gutride's fate was the most tragic among the city's teachers accused of being Communists, countless others were also casu-alties of the city's drive to rid the schools of radical teachers. Although only 38 of the city's teachers had been dismissed after trials by the end of the 1950s, another 283 had resigned or retired before or after being interrogated. A further 126 publicly recanted their membership in the Communist party, making a total of 447 New York City teachers who directly experienced the Board of Education's purges. This total was a small percentage of all city teachers, but the anxiety of being accused of being Communists and then publicly fired during an age of great suspi-cion had a ripple effect on members of the teaching staff.[75]

We will never know how many others resigned, rather than wait to be charged; and we can never know the trepidation under which these teachers lived. "Fear," as David Caute observed, "is contagious, particularly among the children of immigrants who feel themselves to be ethnically or economically insecure," especially among this generation of teachers who had come of age during the Depression years.[76] Former teachers claim that almost all Jewish teachers, Communists or not, believed themselves to be potential suspects. It was no mere coincidence to them that almost all of the accused were both Jewish and activists in the Teachers Union, a party stronghold. All thirty-three of the teachers dismissed during the purges and who finally had their pension rights restored in 1972 were Jews.[77]

As movers and shakers, the teachers who were fired had continually agitated for improvements in the schools, and had constantly carped at the Board of Education. Therefore, the activities of these teachers affiliated with radical causes hardly went unnoticed by officialdom. Bella Visonti Dodd, a former Communist who had once served as legal representative of the Teachers Union, estimated that as many as one thousand city teachers belonged to the party. However, Dodd, who had disavowed Communism and became a professional witness at anti-Communist showcase trials, was prone to exaggeration. Only 4,000 of the city's 35,000 public schoolteachers were members of the Teachers Union in 1941. Therefore, other estimates that claim that only about five hundred of these teachers actually belonged to the party seem more plausible.[78] According to Fanny Stein, a sizable segment of Communist teachers had left the Communist Party of the United States of America in 1939, in dismay over the alliance between the Soviet Union and Germany. "Yet they all knew that their previous membership would be damaging to their careers," Stein added. Moreover, many of the interviewees said that even if they personally had never joined the Communist party, they all knew someone who was a member, and dreaded being put into a position where they might have to testify against that person.[79] In addition, as Myn Silverman explained, "everyone signed some sort of petition or joined some sort of organization later ruled subversive, which would tinge us with Red paint."

By succumbing to the hysteria of the McCarthy witch-hunts, the city school system lost some of its most idealistic, effective, and devoted teachers. Some were lost through their dismissal or resignation. Others, overcome with anxiety, muted their activism, hoping only to survive the inquisition until they attained retirement. Those who lost the most were

New York City's ghetto children who no longer had teachers like Alice Citron, whose personal crusade was to demonstrate the capabilities of African Americans, both to themselves and to the world at large. These children missed having teachers, most of whom were both Jewish and Communists, who approached the education of African Americans "as a mission of special importance." The schools forfeited the services of teachers like Mildred Flacks, who was said to have "had the love of the children at heart."[80] It would be a long time, perhaps until the city committed itself to recruiting minority teachers, until these children would have a teacher like Flacks, who passed up many offers to transfer to so-called "better" schools, and had remained in Bedford-Stuyvesant because she believed "the most satisfactory moments of my career were spent with the underprivileged children of this Negro community."[81] Alice Citron's assessment of her own career was similar: she was convinced that instilling the children she taught with the belief that "they were people" was her greatest achievement, and her greatest pride was that many of her pupils went on to become teachers and professionals.[82]

As Mark Naison has observed, activism was a trademark of Communist teachers, "who displayed an idealism and enthusiasm in dealing with black children that deeply impressed blacks who worked with them." According to the Reverend David Licorish, these teachers "were much more dedicated to teaching black children the way out of the crucible of American life than the teachers we have now. When they left, Harlem became a worse place. They stayed after school with the children and gave them extra curricular attention to bring them up to level. You didn't have these reading problems like you have today. These people were dedicated to their craft."[83]

These were teachers who were noteworthy for their devotion to teaching throughout some of the most difficult decades in the history of the city's school system. For most, it had been an arduous task to endure as substitute teachers before finally achieving a permanent position during the hiring freeze of the thirties; and it had been difficult, as well, to survive and to teach effectively in schools crippled by budgetary cuts. During the forties, they were overworked because of the teacher shortage caused by the war. In the fifties, they were confronted with overcrowding and an entirely different set of problems arising from changes in the city's population. Yet most teachers, and especially the Jewish teachers who fell victim to McCarthyism, gave unstintingly of themselves physically, emotionally, and intellectually in the interests of their pupils. As Stella Eliashaw, one of the Jewish women fired during the 1950s, noted, teaching was more than a profession to her. Even with all the burdens that she had faced resulting from overcrowding and retardation, she still loved to teach. "In the truest possible sense," she asserted, she had "kept faith" with her students.[84]

Most of the interviewees expressed similar sentiments when assessing their careers. It has been particularly distressing to them that although the majority of their generation of teachers retired during the 1960s, they believe they have suffered from being characterized as racists. Despite their demonstrated commitment to minority children, during the city's decentralization controversy of the 1960s, this group of teachers was accused of setting precedents for bigotry among the next generation of New York City teachers.[85] In one of the ironies of change, the current group of Jewish teachers are in the same position as Irish and Yankee teachers were during the interwar years. New York City public school students are now primarily African American and Hispanic, with a sizable non-English-speaking immigrant component. Their teachers are mostly Jewish, and these teachers do not live in the same neighborhoods as their pupils. Therefore, many of the same problems of identity and understanding that existed during the interwar years are present today, as well.

Nevertheless, the daughters of Jewish immigrants who entered the city's teachng staff in the years between the two world wars represent a unique contingent in the history of women, immigrants, and urban education. They deserve scholarly attention because as public school teachers they are the forgotten element in the history of education and because the full picture of women cannot be complete unless it includes women of diverse socioeconomic, cultural, and educational backgrounds.

In part, these women replicated the familiar cycle of their mothers' lives. They went to work to help provide for their families, participated in the union movement, married, and had children, yet they deviated from their mothers. In ways characteristic of the New Woman, as described by Nancy F. Cott in *The Grounding of Modern Feminism,* they wanted to be modern, well informed, competent and effective in their profession, and productive, contributing members of society.[86] They also differed from their mothers in that they were able to take full advantage of the free education offered them by New York City's public schools. They did not have to be the unskilled workers their mothers were, but were trained professionals with job security and a prestigious position, an impossible situation for their mothers when they were laboring in the sweatshops. As professionals, they would not leave work upon marriage and motherhood, as their mothers had, for the daughters considered teaching a lifelong career.

Just as they veered from the path taken by their mothers, these teachers also diverged in several ways from the New Woman. In the post-suffrage era, they did not consider themselves feminists, and were not recognized as such by others, despite their public behavior. Like their mothers had before them, they continued to work within such male-dominated organizations as the public school administration, the unions, and the political parties, where women were considered irrelevant. As educated professionals, they did not pursue gender-specific objectives, but sought partnership with men along their common interests. Moreover, they fashioned a particularly Jewish version of the modern, twentieth-century woman, both because they were anxious to be perceived as modern *American* women and because their world continued to be that of their families. Unlike the typical New Woman, they did not intend their careers to endow them with economic independence, but to provide themselves and their families with economic stability. The sense of self-respect a teaching position brought them, and its concomitant prestige for all concerned, was perceived as an added bonus. They also believed that like their mothers had done before them, they too left their mark in important and innovative ways.

CHAPTER

10

AFTERWORD

IF THERE IS ONE paramount lesson I have learned from my encounters with the former teachers who served as interviewees for this study, it is the validity of the aphorism "Once a teacher, always a teacher." Beyond the most tangible components of this adage, as manifested during the interview process, where a definite pupil–teacher relationship usually developed between interviewer and interviewee, is the continuing concern for education that these retired teachers demonstrate time and again, along with unshaken notions of what is wrong and a few ideas on how to rectify it. In addition, they also display their enduring ability and desire to teach. During interviews, each former teacher felt compelled to offer her thoughts and observations on the current state of public school education, with special reference to New York City conditions. Many of these women have been anxious to continue offering their educational opinions to me, years after their interviews have been concluded. Any time the newspapers print a story on education, especially about the city, and every time a televised newscast features a scandal involving city schools, several of the interviewees regularly telephone me to be certain I am aware of the news. Although their comments invariably contain the phrase "In my day," some of their reactions are worth noting here.

Certain themes recur in what these former teachers choose to mention, such as their dismay that the more things change, the more they remain the same. A recent piece in the *New York Times* by an active high school teacher delineating an average day, replete with minutiae of extra-professional details identical to those that plagued their own teaching years, brought a spate of telephone calls from these women, who waxed irate that conditions had not improved.¹ Reports on the Board of Education, with its Byzantine bureaucracy riddled with theft, waste, corruption, inefficiency, delays, paperchasing, discrimination, and incompetency remind them of the behemoth with which they had dealings during the interwar years. This leitmotif is carried over to articles depicting old, overcrowded, dilapidated buildings crammed with students who are immigrants or the children of immigrants, coming from homes scarred by poverty, with families on public assistance and unable to speak English.

They may debate whether conditions are actually worse than in their day or not, but they are uniform in their belief that public education does not matter to New York City officials. When a television report recently showed a collapsed ceiling in a Harlem classroom, Anne Kuntsler, who had taught there during the Depression, said that this school had had falling ceilings since the thirties. She then went on to complain that the city had allocated approximately one hundred million dollars to erect a new building for Stuyvesant High School, one of the city's elite schools which is noted for producing so many Westinghouse scholars and other prizewinning students. "By not providing *all* children with safe and pleasant surroundings," she insisted, "the city continues to send them the message that it just doesn't care about *all* of its pupils, especially not those from the inner city."

Yet these former teachers agree that in some respects teachers, and the schools in general, are in far worse shape than when they were in their classrooms. They are appalled by the number of arrests of teachers and other school officials who have been charged with drug possession. Even though the schools are racked with problems emanating directly from the citywide drug epidemic, they are nevertheless shocked that "teachers, professionals, would ever stoop so low," as Dora Fein put it. She further claimed that besides the schools being drug free when she taught, "in my day, children did not have children of their own. Nor were they violent." The presence of guards and metal detectors in many city schools is quite distressing to these former teachers, but most horrifying to them is the crime rate in the schools themselves. They are astounded by crimes committed by children in lower grades, as well as the escalation of violence directed at teachers.² Evelyn Weiss taught for years in a high school in the Red Hook section of Brooklyn, which she claimed was "one of the toughest areas in the city then, with the toughest children. But I never feared any pupil in school. At their worst, their behavior took the form of some backtalk, quite mild by present-day standards," she said, adding in dismay that she "recently saw on the news where an elementary school pupil brought a gun to school. Such a thing never happened in my day!"

However they lament the malaise of American public education today, what these retired teachers find most deplorable is society's refusal to encourage and value public school teachers as professionals.[3] Interviewees constantly remind me that when they joined the profession, it was one of great prestige, especially in their immigrant milieu, "where you cannot imagine the high regard people had for teachers," according to Myn Silverman. "Most of our pupils' parents were unable to attain the education they desired for various reasons, and had such high regard for us," adding that today, her daughter teaches in "an affluent area where all the parents are college graduates who have taken child psychology courses, which makes *them* the experts. They question the teacher's expertise and authority, and respect only those professions that command the most money."

Other informants have told me how resentful they are of the saying "Those who can, do. Those who can't, teach." Moreover, they tend to bristle whenever they hear someone claim that they became teachers during the interwar years because it was one of the few professions available to women, for many insist they never wanted to be anything but classroom teachers. "Despite everything, teaching still holds an attraction for many young women," according to Frances Levy, who then related how she surveyed her seder table this year, noting with great pride and satisfaction that twelve of the twenty family members present were teachers. They encompassed three generations, and are moving into a fourth, for she has a great-granddaughter currently enrolled in a teacher education program at a state university.

While these former teachers offer no panacea for elevating the status of teachers, or for providing quality public education, they do possess an unshaken conviction that there are still schools with special teachers who practice the art and craft of teaching against all apparent odds. They have cited P.S. 94 in the Bronx, an elementary school that was the focus of an ongoing series in the *New York Times* during the spring of 1990. In this school, caring, determined, and committed teachers and supervisors were educating disadvantaged and ill-prepared children in the face of seemingly insurmountable obstacles.

The depiction in a new book written by a journalist of another dedicated and driven New York City teacher who has managed to reach her students was brought to my attention recently by Esther Rubin.[4] Rubin and I had discussed at length the futile task of evaluating the effect of her generation of teachers on their students and on public school education in New York City. Mistrusting the statistics and reports provided by education officials, I also found the informants' self-assessments so positive that they constituted an encomium, which caused me to doubt their credibility as well, in this area. However, when Rubin phoned me about the newly published book, she exclaimed excitedly that its title, *Small Victories,* summed up the classroom teacher's impact on students. "We achieved small victories," she explained. "No teacher single-handedly raises reading scores. But we each have had our small victories: bringing one pupil up to age level in math; persuading a child that he is smart and capable; inspiring another to remain in school; helping another gain admission to college." Rubin further expounded that every teacher she knew had her success stories, "her small victories. I fervently believe that each of us has made a difference in the lives of some of our pupils, which I believe counts for something."

NOTES ON SOURCES

Oral Interviews

The experience and viewpoint of teachers are neglected aspects of standard histories of education, yet the female classroom teacher forms the nucleus of any school system. Because she has been overlooked in most studies, it is especially crucial for her voice to be heard in a work that places the schoolteacher as its central focus. The best possible way to allow those hitherto omitted from accounts to have their say is through oral histories, the methodology that invites people into a place where they have been left out. The interview process also provides a more realistic and fair reconstruction, as well as a challenge to established accounts.

Sixty-one women were interviewed for this study. The only criteria for their selection as interviewees were that they be the daughters of Jewish immigrants and that they entered the teaching staff of New York City's public schools between 1920 and 1940. The years of birth for those chosen for interviews ranged from 1905 to 1919. All were educated in the city's public school system, and all received their teacher training at a municipal institution. Nine were trained at The Manhattan Teacher Training School; fourteen at The Maxwell Teacher Training School; fifteen at Brooklyn College; and twenty-three graduated from Hunter College. All but one married, and all but two had children. The total number of children among these former teachers is 111. Reflecting the preponderance of elementary school teachers among the teaching staff, 45 taught the lower grades; 4 taught in junior high schools; and 12 were high school teachers. All of the interviewees taught in the city until retirement, with the majority retiring during the 1960s.

Because research for this work began in college archives, where I learned of an unusual amount of political activism engaged in by women students during the 1930s, an attempt was made to locate and interview former student activists. On the basis of a newspaper advertisement seeking such women, forty-five were chosen to be interviewed. Forty of these women were later included as subjects for further interviews on their teaching experience. Therefore, the interview subjects in this work are somewhat skewed toward women whose politics were left wing, and who tended toward political and social activism during their careers. However, this has significance for chapters 3 and 4 exclusively. In all other respects, these women conformed to the prerequisites, and exhibited no striking differences from the other respondents.

The rest of the interviewees were located through friends, recommendations from the initial group of informants, and through the Retired Teachers' Association. Interviews were conducted from 1983 to 1986 in New York City and on Long Island, in the subjects' homes, in senior citizen centers, and in the Retired Teachers' lounge at UFT headquarters in Manhattan. Interview time durations varied from two hours to fifteen, and interviews were usually conducted in several sessions. Notes were always taken (former teachers heartily approve of note-taking!) and sometimes supplemented by a tape recorder, depending on the subject's whim and the interviewer's mechanical ability on any given day.

While conventional wisdom and the advice of most oral history experts dictate that the interviewer have prearranged questions on hand, and that the interviewer maintain control over the process, other practitioners have called for a more open and accommodating relationship between informant and interviewer.[1] Sherna Gluck's observations on some of the more difficult and frustrating tasks of the interview process, especially those considerations arising from interviewing the elderly, replicate many problems personally encountered. In addition, there were problems undoubtedly unique to encounters with former schoolteachers, such as convincing them that asking questions should not be considered an intrusion upon the mode some of them preferred, namely that of the monologue.[2]

Two aspects of my oral interviews pose special problems. The first arises from the fact that some of these former teachers, especially those among the student activist group, had been members of the Communist party and other leftist organizations, living through periods when discovery of their membership would have meant dismissal from their jobs, loss of pension, and other reprisals. The informants' perceptions place the sensitivity of their political information within a nexus of fear that may seem unbelievable after so many years, but is quite real and palpable to them. Although they were not reticent about discussing their involvement in leftist causes, most were adamant that their identities not be revealed. Apparently, these concerns are common to radicals of their generation; all of the archivists whose holdings include material about left-wing teachers also insist on confidentiality for the participants. Because I promised to protect their identities, it became clumsy and confusing when footnoting their information, stating which was an assumed name and which was an actual one. Their wishes, of course, will be honored, and in the interest of clarity and uniformity, I have chosen anonymity for all interviewees by changing the names of all informants.

The next problem is that I conducted sixty-one interviews, a rather large number for a social history that utilizes the methodology of oral histories. While human memory often provides a selective record, I have sought shared experiences and viewpoints that would permit me to compare these with other sources, and then to form generalizations or state disagreements. To cite each interviewee is just too unwieldy and produces far too many citations per paragraph. However, I have attributed statements to either collective or individual interviews. Those real names that are cited in this study have been in print previously and are so noted.

The informants were not only generous with their time and attention, but demonstrated an understanding and commitment to historical integrity and truth that convinces me of the reliability and validity of the interviews.

Methodology Employed for Quantitative Material

The following is an explanation of the methodology employed for the quantitative study of New York City teachers, especially in regard to chapter 8:

The *Journal of the Board of Education* published the names and dates of every female employee who applied for the mandatory maternity leave of absence. It must be noted here that while it is quite possible that some women resigned from teaching altogether, without ever applying for maternity leave, the *Journal* did not list the reason for a teacher's resignation. However, I do not believe this was a common occurrence. The average number of resignations from service rarely exceeded 80 each year, and about one-quarter of those resigning were males.

Every name listed from 1920 to 1940 was copied, totalling 4,145, along with the leave dates, and then typed into a computer. After having these names sorted into alphabetical order, I observed that many names were duplicated, although the dates were different. Realizing that these were women who applied for more than one leave, I adjusted my list.

This list was taken to the New York City Board of Education's Bureau of Teachers' Records, Division of Personnel, in Brooklyn, where Teacher Personnel Cards and Teachers' Record Department files are stored in the depths of their subterranean basements. This area holds all records of teachers who left the system between the 1930s and late 1970s. The records of teachers whose service ended prior to the thirties have been microfilmed and are in the Board of Education Collection of the Special Collections at Milbank Library, Teachers College, Columbia University. The Board of Education has placed the records of all teachers who left the teaching staff after the late 1970s on microfilm, and they are held at the Board's headquarters in Brooklyn.

The Board of Education kindly allowed me permission to work with the Teacher Personnel cards, which are stored in cardboard boxes on top of the file cabinets that hold Teachers' Record Department files. As the first person to ever utilize these records, I found that there was not much semblance of order to the filing system; countless cards were not in proper alphabetical sequence. Moreover, the cards are badly deteriorating, and many just disintegrated at touch. The Board of Education preferred that I not consult their Teachers' Record Department files. However, they did oblige my request to sample a few, so that I could see what kind of material they contained. They also granted my request to examine a few files: I specified those of teacher activists, such as two of those interviewed, along with those of Alice Citron and several other teachers later dismissed from service.

For reasons the Board was unable to explain, many cards of the women on my maternity leave list could not be located. The possibility of remarriages and name changes do not fully explain why so many could not be found, because I was also unable to locate the cards of four of the sixty-one women interviewed for this study. In each case I had the interviewee's correct married name, under which her card should have been filed. I also found that in many cases, the pregnancy for which leave was requested was terminated because of miscarriage, with no other births recorded; these women were not included in this study. In addition, I soon realized that the *Journal* recorded the leave applications for all female employees of the Board of Education, including school nurses, and supervisory and clerical staffs. Therefore, I omitted their names as well. The method that was finally adopted was to take every third name on the list and attempt to locate it. If that name could not be found, I moved on to the name just after the missing one. In all, I scrutinized 1,212 cards, or approximately one-third of the total on my list.

The personnel cards listed teachers' names: birth names, name changes, and married names, including subsequent marriages. Having all this information facilitated determination of the woman's ethnicity. Whereas others who have studied various listings of teachers in the *Journal* might have assumed that "Sally Brown" was not Jewish and would therefore not be counted as such, her card would indicate that she had changed her name from "Sarah Bernstein," an obviously Jewish name. Also, when a name like "M. B. Smith" is listed in the *Journal*, it is difficult to guess the woman's ethnic background, but her card might read "Maureen Bridget," and the researcher can then safely count her as an Irish American. In studying the names on these cards, I made every attempt to discern the teachers' ethnicity, looking specifically for Irish, Italian, and Jewish names. All other names, including those I could not reasonably determine to be any of the aforementioned three, were considered as "other," whether they appeared to be Anglo-Saxon or Hungarian or German, and so on. The cards do not state a teacher's race; therefore, I could not tell how many of these women were African Americans. Less than ten of the cards studied indicated that the teacher trained at traditional African-American schools like Howard University.

Birth dates and marriage dates were supposed to be placed on each card. Although the teacher's married name was always listed, there were too many instances where birth and marriage dates were omitted for them to be included in this study. The institution or college where the teacher trained is listed, as well, and was noted for this study.

Other pertinent items of information that I gathered are: the dates when maternity leaves were granted and the dates when the teacher returned to service; other leaves of absence, such as for care of child or for family illness; and any sabbaticals taken. Also indicated is the date when service was terminated, and whether the teacher retired, resigned, was fired, or died before retirement.

Other data available on these cards, but not noted for this research, are: the date of entry into the system; probationary period served; date of grant of license, license examination standing; where the teacher taught and at what grade level; salary schedule; and promotions. Accompanying each teacher's card are cards that list every absence and lateness for each year. These cards also record teachers' twice-yearly ratings, along with supervisors' comments on satisfactory and unsatisfactory service. Although the cards provided equal amounts of space for both type of service, notations of unsatisfactory service were infrequent, and almost nonexistent for the interviewees.

A second study was carried out by examining five hundred cards of both men and women to compare their attendance records. The findings are discussed in chapter 8.

Obviously, teacher personnel cards are a mine of information. They contain data about teachers and their working conditions that is usually unavailable. It is hoped that this use of personnel cards will inspire other scholars to consider utilizing them as a viable historical source. We greatly need more case studies of teachers in various time periods and locations to allow us to have the most complete view of the teaching profession as is possible.

NOTES

Abbreviations

Agencies and Associations

ACLU	American Civil Liberties Union
BE	Board of Education of The City of New York
NEA	National Education Association
TG	New York Teachers Guild
TU	Teachers Union of New York City

Archival Sources

ACLU	American Civil Liberties Union papers, Princeton University Library, Princeton University.
AJA	American Jewish Archives, Cincinnati, Ohio
BAR	Barnard College Archives, Woolman Library, Barnard College, Columbia University
BC	Brooklyn College Archives, Brooklyn College Library, Brooklyn College
BE	The Board of Education of The City of New York, Bureau of Teachers' Records, Division of Personnel, Brooklyn, New York
CC	City College Archives, City College Library, City College of New York
CLMDC	Cornell Labor-Management Documentation Center, M. P. Catherwood Library, Cornell University
HC	Hunter College Archives, Wexler Library, Hunter College
TC	Special Collections, Milbank Library, Teachers College, Columbia University
WLA	Robert F. Wagner Labor Archives of the Tamiment Institute Library, Elmer Holmes Bobst Library, New York University

Chapter 1: From Mother's Kitchen to Teacher's Desk

1 Thomas Sowell, *Ethnic America*, 98; Milton M. Gordon, *Assimilation in American Life: The Role of Race, Religion, and National Origins*, 185–187; Stephen Steinberg, "The Rise of the Jewish Professional: Case Studies of Intergenerational Mobility"; Selma C. Berrol, "Education and Economic Mobility: The Jewish Experience in New York City, 1880–1920."

2 For studies of discriminatory admission practices employed against Jews, see Harold S. Wechsler, *The Qualified Student: A History of Selective College Admission in America;* "The Rationale for Restriction: Ethnicity and College Admission in America, 1910–1980"; Marcia Graham Synnott, *The Half-Opened Door: Discrimination at Harvard, Yale, and Princeton, 1900–1970;* "Anti-Semitism and American Universities: Did Quotas Follow the Jews?"; David O. Levine, *The American College and the Culture of Aspiration, 1915–1960;* Dan A. Oren, *Joining the Club: A History of Jews and Yale.*

3 Stephen Cole, *The Unionization of Teachers: A Case Study of the UFT,* 95. Cole's figures were derived from the names of newly appointed teachers as provided by Board of Education, City of New York, Office of the Superintendent of Schools, *Journal of the Board of Education*, TC, for

the years between 1920 and 1940, counting only obviously Jewish names. However, the *Journal* also lists many teachers who changed their names, a fairly common practice during the interwar years. In addition, close scrutiny of the names on more than one thousand Teacher Personnel Cards, BE, taking into account both birth and marriage names and noting name changes that appear on these cards, indicates that Cole's estimate may have been somewhat low.

4   Nathan Glazer and Daniel Patrick Moynihan, *Beyond the Melting Pot: The Negroes, Puerto Ricans, Jews, Italians, and Irish of New York City,* 146. Because the Board of Education kept no statistics regarding its employees' religion, all estimates of the numbers of Jewish teachers have been based on teachers' names, usually those printed in the Board's journal. However, a study of teacher personnel cards on file at the Board of Education makes it obvious that these estimates have been low, because far more information is provided on the cards than merely the names that appear in the *Journal.* Often a name in print is ambiguous as to ethnicity and therefore cannot be considered in making estimates, but the personnel cards indicate birth, as well as married names, along with name changes. See Notes on Sources: Methodology for further discussion of this subject.

5   Joan Jacobs Brumberg and Nancy Tomes, "Women in the Professions: A Research Agenda for American Historians," 282.

6   For studies of Jewish immigrant women, see Charlotte Baum, Paula Hyman, and Sonya Michel, *The Jewish Woman in America;* Elizabeth Ewen, *Immigrant Women in the Land of Dollars: Life and Culture on the Lower East Side, 1890–1925;* Sydney Stahl Weinberg, *The World of Our Mothers: The Lives of Jewish Immigrant Women;* Neil M. Cowan and Ruth Schwartz Cowan, *Our Parents' Lives: The Americanization of Eastern European Jews;* and Susan A. Glenn, *Daughters of the Shtetl: Life and Labor in the Immigrant Generation.*

7   Barbara Finkelstein, *Governing the Young: Teacher Behavior in Popular Primary Schools in Nineteenth-Century United States* (New York: Falmer Press, 1989) examines schooling from teachers' perspectives through the use of reminiscences and autobiographies. Unfortunately, only two of the twenty-seven selections in this book are written by women. Redding S. Sugg, Jr., *Motherteacher: The Feminization of American Education* (Charlottesville: University Press of Virginia, 1978) complains about the feminization of teaching.

8   *Notable American Women, 1607–1950: A Biographical Dictionary.* Edited by Edward T. James. See also *Notable American Women: The Modern Period.* Edited by Barbara Sicherman and Carol Hurd Green.

9   See Dan C. Lortie, *School-Teacher: A Sociological Study.*

10   Nancy Hoffman, *Woman's "True" Profession: Voices from the History of Teaching* (Old Westbury, N.Y.: Feminist Press, 1981); Frances R. Donovan, *The Schoolma'am.*

11   Brumberg and Tomes, "Women in the Professions," 278. The neglect of teachers is only just beginning to be remedied. A valuable step in this direction is the collection of articles recently published under the auspices of the American Educational Research Association. See Donald Warren, ed., *American Teachers: Histories of a Profession at Work.* Another step is an ongoing research project designed to study the social origins, demographic characteristics, and labor market experiences of American teachers from 1860 to 1940, utilizing manuscript censuses and published school reports, as outlined in Joel Perlmann and Robert Margo, "Who Were America's Teachers? Toward a Social History and a Data Archive."

12   Mark Zborowski and Elizabeth Herzog, *Life is With People: The Jewish Little-Town of Eastern Europe,* 124–129.

13   U.S. Department of Labor, *The Economic Condition of Jews in Russia,* prepared by Israel Rubinow; bulletin no. 72 (Washington, D.C.: GPO, 1907), 578.

14   See Notes on Sources.

15   New York Cities Census Committee, *Population of the City of New York, 1890–1930* (New York: Cities Census Committee, 1932); U.S. Bureau of the Census, *Thirteenth Census of the United States: 1910. Vol. 3: Population,* 240; *Fifteenth Census of the United States: 1930. Vol. 3: Population,* 290; *Abstract of the Fourteenth Census of the United States,* 50.

16   Quoted in Selma Cantor Berrol, "Immigrants at School: New York City, 1898–1914," 41.

17   U.S. Congress. Senate Immigration Commission, *Children of Immigrants in School,* 61st Congress, 3rd Session, 1911 (Washington, D.C.: GPO, 1911), 4:626.

18   Ibid.; Berrol, "Education and Economic Mobility"; Moses Rischin, *The Promised City: New York's Jews, 1870–1914,* 200; Selma C. Berrol, "Public Schools and Immigrants: The New York City Experience," 38.

19   Michael R. Olneck and Marvin Lazerson, "The School Achievement of Immigrant Children: 1900–1930," 463–464.

20   New York Cities Census Committee, *Population of the City of New York,* table 18, 300–301.

21   Mario Puzo, *The Fortunate Pilgrim* (New York: Fawcett Crest, 1964), 15; Thomas Kessner, *The Golden Door: Italian and Jewish Immigrant Mobility in New York City, 1880–1935,* 84; Maxine Seller, "The Education of the Immigrant Woman, 1900–1935," 317–318; Miriam Cohen, "Changing Education Strategies Among Immigrant Generations: New York Italians in Comparative Perspective."

22   Immigration Commission, *Children of Immigrants in School,* 54–55; Only 35 women with obviously Italian names were found among the more than 1000 personnel cards of women teaching in the city's schools during the interwar years. BE.

23   Fannie Schapiro is quoted in Sydelle Kramer and Jenny Masur, eds. *Jewish Grandmothers,* 10, 13. Also see: Abraham Cahan, *The Rise of David Levinsky* (New York: Harper and Brothers, 1917); Anzia Yezierska, *Children of Loneliness: Stories of Immigrant Life in America* (New York: Funk and Wagnalls, 1923); Weinberg, *World of Our Mothers.*

24   Berrol, "Education and Economic Mobility," 264–265; "From Compensatory Education to Adult Education: The New York City Evening Schools, 1825–1935," 212–214; Kramer and Masur, *Jewish Grandmothers,* 11.

25   Weinberg, *World of Our Mothers,* xx:241–242.

26   Ibid., 151–152.

27   Joseph King Van Denburg, *Causes of the Elimination of Students in Public Secondary Schools of New York City,* 35, 80.

28   Interview in Kramer and Masur, *Jewish Grandmothers,* 97; Anna Quindlen, "Brooklyn College's Class of '33 Relives the Honor."

29   Weinberg, *World of Our Mothers,* 152, 175.

30   Berrol, "Immigrants at School," 43, 62; "Public Schools and Immigrants," 30.

31   See Myra Kelly, *Little Aliens* (New York: McClure, 1910); *Little Citizens* (New York: McClure, 1904).

32   Full-length accounts of the education of Jewish immigrant children in New York City can be found in Berrol, "Immigrants at School"; Stephan F. Brumberg, *Going to America, Going to School: The Jewish Immigrant Public School Encounter in Turn-of-the-Century New York City.*

33   Irving Howe, *World of Our Fathers,* 273.

34   Glenn, *Daughters of the Shtetl,* 3.

35   Mary Antin, *The Promised Land* (Boston: Houghton Mifflin, 1912); Berrol, "Public Schools and Immigrants," 39.

36   Cowan and Cowan, *Our Parents' Lives,* 96–98.

37   Carl F. Kaestle, *Pillars of the Republic: Common Schools and American Society, 1780–1860* (New York: Hill and Wang, 1983), 123–127.

38   Quoted from Catharine Beecher's *True Remedy,* in Thomas Woody, *A History of Women's Education in the United States,* 2:462.

39   NEA, "The Status of the Teaching Profession," 55.

40   Bureau of the Census, *Children of Immigrants,* 54–55; Hasia R. Diner, *Erin's Daughters in America: Irish Immigrant Women in the Nineteenth Century* (Baltimore: Johns Hopkins University Press, 1983), 96–97; Geraldine Jonçich Clifford, "'Marry, Stitch, Die, or Do Worse': Educating Women for Work," in *Work, Youth, and Schooling: Historical Perspectives on Vocationalism in American Education,* ed. Harvey Kantor and David B. Tyack (Stanford, Calif.: Stanford University Press, 1982), 253.

41   See Polly Welts Kaufman, *Women Teachers on the Frontier* (New Haven: Yale University Press, 1984); Diane Manning, ed., *Hill Country Teacher: Memories from the One-Room School and Beyond* (Boston: Twayne, 1989); Jacqueline Jones, *Soldiers of Light and Love: Northern Teachers and Georgia Blacks, 1865–1873* (Chapel Hill: University of North Carolina Press, 1980); Robert C. Morris, *Reading, 'Riting, and Reconstruction: The Education of Freedmen in the South, 1861–1870*

(Chicago: University of Chicago Press, 1981); Ronald E. Butchart, *Northern Schools, Southern Blacks, and Reconstruction: Freedmen's Education, 1862–1875* (Westport, Conn.: Greenwood 1980).

42   Woody, *History of Women's Education*, 2:496–498.

43   Studies of women and teachers' unions are noted in chapter 9.

44   Sally Schwager, "Educating Women in America."

45   Berrol, "Immigrants at School," 64; John Higham, *Send These to Me: Immigrants in Urban America*, rev. ed. (Baltimore: Johns Hopkins University Press, 1984), 191; Cole, *Unionization of Teachers*, 95.

46   Selma C. Berrol, "School Days on the Old East Side: The Italian and Jewish Experience," 212. Berrol has written about Richman and her work with immigrant children in "Julia Richman: Agent of Change in the Urban School"; "When Uptown Met Downtown: Julia Richman's Work in the Jewish Community of New York, 1880–1912."

47   Berrol, "Immigrants at School," 119–120; Brumberg, *Going to America*, 138.

48   Kate Simon, *Bronx Primitive: Portraits in a Childhood*, 48.

49   Paula E. Hyman, "Culture and Gender: Women in the Immigrant Jewish Community," 161, Howe, *World of Our Fathers*, 266.

50   Interview in Kramer and Masur, *Jewish Grandmothers*, 20. Also, see Weinberg, *World of Our Mothers*, 242; Baum et al., *Jewish Woman in America*, 125.

51   Joyce Antler, "Culture, Service, and Work: Changing Ideals of Higher Education for Women," in *The Undergraduate Woman: Issues in Educational Equity*, ed. Pamela J. Perun (Lexington, Mass.: Lexington Books, 1982), 29–30.

52   *New York Times*, 20 July 1986, 21.

53   Brumberg, *Going to America*, 146–147.

54   Perlmann and Margo, "Who Were America's Teachers?" 70.

55   Donovan, *The Schoolma'am*, 34–35.

56   Catharine Beecher, *Suggestions Respecting Improvements in Education, Presented to the Trustees;* quoted in Kathryn Kish Sklar, *Catharine Beecher: A Study in American Domesticity* (New Haven: Yale University Press, 1973), 97.

57   Kessner, *Golden Door*, 91.

58   Ewen, *Immigrant Women*, 193.

59   Glazer and Moynihan, *Beyond the Melting Pot*, 147.

60   J. X. Cohen, *Jews, Jobs, and Discrimination: A Report on Jewish Non-Employment*, 12–19; *Towards Fair Play for Jewish Workers: Third Report on Jewish Non-Employment*, 16–19, 28, 31–35; Brumberg, *Going to America*, 145.

61   William Toll, *The Making of an Ethnic Middle Class: Portland Jewry Over Four Generations* (Albany: State University of New York Press, 1982), 64–66, 72, 75.

62   Norma Fain Pratt, "Immigrant Jewish Women in Los Angeles: Occupation, Family and Culture," in *Studies in the American Jewish Experience*, ed. Jacob R. Marcus and Abraham J. Peck (Cincinnati: American Jewish Archives), 82.

63   *School and Society* XXII (3 October 1925): 429–430; New York State Department of Education, *Report of a Study of New York City Schools, Part I, The Administrative-Supervisory Organization*, prepared by Frank Pierrepont Graves, 39, TC.

64   Department of Education, *Report of a Study of New York City Schools*, 38–39, TC; Harold G. Campbell, "America's Largest City School System," 178.

65   Alice Kessler-Harris, *Out to Work: A History of Wage-Earning Women in the United States*, 226.

Chapter 2: Subway Scholars at Concrete Campuses

1   For discussions of the discriminatory admissions policies at women's colleges, which kept Jewish enrollment low, see Helen Lefkowitz Horowitz, *Alma Mater: Design and Experience in the Women's Colleges from Their 19th-Century Beginnings to the 1930s*, 158–159; Lynn D. Gordon, "Annie Nathan Meyer and Barnard College: Mission and Identity in Women's Higher Education

1889–1950," 513–517; Barbara Solomon, *In the Company of Educated Women: A History of Women and Higher Education in America*, 143–144; Louise Blecher Rose, "The Secret Life of Sarah Lawrence"; Synnott, "Anti-Semitism and American Universities," 249–250; Stanley Feldstein, *This Land That I Show You: Three Centuries of Jewish Life in America*, 288–292.

2   *Columbia University Bulletin of Information, Barnard College Announcement, 1935–1936*, 32, 34, 118, BAR.

3   Jurgen Herbst, *And Sadly Teach: Teacher Education and Professionalization in American Culture*, 181. Jewish women tended to take its graduate courses during summer sessions. During the 1930s, many women teachers took extension courses there as part of their required in-service training.

4   Lee J. Levinger, *The Jewish Student in America*, 42.

5   Queens College is not discussed either in this or in subsequent chapters for two reasons. The more obvious is that because Queens College did not graduate its first class until 1941, it is therefore beyond the time period of this study. Second, the borough of Queens had a relatively small Jewish population, especially in contrast to Manhattan, the Bronx, and Brooklyn during the interwar years; therefore, the majority of its students were not Jewish. Moreover, none of the sixty-one women interviewed for this study attended Queens College; nor have I located anyone who attended the college during this period.

6   Founded in 1885 as The Brooklyn Training School; its name was changed in 1920 to The Maxwell Training School for Teachers in honor of William Maxwell, Superintendent of Schools of the City of New York, 1898–1918. *Journal of the New York City Board of Education, 1920*, 1060, TC.

7   *Annual Report of the City Superintendent of Schools, New York City, 1931*, 803, TC.

8   In 1930 over 8 percent of the students in the three schools were male, and by February of 1933 their enrollment reached an all-time high of over 16 percent of students in the city's teaching colleges. Arthur Mallon, "The Development of the Municipal Teacher Training Colleges in New York City," 201.

9   M'Ledge Moffett, *The Social Background and Activities of Teachers College Students*, 20–21; Verne McGuffey, "Some Elements in the Cultural Background of Students in One of the New York City Training Schools for Teachers," 280.

10   Moffett, *Social Background*, 33; Levinger, *Jewish Student in America*, 44.

11   Levinger, *Jewish Student in America*, 8, 42.

12   Stephen Steinberg, *The Academic Melting Pot: Catholics and Jews in American Higher Education*, 9; Thomas Evans Coulton, *A City College in Action: Struggle and Achievement at Brooklyn College, 1930–1955*, 6, 8.

13   Nettie Pauline McGill, "Some Characteristics of Jewish Youth in New York," 257; Mabel Newcomer, *A Century of Higher Education for American Women*, 46.

14   A 1935 survey of New York City's Jewish youth found that 83 percent of those 16 to 24 years of age reported parents born in Eastern Europe, and another 8 percent had one foreign-born parent. More than one half of their parents had been born in Russia. McGill, "Some Characteristics of Jewish Youth," 252.

15   William L. Ettinger, "America Calls: Will *You* Answer the Call?" Presented to the author by a 1925 graduate of The Maxwell Training School for Teachers.

16   Ibid.

17   *Annual Report of the City Superintendent, 1931*, 803, TC. See also Willard S. Elsbree, *The American Teacher: Evolution of a Profession in a Democracy*, 324.

18   Mallon, "Development of Teacher Training Colleges," 124.

19   Teachers' Record Department File 94464, BE.

20   *Annual Report of the City Superintendent, 1931*, 803, TC.

21   Mallon, "Development of Teacher Training Colleges," 167.

22   Ibid., 162–164.

23   Ibid., 127, 164.

24   Elsbree, *American Teacher*, 324–325; U.S. Office of Education, *National Survey of the Education of Teachers, Summary and Interpretation*, prepared by E. S. Evenden, 37.

25   Mallon, "Development of Teacher Training Colleges," 165–166.

26   *New York Sun,* 17 June 1932, 8.

27   *School and Society* 37 (21 January 1933): 87.

28   Samuel White Patterson, *Hunter College: Eighty-Five Years of Service,* 3, 30, 113; Elizabeth Vera Loeb Stern, "A History of Hunter's Splendid Century," 16.

29   Department of Education, *Report of A Study of New York City Schools,* 38, TC. College degrees were mandatory for teachers in the secondary schools in New York City when, as late as 1930, only 77 percent of the nation's high school teachers were college graduates. U.S. Bureau of the Census, *Education of the American Population: A 1960 Census Monograph,* prepared by John K. Folger and Charles B. Nam, 84.

30   George N. Shuster, *The Ground I Walked On: Reflections of a College President,* 107.

31   Teachers' Record Department File 126526, BE.

32   *New York Sun,* 5 April 1939, 38.

33   Bel Kaufman, *Up the Down Staircase; "Mihi Cura Futuri,"* 7.

34   Brooklyn College, Graduate Survey Group, Bureau of Economic Research, *The Brooklyn College Graduate (1932–1939): Complete Report of Findings and Conclusions,* prepared by Edwin H. Spengler, 24, BC.

35   Patterson, *Hunter College,* 130–131.

36   *Hunter College Bulletin,* 5 November 1934, 1, HC.

37   *New York Sun,* 5 April 1939, 38.

38   Stern, "History of Hunter's Splendid Century," 14, 18.

39   *The Wisterian, 1929,* 8, HC.

40   Helen Hochfelder Taffel, "Reminiscences of the Depression Years," 13.

41   Murray M. Horowitz, *Brooklyn College: The First Half-Century,* 4, 7, 43.

42   *New York Times,* 2 October 1938, II, 2.

43   For a discussion of Jewish residential patterns in New York City during the 1920s and 1930s, see Deborah Dash Moore, *At Home in America: Second Generation New York Jews,* 19–58; and J. B. Maller, "A Study of Jewish Neighborhoods in New York City," 271–272.

44   Thomas Kessner, "The Selective Filter of Ethnicity: A Half Century of Immigrant Mobility," 178–179; "Jobs, Ghettoes and the Urban Economy, 1880–1935," 234. See also Feldstein, *This Land That I Show You,* 310.

45   Kessner, "Jobs, Ghettoes and the Urban Economy," 236; Brooklyn College, Graduate Survey Group, *Brooklyn College Graduate,* 13, BC.

46   William J. O'Shea, *Progress of the Public Schools, May 1, 1924–July 31, 1929,* 5–7, 12, TC.

47   Ibid., 17–20.

48   *New York Teacher* V (December 1939): 21.

49   *New York Sun,* 19 May 1932, 38.

50   Ibid., 13 June 1932, 34.

51   Ibid., 3 October 1932, 29.

52   *Hunter College Bulletin,* 31 October 1933, 4, HC; *The Broeklundian, 1933,* 237, BC.

53   Personal interviews as well as polls conducted periodically by the colleges during the 1930s attest to the overwhelming popularity of teaching as the career goal of its students. See Horowitz, *Brooklyn College,* 9; *Brooklyn College Vanguard,* 12 November 1937, 5, BC; *New York Times,* 3 January 1933, 18; 3 March 1935, II, 5; *Wisterian, 1931,* 28; *Hunter College Bulletin,* 22 June 1931, 5; 31 October 1933, 4; 20 February 1934, 1; 5 October 1936, 1, HC.

54   McGill, "Some Characteristics of Jewish Youth," 264; Cohen, *Towards Fair Play,* 28.

55   Irving Howe, *A Margin of Hope: An Intellectual Autobiography,* 10.

56   *New York Times,* 6 October 1935, II, 9; *Brooklyn College Vanguard,* 15 May 1936, 1, BC; Margaret Herbst, "Reminiscences of the Depression Years."

57   Kaufman, *"Mihi Cura Futuri ,"* 7; *The Wisterian, 1937,* unpaged, HC.

58   *Brooklyn College Handbook,* 1937–38, 38, BC; Horowitz, *Brooklyn College,* 13; Shuster, *Ground I Walked On,* 53.

59   Quoted by Hal Draper, "The Student Movement of the Thirties," in *As We Saw the Thirties: Essays on Social and Political Movements of a Decade,* 156.

60   Shuster, *Ground I Walked On,* 55.

61   Herman Wouk, *Marjorie Morningstar,* 56.

62   Brooklyn College, Graduate Survey Group, *Brooklyn College Graduate,* 2, BC.
63   *Hunter College Bulletin,* 15 November 1937, 2, HC.
64   Shuster, *Ground I Walked On,* 104.
65   Horowitz, *Brooklyn College,* 7, 9.
66   Ibid.
67   Kaufman, *"Mihi Cura Futuri,"* 6; Kate Simon, *A Wider World: Portraits in an Adolescence,* 11; Wouk, *Marjorie Morningstar,* 56.
68   Shuster, *Ground I Walked On,* 104.
69   See Ewen, *Immigrant Women in the Land of Dollars,* chapter 12.
70   Henry L. Feingold, "Investing in Themselves: The Harvard Case and the Origins of the Third American-Jewish Commercial Elite," *American Jewish History* LXXVII (June 1988): 530–553.
71   Ibid., 545. See also Sherry Gorelick, *City College and the Jewish Poor: Education in New York, 1880–1924,* 179.
72   Simon, *Wider World,* 170.
73   Morris Raphael Cohen, *A Dreamer's Journey* (Glencoe, Ill.: Free Press, 1949), 184–185.
74   Gertrude Himmelfarb, "Reflections of a Provincial," *Nocturne* IX, Book I (March 1957), 8, BC; Norman Rosten, "A Reminiscence With Some Nostalgia." *Nocturne* IX, Book I (March 1957), 13, BC.
75   *City College Bulletin,* 1 January 1935, 13, CC.
76   Cohen, *Dreamer's Journey,* 5.
77   *Report of the New York City Subcommittee of Rapp-Coudert Committee of the New York State Legislature,* 1944, cited in Eileen Eagan, *Class, Culture, and the Classroom: The Student Peace Movement of the 1930s,* 101–102.
78   Ibid., 102.
79   For an account of President Robinson's confrontation with City College students at an anti-Fascist demonstration, during which he called them "guttersnipes" (he was later faced with a large contingent of CCNY students wearing buttons proclaiming themselves "guttersnipes"), see James Wechsler, *Revolt on the Campus,* 395–396; *Hunter College Bulletin,* 29 October 1934, 2, HC.
80   Simon, *Wider World,* 116.
81   Ibid., 112; Kaufman, *"Mihi Cura Futuri,"* 7. Dean Hannah C. Egan chaired Hunter College's Conduct Committee during the thirties.
82   Shuster, *Ground I Walked On,* 55, 104.
83   Kaufman, *"Mihi Cura Futuri,"* 7.
84   *Hunter College Bulletin,* 13 February 1934, 4, HC.
85   Ibid., 13 March 1934, 1.

Chapter 3: Pamphlets, Petitions, and Pickets

1   Although most of the former activists interviewed preferred to remain anonymous, Esther Rubin emphatically requested that her full name be used and provided written permission to do so, although it must be noted that this is her married name (a second marriage) and not the name by which she was known while either a student or a teacher. *Barnard Bulletin,* 17 April 1934, 1, 3, BAR; *Brooklyn College Vanguard,* 14 April 1934, 1, BC; *Hunter College Bulletin,* 17 April 1934, 1, HC.
2   For historical studies of the 1930s' student movements, see Eagan, *Class, Culture, and the Classroom;* Ralph S. Brax, *The First Student Movement: Student Activism in the United States During the 1930s;* and Robert P. Cohen, *Revolt of the Depression Generation,* (New York: Oxford University Press, 1993). For further studies, both contemporary and comparative, see Bibliography.
3   Frederick Rudolph, "Neglect of Students as a Historical Tradition," 47, 53.
4   Eagan, *Class, Culture, and the Classroom,* 61, 42.
5   See Draper, "Student Movement"; Joseph P. Lash, *The Campus Strikes Against War;* and Wechsler, *Revolt on the Campus.*
6   Leila J. Rupp, "Reflections on Twentieth-Century American Women's History."
7   Sara Evans deals with the way the contributions of women activists of the 1960s were

disregarded by their male colleagues in her book *Personal Politics: The Roots of Women's Liberation in the Civil Rights Movement and the New Left* (New York: Alfred A. Knopf, 1979).

8   See Horowitz, *Alma Mater*, 158–159; Gordon, "Annie Nathan Meyer," 513–517; Solomon, *In the Company of Educated Women*, 143–144; Rose, "Secret Life of Sarah Lawrence"; Synnott, "Anti-Semitism and American Universities," 249–250; Feldstein, *This Land That I Show You*, 288–292.

9   Levinger, *Jewish Student in America*, 42.

10   Steinberg, *Academic Melting Pot*, 9; Coulton, *A City College in Action*, 6, 8.

11   Patterson, *Hunter College*, 4; McGill, "Some Characteristics of Jewish Youth," 257; Newcomer, *Century of Higher Education*, 46.

12   Calvin B. T. Lee, *The Campus Scene: 1900–1970*, 43–47; Patti McGill Peterson, "Student Organizations and the Antiwar Movement in America, 1910–1960," 135. For an account of college students during the 1920s, see Paula S. Fass, *The Damned and the Beautiful: American Youth in the 1920s* (New York: Oxford University Press, 1977).

13   Helen Lefkowitz Horowitz, *Campus Life: Undergraduate Cultures from the End of the Eighteenth Century to the Present*, 16.

14   Ralph S. Brax, "When Students First Organized Against War: Student Protest During the 1930s," 229.

15   Virginia Crocheron Gildersleeve, "A Dean's Portrait of the College Girl," 6.

16   Eagan, *Class, Culture, and the Classroom*, 16.

17   Draper, "Student Movement," 188; Patterson, *Hunter College*, 144.

18   *The Broeklundian, 1938,* 134, BC.

19   Lynn D. Gordon, "In the Shadow of SDS: Writing the History of Twentieth-Century College Students," 132–133.

20   *New York Times*, 27 November 1938, 12 November 1939; *Brooklyn Eagle*, 3 December 1939; Scrapbook, BC.

21   *Hunter College Bulletin*, 26 November 1934, 1, HC.

22   Ibid.

23   Lawrence Wittner, *Rebels Against War: The American Peace Movement, 1933–1983*, 6.

24   Draper, "Student Movement," 168.

25   Peterson, "Student Organizations," 140.

26   One of these officers was Molly Yard, who would later serve as president of the National Organization of Women. Solomon, *In the Company of Educated Women*, 249.

27   Harvey Klehr, *The Heyday of American Communism: The Depression Decade*, 317; Eagan, *Class, Culture, and the Classroom*, 14; *The Wisterian, 1937,* unpaged, HC; *Brooklyn College Vanguard*, 12 May 1939, 1.

28   Wechsler, *Revolt on the Campus*, 398.

29   *The Wisterian, 1934*, 117, HC.

30   *Brooklyn College Vanguard*, 6 March 1936, 3, BC.

31   Ibid., 3 March 1940, 2, BC.

32   Ibid., 16 February 1940, 2, BC.

33   *Barnard Bulletin*, 15 December 1933, 1, BAR.

34   *Hunter College Bulletin*, 22 May 1934, 4, HC; *New York Times*, 30 March 1933, 13.

35   Bella Abzug, *Bella! Ms. Abzug Goes to Washington*, 86.

36   *New York Times*, 5 October 1935, 6; *Brooklyn College Handbook, 1938–1939*, 18; *The Broeklundian, 1938*, 124, 134, *Brooklyn College Vanguard*, 1 March 1940, Scrapbook, BC.

37   *Brooklyn College Vanguard*, 21 January 1937, 1; 12 November 1937, 5; *The Broeklundian, 1938*, 134, BC.

38   *Brooklyn College Vanguard*, 14 December 1936, 1, BC; *The Wisterian, 1938*, 169, HC.

39   *Brooklyn College Vanguard*, 14 December 1936, 1, BC. For a discussion of American college students and the Spanish Civil War, see Eagan, *Class, Culture, and the Classroom*, chapter 8.

40   *New York Times*, 11 November 1938, 4; *New York Herald Tribune*, 11 November 1938, Scrapbook, BC.

41   *Hunter College Bulletin*, 27 May 1935, HC.

42   Norman Rosten, "Reminiscence With Some Nostalgia," 11, BC.

43   *Hunter College Bulletin*, 13 March 1934, 2, HC; Kaufman, "*Mihi Cura Futuri*," 6.

44   *Brooklyn College Vanguard*, 6 May 1936, 1, BC.
45   Ibid., 6 November 1938, 11, BC.
46   *New York Herald Tribune*, 7 December 1939, Scrapbook, BC.
47   Horowitz, *Brooklyn College*, 30.
48   *New York Times*, 26 May 1932, 16; 28 May 1932, 8.
49   Ibid., 14 May 1932, 17.
50   Ibid., 26 May 1932, 16.
51   Ibid., 14 May 1932, 17.
52   Ibid., 3 January 1933, 18; *New York Sun*, 3 October 1932; *Hunter College Bulletin*, 31 October 1933, 4, HC.
53   Brooklyn College, Graduate Survey Group, *Brooklyn College Graduate,* 13, BC.
54   Abzug, *Bella!,* 84.
55   *The Wisterian, 1933,* 117, HC.
56   *Hunter College Bulletin,* 31 October 1933, 4, HC; *New York Times,* 6 October 1935, II, 9; *Brooklyn College Vanguard,* 12 November 1937, 5; 16 February 1940, 3, BC.
57   Nettie Pauline McGill and Ellen Nathalie Matthews, *The Youth of New York City,* 338. Another study of Depression-era women high school students in New York City found that Jewish and Irish women who intended to pursue teaching careers were more active in extracurricular organizations than were students of other backgrounds. Paula S. Fass, *Outside In: Minorities and the Transformation of American Education,* 106.
58   Georg Mann, "Two Lefts: A Look Across the Generation Gap," 436. For discussions of the psychological and sociological studies that attest to 1930s student activists taking their direction from adult political movements, see Philip G. Altbach, *Student Politics in America: A Historical Analysis,* 6; and Philip G. Altbach and Patti McGill Peterson, "Before Berkeley: Historical Perspectives on American Student Activism," 4.
59   Oscar Handlin, "The Uses of Adversity," *Nocturne* IX, Book I (March 1957): 15, BC.
60   *The Broeklundian, 1935,* 149, BC.
61   Rosten, "Reminiscence," 11, BC.
62   Ibid.
63   *Hunter College Bulletin,* 14 May 1935, 2; 27 May 1935, 2, 6, HC.
64   Interview with Florence Rossi, 17 March 1982, Oral History of the American Left Collection, WLA.
65   *New York Sun,* 23 August 1938, 1, 11.
66   Peterson, "Student Organizations," 137; Brax, *First Student Movement,* 14; Milton Cantor, *The Divided Left: American Radicalism, 1900–1975,* 139; Harvey Klehr, *Communist Cadre: The Social Background of the American Communist Party Elite,* 5.
67   Shuster, *Ground I Walked On,* 54; *New York Sun,* 23 August 1938, 1.
68   Cantor, *Divided Left,* 138–139; Robert W. Iverson, *The Communists and the Schools,* 140; Irving Howe and Lewis Coser, *The American Communist Party: A Critical History (1919–1957),* 199–204.
69   *Daily Worker,* 8 May 1934, 4; Interview, Florence Rossi, WLA.
70   Rossi, ibid.; Howe and Coser, *American Communist Party,* 201.
71   *Brooklyn College Vanguard,* 20 November 1934, 1, BC.
72   Robert Shaffer, "Women and the Communist Party, USA, 1930–1940," 94.
73   See Ellen Kay Trimberger, "Women in the Old and New Left: The Evolution of a Politics of Personal Life," *Feminist Studies* 5 (Fall 1979): 432–450.
74   For women and the Left during the thirties, see Susan Ware, *Holding Their Own: American Women in the 1930s,* chapter 5. Also see Shaffer, "Women and the Communist Party," 90; and Peggy Dennis, *The Autobiography of an American Communist: A Personal View of a Political Life, 1925–1975* (Westport, Conn.: Lawrence Hill, 1977), 159.
75   Howe, *Margin of Hope,* 43.
76   *Hunter College Bulletin,* 31 March 1931, 1, HC.
77   Gildersleeve, "Dean's Portrait," 6.
78   Similarly, see Howe, *Margin of Hope,* 44; and Ware, *Holding Their Own,* 136.

Chapter 4: Repression and Punishment

1   Eagan, *Class, Culture, and the Classroom*, 81, 146–147.
2   Levine, *American College*, 205.
3   Simon, *Wider World*, 123.
4   Georg Mann, "Two Lefts," 433–434; Thomas Evans Coulton, *A City College in Action*, 14.
5   See Wechsler, *Revolt on the Campus*, 373–396. From 1932 to 1934, 42 students were expelled from CCNY for student activism. *Hunter College Bulletin*, 19 November 1934, 2, HC.
6   Also mentioned by Florence Rossi, interview, WLA.
7   Wechsler, *Revolt on the Campus*, 398.
8   *Regular Meeting of the Faculty*, 9 May 1934, 901, HC.
9   Wechsler, *Revolt on the Campus*, 398–399.
10   *Hunter College Bulletin*, 27 May 1935, 5–6, HC.
11   Wechsler, *Revolt on the Campus*, 401.
12   *New York Times*, 1 May 1935, 23.
13   *Hunter College Bulletin*, 6 May 1935, 7, HC.
14   Ibid., 27 May 1935, 2, HC.
15   Levine, *American College*, 195–197.
16   U.S. Office of Education, *Federal Student Aid Program*, prepared by Fred J. Kelly and John H. McNeely. Bulletin No. 14 (Washington, D.C.: GPO, 1935), 29.
17   *Hunter College Bulletin*, 18 March 1935, 2; 1 April 1935, 1–2, HC.
18   *Barnard Bulletin*, 15 December 1933, 1, BAR; *Hunter College Bulletin*, 19 November 1934, 1, 5, HC.
19   *Hunter College Bulletin*, 19 November 1934, 5, HC.
20   Ibid.,16 October 1934, 2, HC.
21   Interview, Florence Rossi, WLA.
22   *Hunter College Bulletin*, 19 November 1934, 2, HC.
23   *New York Sun*, 19 July 1937, 28.
24   Sidney C. Gould, "The Freedom of Teachers in New York City's Public Elementary and Secondary Schools From 1932–1952," 598.
25   *New York Sun*, 31 May 1939, 38.
26   Lash, *Campus Strikes Against War*, 8.
27   Telephone conversation with the author, 29 January 1988.
28   *Mortarboard, 1935*, 120, BAR.
29   *Barnard Bulletin*, 17 October 1933, 1; 14 November 1933, 1, BAR.
30   Ibid., 28 November 1933, 1; 8 May 1934, 1, BAR.
31   Edward S. Canning, BE, Office of the Board of Examiners to Gertrude Epstein, 10 July 1936, ACLU.
32   *New York Sun*, 7 August 1936, 23.
33   *New York World Telegram*, 6 August 1936. ACLU papers, 1936, vol. 868.
34   Katharine S. Doty to Board of Examiners, 10 January 1935, ACLU papers, 1937, vol. 958.
35   Katharine S. Doty to Board of Examiners, 10 June 1935, ACLU papers, 1937, vol. 958.
36   Exhibit "D," statement by Katharine S. Doty. Petition of Gertrude Epstein to the Supreme Court of the County of New York for an Order against The Board of Examiners of the Board of Education of the City of New York, 18 November 1937, ACLU papers, 1937, vol. 958. (Hereafter referred to as Epstein Petition.)
37   Katharine S. Doty to Virginia C. Gildersleeve, 5 May 1937, Dean's Office Correspondence, File 17DF, BAR.
38   Epstein Petition, 19 November 1937, 5, ACLU papers, 1937, vol. 958.
39   Gertrude Epstein to Dean Virginia C. Gildersleeve, 5 May 1937, Dean's Office Correspondence, File 17DF, BAR.
40   Virginia C. Gildersleeve to Gertrude Epstein, 6 May 1937. Dean's Office Correspondence, File 17DF, BAR.
41   *New York Herald Tribune*, 7 August 1936, ACLU papers, 1936, vol. 868.

42   Virginia C. Gildersleeve to Gertrude Epstein, 6 May 1937. Dean's Office Correspondence, File 17DF, BAR.

43   Gertrude Epstein to Dean Virginia C. Gildersleeve, 7 May 1937. Dean's Office Correspondence, File 17DF, BAR.

44   News release, ACLU, 21 August 1936, ACLU papers, 1937, vol. 958.

45   Virginia C. Gildersleeve to William J. McGrath, 6 May 1937. Dean's Office Correspondence, File 17DF, BAR.

46   William J. McGrath to Dean Virginia C. Gildersleeve, 7 May 1937. Dean's Office Correspondence, File 17DF, BAR.

47   Virginia C. Gildersleeve to Gertrude Epstein, 15 May 1937. Dean's Office Correspondence, File 17DF, BAR.

48   Gertrude Epstein to Dean Virginia C. Gildersleeve, 24 May 1937. Dean's Office Correspondence, File 17DF, BAR.

49   News release, ACLU, 17 August 1936, ACLU papers, 1936, vol. 868.

50   Epstein Petition, 19 November 1937, 4, ACLU papers, 1937, vol. 958. Although this case was first heard in New York City in April 1936, the material cited is that of Epstein's final appeal to the commissioner of education in Albany in 1938. Since the material quoted is a duplication of the material provided for the two previous cases, these constitute the only documents retained by the ACLU in its archives.

51   Ibid., 5.

52   Ibid., 1–2. *Barnard Bulletin*, 19 January 1934, 1, 3–4; 20 February 1934, 1–2, 4, BAR.

53   Exhibit "K," Epstein Petition, 19 November 1937, ACLU papers, 1937, vol. 958.

54   Epstein Petition, 19 November 1937, 8, ACLU papers, 1937, vol. 958.

55   Exhibit "G," William Haller "to whom it may concern," 14 May 1937; and Exhibit "H," Mabel Foote Weeks "to whom it may concern," 14 May 1937. Epstein Petition, 18 November 1937, ACLU papers, 1937, vol. 958.

56   *New York Sun*, 5 November 1937, 38.

57   Press release, ACLU, 29 April 1938, ACLU papers, 1938, vol. 1070.

58   Annette K. Baxter, "Virginia Crocheron Gildersleeve," 274.

59   Gildersleeve, "Dean's Portrait," 7.

60   *Barnard Bulletin*, 17 April 1934, 2, BAR.

61   See Eagan, *Class, Culture, and the Classroom*, 43–44, 142.

62   Brax, "When Students First Organized," 244. Eileen Eagan provides an account of the expulsion of Reed Harris, editor of the Columbia *Spectator,* in *Class, Culture, and the Classroom*, 40–47.

63   *New York Teacher* I (November 1936): 5.

64   Mary V. Libby to Dean Virginia C. Gildersleeve, 2 February 1931, and 4 February 1931; Virginia C. Gildersleeve to Wilfred M. Aikin, 18 December 1935. Dean's Office Correspondence, folder 12c, BAR.

65   Virginia C. Gildersleeve to Mrs. Alfred Meyer, 12 January 1932 and 30 March 1933. Annie Nathan Meyer papers, box 7, folder 1, AJC.

66   *New York Sun*, 18 June 1937, 28.

67   Gildersleeve, "Dean's Portrait," 7.

68   Brax, "When Students First Organized," 154. See Howe and Coser, *American Communist Party*, 198; Cantor, *Divided Left*, 138–139; and Klehr, *Heyday of American Communism*, 317.

69   Wechsler, *Revolt on the Campus*, 455; Draper, "Student Movement of the Thirties," 182–188.

70   *The Broeklundian, 1938*, 134, BC.

71   Vivian Gornick, *The Romance of American Communism*, 31; Handlin. "Uses of Adversity," 15, BC; Irving Howe, *Steady Work: Essays in the Politics of Democratic Radicalism, 1953–1966*, 361–352.

72   *The Wisterian, 1933*, 119, HC.

73   Murray Kempton, *Part of Our Time: Some Monuments and Ruins of the Thirties*, 307.

74   Howe and Coser, *American Communist Party*, 203.

Chapter 5: Examinations, Enunciation, and Endurance

1   *"Proposed Requirements for Licenses for Teachers,"* BE 1936, 9–10, TC.
2   *New York Sun,* 10 January 1925, 17.
3   Ibid., 23 November 1934, 27; 22 March 1938, 22; Teacher Personnel Cards, BE.
4   *New York Sun,* 20 July 1937, 34; 6 February 1939, 28.
5   Ibid., 20 July 1937, 34.
6   Ibid., 1 September 1939, 42.
7   *New York Teacher* I (October 1936): 16–17.
8   Kaufman, *Up the Down Staircase,* 126.
9   *New York Sun,* 1 February 1937, 32; 17 January 1925, 15.
10 Ibid., 10 August 1929, 10; Teachers' Record Department File Number 94464, BE.
11 *New York Sun,* 6 May 1935, 30; 2 February 1937, 32.
12 Moore, *At Home in America,* 90.
13 See Madeleine R. Grumet, *Bitter Milk: Women and Teaching* (Amherst: University of Massachusetts Press, 1988), 170.
14 Howe, *Margin of Hope,* 10; Cowan and Cowan, *Our Parents' Lives,* 242.
15 See Cohen, *Jews, Jobs and Discrimination,* 17.
16 *New York Sun,* 11 January 1938, 32; 8 February 1939, 32.
17 Ibid., 8 April 1925, 29.
18 Ibid., 20 December 1932, 37.
19 Ibid., 16 December 1931, 50; 11 July 1932, 28.
20 Ibid., 24 April 1931, 42.
21 Ibid., 17 September 1935, 33.
22 Ibid., 2 December 1935, 40; 14 March 1936, 39.
23 Teachers' Record Department File Number 99362, BE.
24 David Tyack, Robert Lowe, and Elisabeth Hansot, *Public Schools in Hard Times: The Great Depression and Recent Years,* 129–131.
25 *New York Sun,* 7 September 1935, 12; *New York Teacher* II (May 1937): 8.
26 *New York Sun,* 7 September 1935, 12.
27 Ibid., 14 January 1937, 34; 18 January 1937, 36.
28 Ibid., 26 January 1938, 2.
29 Ibid., 4 February 1937, 34; 28 May 1937, 30.
30 BE, *Journal of the Board of Education of the City of New York, 1938,* 2:1334, TC.
31 *New York Sun,* 9 November 1938, 38.
32 Cohen, *Jews, Jobs and Discrimination,* 17.
33 *New York Sun,* 4 November 1938, 40; *New York Times,* 19 March 1939, II, 5. For a detailed discussion of unequal opportunities for female administrators in public schools in the United States, see David Tyack and Elisabeth Hansot, *Managers of Virtue: Public School Leadership in America, 1820–1980,* 180–201; and Myra H. Strober and David Tyack, "Why Do Women Teach and Men Manage? A Report on Research on Schools."
34 *New York Teacher* V (December 1939): 21.
35 *New York Sun,* 4 February 1938, 34.
36 Ibid.
37 Ibid., 4 February 1938, 34; 12 April 1938, 34.
38 Charles J. Hendley to Dr. Joseph K. Van Denburg, 15 March 1938. TU, Local 5 papers, Box 70, File 8, CLMDC.
39 *New York Sun,* 16 November 1938, 40; 25 January 1939, 28; 3 March 1939, 36; 18 September 1940, 32.
40 Ibid., 10 August 1938, 29; *New York Teacher* II (April 1937): 5; U.S. Office of Education, *Biennial Survey of Education in the United States: Statistical Summary of Education, 1939–40,* 2:34.
41 *New York Sun,* 11 March 1938, 36; 10 August 1938, 29.
42 Ibid., 26 August 1938, 17; 11 March 1938, 36; *New York Times,* 11 March 1938, 21.
43 Unemployment Committee of the TG, *Teachers Stand in Line: Analysis and Forecast of*

eacher Unemployment in the New York City School System, 9, WLA; *New York Teacher* V (December 1939): 21.

4 Unemployment Committee, *Teachers Stand in Line,* 10.

5 *New York Sun,* 20 July 1929, 22; 8 November 1938, 32.

6 Ibid., 7 January 1931, 1, 39; 8 January 1931, 38.

7 Ibid., 19 January 1931, 32.

8 Thomas Brooks, *Towards Dignity: A Brief History of the UFT,* 56-57.

9 Kathleen Murphey, "Boston Teachers Organize, 1919-1965," 100.

0 BE, *A Survey of the Substitute Teachers in the Public Schools of the City of New York,* repared by Daniel Paul Higgins, TC.

Chapter 6: Inside the School

1 Victor Bernstein, "Teacher Goes Modern," *New York Times,* 2 February 1936, IX, 11. For discussions of negative stereotypes of the schoolteacher, see Donovan, *The Schoolma'am,* 15-16; nd Kenneth H. McGill, "The School-Teacher Stereotype."

2 Bernstein, "Teacher Goes Modern"; U.S. Bureau of the Census, *Education of the American Population,* 82; Benjamin W. Frazier, "Comparing Typical Teachers," 261.

3 BE, *Official Directory of the Board of Education of the City of New York, 1938,* 4, TC; NEA, The Status of the Teaching Profession," prepared by E. S. Evenden, 61; William H. Chafe, *The merican Woman: Her Changing Social, Economic, and Political Role, 1920-1970,* 61.

4 BE, *All the Children: Forty-Third Report of the Superintendent of Schools, City of New York, 939-40,* 86, 117, 145-146, TC.

5 For studies of how Progressive reformers applied efficiency experts and scientific management to public schools, see Raymond E. Callahan, *Education and the Cult of Efficiency: A Study of he Social Forces That Have Shaped the Administration of the Public Schools* (Chicago: University f Chicago Press, 1962); Lawrence A. Cremin, *American Education: The Metropolitan Experience, 876-1900* (New York: Harper and Row, 1988); *The Transformation of the School: Progressivism 1 American Education, 1876-1957.* It has not been possible to ascertain the precise date of the nstallation of time clocks in New York City public schools. Most probably, they were put into use n the years immediately following World War I. Several of the interviewees have said that time locks were present in the schools in which they taught during the 1920s. According to Robert ertes of the Public Affairs Office of New York's BE, these clocks are still being used in some city chools, at the discretion of the principals in charge, despite efforts by the United Federation of eachers and recent school chancellors to have them removed.

6 Larry Cuban, *How Teachers Taught: Constancy and Change in American Classrooms, 1890- 980,* 49; Adele Marie Shaw, "The True Character of the New York Public Schools," *The World's Vork* 7 (December 1903): 4204-4221.

7 Bronx Council, *Study of the Lower Bronx* , 113.

8 *New York Sun,* 2 March 1925, 22.

9 Bronx Council, *Study of the Lower Bronx,* 121.

0 *New York Sun,* 17 September 1938, 26.

1 Ibid., 22 April 1931, 50.

2 BE, *All the Children: Thirty-Eighth Report, 1935-36,* 39, TC.

3 For a discussion of autonomy in the semi-professions, see Barbara Melosh, *"The Physicians's land": Work Culture and Conflict in American Nursing* (Philadelphia: Temple University Press, 982), chapter 1.

4 "A Teacher's Diary," *New York Sun,* 4 March 1940, 28; 11 March 1940, 30.

5 Ibid.

6 "My Day: By a Junior High School Teacher."

7 Ibid.; BE, *The Teacher's Handbook: A Guide for Use in the Schools of the City of New York,* 7, 44; "Practical Suggestions for Teachers: Prepared for the Public School Teachers of the Bronx," 6, TC.

18   Anne M. Limpus, "Getting Ready for the New Class"; "Getting Ready for New Term."
19   "My Day," 26.
20   Ibid; "Bricks Without Straw."
21   "My Day"; BE, *Teacher's Handbook,* 19–20; "Practical Suggestions for Teachers," 18.
22   "My Day," 27; Kaufman, *Up the Down Staircase*; Tracy Kidder, *Among Schoolchildren*; Samuel G. Freedman, *Small Victories: The Real World of a Teacher, Her Students and Their High School.* Also, see Arthur T. Costigan, "Even Socrates Couldn't Teach in N.Y.C. Schools."
23   BE, *All the Children: Forty-Third Report,* 1–53, TC. As a matter of fact, the *New York Sun,* which gave daily coverage to public schools and regularly contained photographs of school events, teachers, and administrators, contained not one single picture of African Americans in the years between 1920 and 1940.
24   Robert A. Davis, "The Teaching Problems of 1,075 Public School Teachers."
25   BE, *All the Children: Forty-Third Report,* 1–53, TC.
26   BE, *Report of Survey of Public School System, City of New York, 1924,* 306, TC.
27   Progressive education, which sprang from the reform impulses of the Progressive era, contained three basic elements: vocational training (or education for life), social reform, and child-centered schooling. The latter, as espoused by John Dewey, was based on a concern for all the complexities of a child's learning. After 1910, progressive education became more diffused as William H. Kilpatrick stressed education through problem-solving, and Harold Rugg emphasized the child-centered school. Patricia Albjerg Graham, *Progressive Education: From Arcady to Academe: A History of the Progressive Education Association, 1919–1955* (New York: Teachers College Press, 1967), chapter 1; John Dewey, *How We Think: A Restatement of the Relation of Reflective Thinking to the Educational Process* (Boston: Heath, 1910, revised ed., 1933) and Dewey, *Democracy and Education* (New York: Macmillan, 1916); William H. Kilpatrick, ed., *The Educational Frontier* (New York: Century, 1933); Harold Rugg and Ann Shumaker, *The Child-Centered School* (Yonkers-on-Hudson, N.Y.: World Book, 1928); *New York Sun,* 26 January 1925, 23.
28   BE, *The First Fifty Years: A Brief Review of Progress, 1898–1948,* 126–127, TC.
29   Cuban, *How Teachers Taught,* 3.
30   Ibid.
31   BE, *First Fifty Years,* 127–129, TC.
32   Cuban, *How Teachers Taught,* 65, 67.
33   Simon, *Wider World,* 8, 10.
34   Larry Cuban did not find much evidence of change in classroom practices; *How Teachers Taught,* 2. Those who believe progressive theories were practiced inside the classroom are Cremin, *Transformation of the School,* and Silberman, *Crisis in the Classroom.* Among those who assert that progressive practices did not find their way into the classroom are David B. Tyack, *The One Best System: A History of American Urban Education*; Robert S. Lynd and Helen Merrell Lynd, *Middletown in Transition: A Study in Cultural Conflicts,* 241.
35   C. A. Bowers, *The Progressive Educator and the Depression: The Radical Years,* 80–87, 29–30, 98; George S. Counts, *School and Society in Chicago* (New York: Harcourt, Brace, 1928), 357. Also see Counts, *Dare the School Build a New Social Order?* (New York: John Day, 1932).
36   Tyack et al., *Public Schools in Hard Times,* 57, 197–198.
37   "Bricks Without Straw."
38   Martin Denscombe, "The 'Hidden Pedagogy' and Its Implications for Teacher Training," 249–250.
39   Cuban, *How Teachers Taught,* 51; Lortie, *School-Teacher,* 9.
40   Kidder, *Among Schoolchildren,* 52–53.
41   See Kaufman, *Up the Down Staircase.* A centerpiece of this novel, by one who once taught in New York's public schools, is the guidance and advice provided a new teacher by an older and more experienced one.
42   Ibid. Also see Freedman, *Small Victories.*
43   NEA, "Status of the Teaching Profession," 63.
44   NEA, "The Teacher Looks at Teacher Load," 230.
45   BE, *All the Children: Forty-Third Report,* 55, TC.

46   Donovan, *The Schoolma'am*, 234; Kathleen Brady, "The Depression and the Classroom Teacher," 264.

47   BE, *Teacher's Handbook*, 41, TC.

48   *New York Sun*, 4 June 1936, 30; Dale Zysman, "Dear Sir: An Extract from an Open Letter to Superintendent Bayne," 20–21.

49   *New York Teacher* V (December 1939): 15.

50   NEA, "Status of the Teaching Profession," 63.

51   Ibid.; *New York Sun*, 4 February 1925, 27; 2 June 1936, 35.

52   *New York Sun*, 22 September 1936, 26.

53   Ibid., 2 June 1936, 35.

54   Lynd and Lynd, *Middletown in Transition*, 224.

55   BE, *First Fifty Years*, 115, TC; Cole, *Unionization of Teachers*, 26. However, their plight did not compare to the situation in Chicago where 13,000 teachers went unpaid for almost a year. *New York Sun*, 20 October 1931, 42.

56   Brady, "Depression and the Classroom Teacher," 264; William W. Wattenberg, *On the Educational Front: The Reactions of Teachers Associations in New York and Chicago*, 28–29; NEA, "Teacher Looks at Teacher Load," 249.

57   *New York Teacher* I (3 March 1936): 77.

58   For a thorough depiction of the effect of the Depression on public education, see Tyack et al., *Public Schools in Hard Times*, chapter 1.

59   Edward A. Krug, *The Shaping of the American High School: 1880–1920*, 2 vols. (Madison: University of Wisconsin Press, 1969), I:247–248; Fass, *Outside In*, 71–73; David Nasaw, *Schooled to Order: A Social History of Public Schooling in the United States*, 163.

60   Tyack, *One Best System*, 146–150; BE, *Thirty-Sixth Annual Report of the Superintendent of Schools, City of New York, Part II*, 189; *All the Children: Forty-Third Report*, 13, *First Fifty Years*, 120–121, TC; William B. Sears, Jr., "The Schools and the Depression," 501.

61   BE, *Thirty-Sixth Annual Report*, 79, TC.

62   Brady, "Depression and the Classroom Teacher," 263.

63   BE, *First Fifty Years*, 138–139, TC.

64   Paul L. Benjamin, "The Family Society and the Depression," 142.

65   BE, *All the Children: Forty-Third Report*, 47, 50–54, TC.

66   BE, *Teacher's Handbook*, 22–31; BE, *First Fifty Years*, 144, TC.

67   Personnel files, Teachers' Record Department File Number 72304, BE.

68   *New York Sun*, 3 June 1935, 34.

69   NEA, "Teacher Looks at Teacher Load," 235.

70   *New York Sun*, 1 October 1936, 42; 19 May 1938, 34.

71   Ibid, 4 March, 1925, 31.

72   NEA, "Teacher Looks at Teacher Load," 236.

73   Gould, "Freedom of Teachers," 570–571.

74   *New York Times*, 19 May 1934, 15.

75   Samuel Tenenbaum, "Supervision: Theory and Practice."

76   Howard K. Beale, *A History of Freedom of Teaching in American Schools*, 589.

77   Moore, *At Home in America*, 97–99; Alter F. Landesman, *Brownsville: The Birth, Development and Passing of a Jewish Community in New York*, 56, 59.

78   Arthur T. Jersild, "Characteristics of Teachers Who Are 'Liked Best' and 'Disliked Most.'"

79   *New York Times*, 20 July 1986, 20.

80   Simon, *Wider World*, 10; Howe, *Steady Work*, 350; Howe, *Margin of Hope*, 28–30; Alfred Kazin, *A Walker in the City* (New York: Harcourt, Brace and World, 1951), 18, 91.

81   BE, *First Fifty Years*, 122, TC.

82   Berrol, "Public Schools and Immigrants," 40; Sol Cohen, *Progressives and Urban School Reform: The Public Education Association of New York City, 1895–1954*, 151; Diane Ravitch, *The Great School Wars, New York City, 1805–1973: A History of the Public Schools as Battlefield of Social Change*, 239.

83   Moore, *At Home in America*, 96.

Chapter 7: A Very Long Day

1   BE, "Practical Suggestions," 13, TC.
2   *New York Sun*, 4 June 1936, 30; BE, *All the Children: Forty-Third Report,* 55, TC; Zysman, "Dear Sir," 20–21; *New York Teacher* V (December 1939): 15.
3   "Teacher or Factory Hand?" 171.
4   Zysman, "Dear Sir," 21; *New York Teacher* V (December 1939): 15.
5   "Teacher or Factory Hand?" 171.
6   BE, *All the Children: Forty-Third Report,* 24, 29, TC.
7   BE, *First Fifty Years,* 96, TC.
8   BE, *All the Children: Forty-Third Report,* 55, TC.
9   *School and Society* 36 (12 November 1932): 624; 38 (19 August 1933): 239; 39 (6 January 1934): 7.
10   Howard K. Beale, *Are American Teachers Free? An Analysis of the Restraints Upon the Freedom of Teaching in American Schools,* 393.
11   *New York Sun,* 30 December, 1931, 22; BE, *Journal of the New York City Board of Education, 1932,* I:128, TC.
12   BE, *First Fifty Years,* 115, TC; *School and Society* 38 (19 August 1933): 239; Bronx Council, *Study of the Lower Bronx,* 27.
13   *New York Sun,* 30 December 1931, 22; 22 May 1940, 30.
14   BE, *All the Children: Forty-Third Report,* 7, TC.
15   *New York Sun,* 17 January 1938, 28.
16   See chapter 9.
17   See BE, *All the Children: Forty-First Report,* 1–58; BE, *First Fifty Years,* 126, TC.
18   BE, *First Fifty Years,* 117, TC.
19   BC, *All the Children: Forty-First Report,* 7, 8, 45, TC.
20   Elwood Cubberly, editor's introduction, Elbert K. Fretwell, *Extra-Curricular Activities in Secondary Schools* (Boston: Houghton Mifflin, 1931), v; Charles R. Foster, *Extra-Curricular Activities in the High School* (Richmond, Va.: Johnson, 1925), 5.
21   Eugene S. Briggs, "The Demand for Teachers Prepared to Guide and Direct Extra-Class Activities," *School and Society* 45 (15 May 1937): 696.
22   NEA, "Teacher Looks at Teacher Load," 230.
23   BE, *All the Children: Forty-Third Report,* 32, TC.
24   Samuel P. Abelow, "What New York City Teachers Do for Schools During Their Leisure Moments," 165–166; *New York Times,* 14 December 1930, II, 3.
25   *New York Sun,* 22 May 1940, 30.
26   BE, *All the Children: Forty-Third Report,* 28–29, 63, TC.
27   See Lortie, *School-Teacher,* 92–93.
28   The New York Association of Teachers of English arranged with unions and producers for senior high school students to see current plays at prices as low as five cents. BE, *All the Children: Forty-Third Report,* 27, TC.
29   Moore, *At Home in America,* 98–99. For a discussion of first- and second-generation immigrants' encounters with schooling and teachers, see Tyack, *One Best System,* 229–255.
30   Fass, *Outside In,* 79–80.
31   Moore, *At Home in America,* 99; BE, *All the Children: Forty-Second Report,* 8, 29, 38, TC.
32   BE, *All the Children: Forty-Third Report,* 51, 53–54; Principals of Districts 23 and 24, Bronx, New York, "Working Together: A Ten Year Report," unpaged, TC.
33   See Moore, *At Home in America,* 99.
34   Principals, "Working Together"; BE, "Program of In-Service Courses for Teachers Offered by Board of Superintendents of Public Schools of The City of New York"; BE, *First Fifty Years,* 129–130, TC.
35   BE, "Program of In-Service Courses"; BE, *First Fifty Years,* 129–130, 144–145, TC.
36   *New York Sun,* 8 May 1934, 38.
37   Ibid., 9 February 1940, 34.
38   Ibid.; BE, *First Fifty Years,* 129–130, TC.

39   Abelow, "What New York City Teachers Do," 164–165; *New York Sun*, 15 July 1940, 20.

40   Wattenberg, *On the Educational Front*, 4–5, 50–51; Abelow, "What New York City Teachers Do," 165.

41   For the struggle to obtain equal salaries for men and women teachers in New York City, see Grace Strachen, *Equal Pay for Equal Work* (New York: B. F. Buck, 1910); Robert E. Doherty, "Tempest on the Hudson: The Struggle for 'Equal Pay for Equal Work' in the New York City Public Schools, 1907–1911," *History of Education Quarterly* 19 (Winter 1979): 413–434.

42   Cole, *Unionization of Teachers*, 15; Wattenberg, *On the Educational Front*, 45, 58–59.

43   Brooklyn Teachers Association, "Fifty-First Annual Report, 1924–25," 8, 11–12, 17, TC; Wattenberg, *On the Educational Front*, 46–47, 81.

44   Wattenberg, *On the Educational Front*, 126, 57, 55.

45   Ibid., 55–56; BE, *First Fifty Years*, 143, TC.

46   Wattenberg, *On the Educational Front*, 47, 49–50; BE, *First Fifty Years*, 110, TC.

47   *New York Sun*, 16 March 1925, 20.

48   Ibid.

49   BE, *First Fifty Years*, 115, TC.

50   Bernstein, "Teacher Goes Modern."

51   Wattenberg, *On the Educational Front*, 86–87.

52   Ibid.

53   Ibid., 81, 45, 88.

54   Lortie, *School-Teacher*, 92–93; Wattenberg, *On the Educational Front*, 100–101; *Guild Teacher* 4 (14 February 1939): 3, WLA.

55   Brooklyn Teachers Association, "Fifty-First Annual Report," 59–60, TC; *New York Sun*, 8 February 1939, 2.

56   *New York Sun*, 5 August 1933, 23.

57   Ibid., BE, *Journal of the Board of Education, 1937*, vol. II, 1946–1948, TC.

58   Leo Gross, "Will You Get Your Increment?" *New York Teacher* V (November 1938): 13; *New York Sun*, 17 May 1938, 32.

59   Mollie Sobol, "News from Abraham Lincoln High School," *New York Teacher* IV (January 1939): 20; *New York Sun*, 19 July 1929, 20.

60   *New York Sun*, 15 March 1935, 27. For further details on community activism among women teachers in New York City, see chapter 9.

Chapter 8: Profession or Procession?

1   Quoted in Dean Lobaugh, "Men Must Teach," 34.

2   Walter Herbert Small, *Early New England Schools* (Boston: Ginn), 114.

3   Murphey, "Boston Teachers Organize," 15–16. France employed a unique administrative policy, established in the 1890s, which encouraged its public school teachers to marry, to choose a colleague as a partner, and to bear and rear children while continuing to teach. Until 1910, when a maternity leave policy was instituted, pregnant teachers could remain in the classroom until childbirth. Leslie Page Moch, "Government Policy and Women's Experience: The Case of Teachers in France," *Feminist Studies* 14 (Summer 1988): 301–302.

4   David Wilbur Peters, "Married or Single? Wedlock's Effect Upon Teaching Ability," *Nation's Schools* 20 (December 1937), 41.

5   Paul N. Garver, "Legal Status of Married Women Teachers," 572–573; David Wilbur Peters, *The Status of the Married Woman Teacher* (New York: Teachers College Press, 1934), 38.

6   BE, "Teacher's Handbook," 49, TC.

7   Garver, "Legal Status," 574–575; *New York Sun*, 8 November 1939, 32; Peters, *Status of the Married Woman Teacher*, 39.

8   Harold H. Punke, "Marriage Rate Among Women Teachers," *American Sociological Review* 5 (August 1940): 511; Samuel Stouffer and Lyle M. Spencer, "Marriage and Divorce in Recent Years," *The Annals of the American Academy of Political and Social Science* CLXXIV (November 1936): 56–69; Viva Boothe, "Gainfully Employed Women in the Family," 82.

9   *New York Sun*, 9 November 1937, 38. About half of these were regular teachers and half were substitutes or women on the eligible lists. Yet the picture is incomplete because only women teachers were required to report their marriages. Kessler-Harris, *Out to Work*, 252.

10   Lois W. Banner, *Women in Modern America: A Brief History*, 196. For working women during the twenties, see Dorothy M. Brown, *American Women in the 1920s: Setting a Course*, chapter 4; and for women at work during the thirties, see Ware, *Holding Their Own*, chapter 2.

11   U.S. Bureau of the Census, *Fifteenth Census of the United States: 1930. Vol. 5: Population, General Report on Occupations*, 47.

12   U.S. Office of Education, *Biennial Survey of Education in the United States, Statistical Summary of Education, 1939–1940*, 2: 34.

13   NEA, "Requirements Affecting Appointment, Retention and Promotion of Teachers," 221; Leo M. Chamberlain and Leonard E. Meece, "Women and Men in the Teaching Profession," 48; *New York Teacher* V (October 1939): 23.

14   Frank Stricker, "Cookbooks and Law Books: The Hidden History of Career Women in Twentieth-Century America," *Journal of Social History* 10 (Fall 1976): 8; Elizabeth L. Woods, "When Wives Teach School: Should Eugenicists Demur?"

15   *New York Sun*, 9 April 1932, 4.

16   M. M. Chambers, "A Plea for Married Women Teachers," 572; Wendell S. Phillips and James E. Greene, "A Preliminary Study of the Relationship of Age, Hobbies, and Civil Status to Neuroticism Among Women Teachers," *Journal of Educational Psychology* XXX (September 1939): 440–441; David Snedden, "Personnel Problems in Educational Administration: Married Women as Public School Teachers," 614–615; Woods, "When Wives Teach School."

17   Florence Hornaday, "An Answer to 'A Plea for Married Women Teachers,'" *School and Society* 30 (21 December 1929): 846; Chamberlain and Meece, "Women and Men," 51; Snedden, "Personnel Problems," 614–615.

18   Chamberlain and Meece, "Women and Men," 51.

19   Floyd F. Goodier, "Another Conclusion Regarding the Married Woman Teacher"; *New York Sun*, 16 July 1934, 15.

20   Chamberlain and Meece, "Women and Men," 51; Goodier, "Another Conclusion," George E. Carrothers, *The Physical Efficiency of Teachers* (New York: Teachers College Press, 1924), 35; Chambers, "Plea for Married Women," 572.

21   *New York Times*, 9 January 1938, II, 1. The Board of Education also noted that 4,000 teachers had perfect attendance records over a ten-year period, and that from 1934 to 1939, 6,000 teachers did not miss a single day.

22   Teacher Personnel Cards, BE.

23   Ibid. A breakdown of leaves granted for the care of sick family members is found in BE, *All the Children: Forty-Third Report*, 41, TC.

24   M. M. Chambers, "Enforced Celibacy in Schools," *Nation's Schools* 18 (July 1936): 32; W. C. McGinnis, "The Married Woman Teacher," *School Executive* 50 (June 1931): 452; Helen Taft Manning, "Should Women Teachers Marry?" *Primary Education—Popular Education* 46 (November 1928): 201; Chambers, "Plea for Married Women Teachers," 572; *New York Times*, 9 January 1938, II, 9.

25   McGinnis, "Married Woman Teacher," 451–453; Logan Abner Waits, "A Study of the Comparative Efficiency of Single and Married Women as Teachers," *Educational Administration and Supervision* 8 (November 1932): 630–633.

26   Beale, *Are American Teachers Free?* 387.

27   Lois Scharf, *To Work and to Wed: Female Employment, Feminism, and the Great Depression*, 75. Scharf provides an excellent rendition of Depression-era prejudice against working wives. For the status of married teachers during the 1930s, see chapter 4.

28   *New York Sun*, 26 June 1939, 26.

29   Scharf, *To Work and to Wed*, 79–80.

30   Cited in Pauline Michel Papke, "Are Married Women People, or Have They Forfeited Democratic Freedom?" *Guild Teacher* 5 (26 September 1939): 11, WLA.

31   *New York Sun*, 2 September 1939, 21; 8 June 1939, 36.

32   Ibid., 7 November 1940, 22.

33   M. Eustace Broom, "Married Teachers," *High School Teacher* 5 (September 1929): 228.
34   McGinnis, "Married Woman Teacher," 452; Chambers, "Plea for Married Women Teachers," 572.
35   Snedden, "Personnel Problems," 614.
36   Lobaugh, "Men Must Teach," 33; McGinnis, "Married Woman Teacher," 452.
37   *New York Times*, 9 January 1938, II, 9.
38   *New York Sun*, 23 December 1937, 24; BE, "Teacher's Handbook," 49; BE, *Journal of the New York City Board of Education, 1937,* 2:1943, TC.
39   Beale, *Are American Teachers Free?* 388.
40   *New York Sun*, 15 July 1929, 37; 27 June 1935, 27.
41   See BE, *Journal of the New York City Board of Education* from 1930 to 1940; BE, *All the Children, Forty-First Report,* 43, TC.
42   *New York Teacher* VI (November 1940): 6.
43   BE, Miscellaneous circular issued by Jacob Greenburg, General Circular #4, 1934–36, Item III, IV A.1.C. (I), TC.
44   *New York Sun*, 6 February 1931, 42; 17 July 1935, 30; BE, General Circular #4; *Journal of the New York City Board of Education, 1935,* 1:928–929, 1194–1196; 1937, 2: 154–156, TC.
45   For an explanation of the methodology employed for this quantitative study, see Notes on Sources: Methodology.
46   In 1940, 81 teachers resigned from service, which was an all-time high. Although they were not required to give a reason, the Board of Education said it believed they were mostly married women who gave up teaching to keep house. *New York Sun*, 26 December 1940, 22.
47   All maternity leaves are listed on the Teacher Personnel Cards. These include the date leave was granted and also list the date of return to the classroom. The cards also specify whether the pregnancy was ended because of miscarriage, and state when the teacher returned to service. While some women undoubtedly circumvented the Board's directive that sabbaticals and other forms of leave were not to be substituted for maternity leave, nevertheless, the Board was so adamant about its policy that I am certain few women did attempt other ploys. Therefore, I argue that the maternity leave information provides reliable figures for the numbers of children born to city teachers. Although the *Journal of the New York City Board of Education*'s listing of maternity leaves was consulted only for the years from 1920 to 1940, all such leaves that appeared on Teacher Personnel Cards were noted. All births were factored into the computations, including those children born during the 1940s.
48   Ben B. Seligman, "The American Jew: Some Demographic Features," *American Jewish Year Book* 51 (Philadelphia: Jewish Publication Society, 1950), 15–17.
49   Ronald Freedman, Pascal Whelpton, and John Smit, "Socio-Economic Factors in Religious Differentials in Fertility," *American Sociological Review* 26 (August 1961): 608; Pascal Whelpton, Arthur Campbell, and John Patterson, *Fertility and Family Planning in the United States* (Princeton: Princeton University Press, 1966), 252.
50   BE, *All the Children: Forty-First Report,* 43, TC.
51   Virginia MacMakin Collier, *Marriage and Careers: A Study of One Hundred Women Who Are Wives, Mothers, Homemakers and Professional Workers,* 19.
52   Leslie Woodcock Tentler, *Wage-Earning Women: Industrial Work and Family Life in the United States, 1900–1930,* 161, 154–155.
53   BE, *First Fifty Years,* 118–119, TC; Bronx Council, *Study of the Lower Bronx,* 36, 104.
54   Boothe, "Gainfully Employed Women," 83–84.
55   Collier, *Marriage and Careers,* 14–24; Tentler, *Wage-Earning Women,* 155–157.
56   Jack Balswick, "Are American-Jewish Families Closely Knit?" *Jewish Social Studies* 28 (July 1966): 167.
57   Ibid.
58   Bernard Farber, Charles H. Mindel, and Bernard Lazerwitz, "The Jewish American Family," in *Ethnic Families in America: Patterns and Variations,* 2nd edition, ed. Charles H. Mindel and Robert W. Habenstein (New York: Elsevier, 1983), 358; Sandra B. Wake and Michael J. Sporakowski, "An Intergenerational Comparison of Attitudes Toward Supporting Aged Parents," *Journal of Marriage and the Family* 34 (February 1972): 46.

59   See Cowan and Cowan, *Our Parents' Lives,* 48–52.
60   See Sara M. Evans, *Born for Liberty: A History of Women in America,* 200; Kessler-Harris, *Out to Work,* 254.
61   Tentler, *Wage-Earning Women,* 149.
62   For a discussion of household work in the interwar years, see Ruth Schwartz Cowan, *More Work for Mother: The Ironies of Household Technology from the Open Hearth to the Microwave* (New York: Basic Books, 1983), 172–181.
63   Collier, *Marriage and Careers,* 24.
64   Anne Byrd Kennon, "College Wives Who Work," *Journal of the American Association of University Women* 20 (June 1927): 104–105.
65   Teacher Personnel Cards, BE; Teachers Union, New York City, Local 5 Collection, Box 8, File 10; Box 52, File 2, CLMD; Celia Lewis Zitron, *The New York City Teachers Union, 1916–1954: A Story of Educational and Social Commitment,* 93.
66   Teacher Personnel Cards, BE; *The Guild Teacher* 4 (6 June 1939): 3, WLA; Brooks, *Towards Dignity,* 60.

Chapter 9: Anti-Unionism, Anti-Semitism, and Anti-Communism

1   For accounts of the great Red scare in New York City's schools, see Iverson, *Communists and the Schools*; David Caute, *The Great Fear: The Anti-Communist Purge Under Truman and Eisenhower*; and Marjorie Murphy, *Blackboard Unions: The AFT and the NEA, 1900–1980,* chapter 9, especially 175–192.
2   Brooks, *Towards Dignity,* 18. For histories of the TU, see Isabella J. W. Lee, "A History of the Labor Union Movement Among New York City Public School Teachers"; Lana D. Muraskin, "The Teachers Union of the City of New York from Inception to Schism, 1912–1935"; Brooks, "Teachers Divided: Teacher Unionism in New York, 1935–1940"; Murphy, *Blackboard Unions.*
3   Muraskin, "Teachers Union," 32, 130.
4   Ibid., 180–181; *New York Teacher* IV (November 1938): 2; Zitron, *New York City Teachers Union,* 30.
5   Cole, *Unionization of Teachers,* 12; Muraskin, "Teachers Union," 123–126, 136.
6   Muraskin, "Teachers Union," 143–144; Cole, *Unionization of Teachers,* 11–12.
7   Lee, "History of the Labor Union Movement," 49.
8   See Jill Bystydzienski, "Women's Participation in Teachers' Unions in England and United States," in *Women Educators: Employees of Schools in Western Countries,* ed. Patricia A. Schmuck (Albany: State University of New York Press, 1987), 162. For studies of the part women played in organizing and leading teachers unions, see Marjorie Murphy, "From Artisan to Semi-Professional: White Collar Women Among Chicago Public School Teachers, 1870–1930"; Murphey, "Boston Teachers Organize"; Steve Trimble, *Education and Democracy: A History of the Minneapolis Federation of Teachers* (Minneapolis: Minneapolis Federation of Teachers, 1979).
9   *New York Teacher* II (June 1925): 8; Box 25, File 9; Box 49, Files 6, 11, TU, Local 5 Collection, CLMD.
10   Box 66, File 8, File 12; Academic Freedom File 9, TU Collection, CLMD.
11   See Box 14, File 1, TU Collection, CLMD; *New York Sun,* 12 October 1935, 38; 6 April 1936, 28; 15 May 1936, 38; 7 October 1940, 24; *New York Teacher* IV (February 1939): 2; *Guild Teacher* 4 (14 February 1939): 3; 5 (26 September 1939): 3, WLA.
12   Brooks, *Towards Dignity,* 54; *New York Teacher* IV (November 1938): 9.
13   Muraskin, "Teachers Union," 86.
14   Brooks, "Teachers Divided," 229.
15   Zitron, *New York City Teachers Union,* 27.
16   *New York Sun,* 16 May 1934, 26; 24 September 1936, 33; 20 August 1937, 23; 27 August 1937, 23; 8 February 1939, 32; *New York Teacher* IV (November 1938): 12–14.
17   ACLU, "What Freedom in New York Schools?" (New York: n.p., 1934), 5, TU Collection, CLMD; Beale, *Are American Teachers Free?* 583.
18   Wayne J. Urban, *Why Teachers Organized,* 90–91; Muraskin, "Teachers Union," 144. See TU

Collection, CLMD; Teachers Guild Collection, WLA. Two particularly noxious examples of anti-Semitic mail received by New York City teachers are reproduced in Zitron, *New York City Teachers Union*, 193; and in Murphy, *Blackboard Unions*.

19   Amitai Etzioni considers teaching, along with nursing and social work, to be a semiprofession, rather than a profession like medicine and law, because teachers' "training is shorter, their status is less legitimized, their right to privileged communication is less established, there is less of a specialized body of knowledge, and they have less autonomy from supervision or societal control than 'the' professions." Preface to *The Semi-Professions and Their Organization: Teachers, Nurses, Social Workers*, ed. Amitai Etzioni (New York: Free Press, 1969), v. For an explication of this theory as it applies to teachers, see Dan C. Lortie, "The Balance of Control and Autonomy in Elementary School Teaching," in Etzioni, *Semi-Professions*, 1–53.

20   Zitron, *New York City Teachers Union*, 16.

21   Muraskin, "Teachers Union," 144.

22   Herbst, *And Sadly Teach*, 192.

23   One woman's file indicates that her principal had her transferred because she used pupils as messengers to send TU materials to other teachers during school hours. However, there is no mention anywhere of her having appealed this decision. Personnel File Number 94464, BE; *New York Teacher* III (May 1937): 12; *New York Sun*, 27 August 1937, 23.

24   *New York Sun*, 24 September 1936, 33; 20 August 1937, 23; 16 May 1934, 26; 8 February 1939, 32; *New York Teacher* IV (November 1938): 12–14.

25   Gould, "Freedom of Teachers," 575.

26   Herman E. Cooper, "Teacher vs the Administrator," *New York Teacher* II (December 1936): 19.

27   *New York Sun*, 18 May 1937, 34.

28   Ibid., 17 July 1936, 24.

29   Beale, *History of Freedom of Teaching*, 239–242.

30   *New York Sun*, 24 October 1935, 33.

31   *New York Times*, 30 May 1934, 3.

32   "Are School Teachers Citizens?" *New Republic* XLIX (1 December 1926): 29.

33   Beale, *History of Freedom of Teaching*, 240.

34   *New York Sun*, 30 November 1938, 33.

35   Iverson, *Communists and the Schools*, 12–13.

36   BE, *Journal of the Board of Education, 1922*, I (8 February 1922): 308; *Minutes of the Board of Education of the City of New York* (23 February 1921): 290–292, TC; Wattenberg, *On the Educational Front*, 16.

37   Beale, *History of Freedom of Teaching*, 267, 274–275.

38   *New York Sun*, 9 September 1940, 1, 20.

39   Beale, *History of Freedom of Teaching*, 55, 90; Wattenberg, *On the Educational Front*, 16.

40   Gould, *Freedom of Teachers*, 55.

41   Celia Lewis, "Schools for Tolerance."

42   Shiebler/Campbell Files, Box 4, Folder 8, TC.

43   Examination of the personnel files stored at the BE indicates that every teacher's file contained the following: her application for license, medical test, college transcript, references, report on probationary training, recommendation for permanent appointment, and notice of prospective retirement. Most files also listed courses and tests taken for advancement. The only other additions to the files are complaints lodged against the teacher, problems brought before supervisors, and appearances before the BE to answer these charges. The only voluminous files appear to be those of the teachers dismissed from service in the 1950s because of alleged membership in the Communist party.

44   Muraskin, "Teachers Union," 142; Marion Milstein and Jenny L. Mayer, "Schools for Tolerance II," *New York Teacher* IV (January 1939): 10–11.

45   Bronx Council, *Study of the Lower Bronx*, 5. For a detailed discussion of anti-Semitism in New York City, see Ronald Howard Bayor, *Neighbors in Conflict: The Irish, Germans, Jews and Italians of New York City, 1929–1941*, especially chapter 8.

46   Zitron, *New York City Teachers Union*, 193.

47 *New York Sun*, 13 May 1940, 30. Religious antagonism in the Chicago teaching staff during the 1930s involved strains between its Catholic and Protestant teachers. Wattenberg, *On the Educational Front*, 127–129.

48 Lewis, "Schools for Tolerance."

49 Bayor, *Neighborhoods in Conflict*, 25–26.

50 Moore, *At Home in America*, 101.

51 Mark Naison, *Communists in Harlem during the Depression*, 216.

52 Teachers' Record Department File Number 107599, BE; Interview, Oral History of the American Left Collection, WLA.

53 Press statement of the Teachers Union Local 555, UPW–CIO, 4 May 1950, TU Collection, Box 19, File 1, CLMD.

54 Because I have not encountered her name in print elsewhere, I shall accede to the wishes of the archivist of the TU Collection at Cornell, where her case is well documented, and protect this teacher's identity.

55 Letter to Assistant Superintendent Dr. Clare C. Baldwin, 7 January 1952, TU Collection, Box 15, File 10, CLMD.

56 Ibid., Box 19, File 1; Box 15, File 10.

57 Ibid., Letter to Assistant Superintendent Dr. Clare C. Baldwin, 7 January 1952, Box 15, File 10.

58 Ibid., Box 15, File 10; "Alice Citron, 'Best of the Best' to Harlem Mothers," (The Teachers Union, Local 555, UPW, November 1950), Box 19, File 1; Zitron, *New York City Teachers Union*, 94–105; Interview with Alice Citron, Oral History of the American Left Collection, WLA.

59 Teachers' Record Department File Number 107599, BE; Naison, *Communists in Harlem*, 216; Iverson, *Communists and the Schools*, 36; Philip Taft, *United They Teach: The Story of the United Federation of Teachers*, 321.

60 *New York Teacher* I (May 1936): 126; "Program of Annual Educational Conference," 1938, 45; 1939, 51–52, TU Collection, CLMD.

61 BE, "Report of the Board of Superintendents, November 23, 1933," TU Collection, CLMD; David Alison, *Searchlight: An Exposé of New York City Schools*, 284.

62 Zitron, *New York City Teachers Union*, 178–180; *New York Teacher News* (27 May 1950): 3; *New York Sun*, 9 March 1935, 38. Despite Board regulations about listing marriages, and despite public knowledge that Isadore Begun was Citron's husband, no mention of this is to be found in her files. Begun is identified as her husband in: Beale, *Are American Teachers Free?* 357; Caute, *Great Fear*, 198; in Alice Citron's obituary, *New York Times*, 23 January 1988, 9.

63 Alison, *Searchlight*, 259.

64 TU Collection, Box 19, File 1; "Teachers Fight for Freedom: Eight New York City Teachers on Trial," 21, TU Collection, CLMD; Teachers' Record Department File Number 107599, BE.

65 TU Collection, Box 15, File 10, CLMD.

66 Ibid., Box 8, File 10; Box 52, File 2; Zitron, *New York City Teachers Union*, 93. Her husband, David Flacks, was dismissed from the teaching staff as well, for refusing to answer when asked whether he was a member of the Communist Party. *New York Teacher News* (15 November 1952): 4.

67 TU Collection, Box 9, File 9; Box 24, File 1, CLMD.

68 Ibid., Box 2, File 7; *New York Teacher News* (15 November 1952): 5.

69 TU Collection, Box 8, File 8, CLMD.

70 *New York Teacher News* (30 April 1949): 1; TU Collection, Box 19, File 1, CLMD.

71 Celia Lewis, "On Your Guard: The Rapp-Coudert Resolution to Investigate the Schools."

72 Box 19, File 1; "Teachers Fight for Freedom: Eight New York City Teachers On Trial," (New York: The Teachers Union, Local 555, UPW, 1950); "Alice Citron," TU Collection, CLMD.

73 Alison, *Searchlight*, 194–196; Zitron, *New York City Teachers Union*, 210.

74 TU Collection, Box 9, File 10, CLMD.

75 Caute, *Great Fear*, 441.

76 Ibid.

77 Ibid., 441–442; 438.

78 Ibid., 432.

79   Klehr, *Heyday of American Communism*, 238, 379.
80   *New York Teacher News*, 15 November 1952, 4.
81   TU Collection, Box 52, File 2, CLMD.
82   Oral History of the American Left Collection, WLA; quoted in Naison, *Communists in Harlem*, 216.
83   Ibid., 321.
84   TU Collection, Box 9, File 10, CLMD.
85   For accounts of this decentralization power struggle, see Carolyn Eisenberg, "The Parents' Movement at IS 201: From Integration to Black Power, 1958–1966," (Ph.D. diss., Teachers College, Columbia University, 1971); Mario Fantini, Marilyn Gittell, and Richard Magat, *Community Control and the Urban School* (New York: Praeger, 1970); Naomi Levine, *Schools in Crisis* (New York: Popular Library, 1969); Ravitch, *Great School Wars*, chapters 29–33.
86   See Nancy F. Cott, *The Grounding of Modern Feminism*.

Chapter 10: Afterword

1   Costigan, "Even Socrates Couldn't Teach."
2   Felicia R. Lee, "New York City's Schools See Crime Rising in Lower Grades," *New York Times*, 24 April 1990, 1, B4.
3   See Herbst, *And Sadly Teach.*
4   Freedman, *Small Victories.*

Notes on Sources: Oral Interviews

1   Margaret Mead and Rhoda Metraux, *The Study of Culture at a Distance* (Chicago: University of Chicago Press, 1953), 144.
2   Sherna Gluck, "What's So Special About Women? Women's Oral History," in *Oral History: An Interdisciplinary Anthology*, ed. David K. Dunaway and Willa K. Baum (Nashville, Tenn.: American Association for State and Local History, 1984), 221–237.

BIBLIOGRAPHY

INTERVIEWS

Interviews with 61 former teachers (See Notes on Sources)

ARCHIVAL SOURCES

Princeton University Library
American Civil Liberties Union papers

American Jewish Archives
Cincinnati, Ohio
Annie Nathan Meyer papers

Barnard College Archives
Woolman Library
Barnard College
Columbia University

Barnard College Bulletin
Columbia University Bulletin of Information, Barnard College Announcement, 1935–1936
Dean's Office Correspondence

The Board of Education of The City of New York
Bureau of Teachers' Records
Division of Personnel
Brooklyn, New York

Teacher Personnel Cards
Teachers' Record Department Files

Brooklyn College Archives
Brooklyn College Library
Brooklyn College

The Broeklundian
Brooklyn College, Graduate Survey Group, Bureau of Economic Research. The Brooklyn College Graduate (1932–1939): Complete Report of Findings and Conclusion. Prepared by Edwin H. Spengler. (Brooklyn: Brooklyn College, 1943).
Brooklyn College Vanguard
Scrapbook containing newspaper clippings on New York City colleges.

BIBLIOGRAPHY

City College Archives

City College Library
City College of New York

City College Bulletin

Cornell Labor-Management Documentation Center

M. P. Catherwood Library
Cornell University

American Civil Liberties Union, "What Freedom in New York Schools?" New York: n.p., 1934.
Teachers Union, New York City, Local Five Collection: Academic Freedom Files.
———. "Alice Citron, 'Best of the Best' to Harlem Mothers." Box 19, File 1.
———. "Program of Annual Educational Conference," 1938, 1939.
———. "Teachers Fight for Freedom: Eight New York City Teachers on Trial." New York: The Teachers Union, Local 555, United Public Workers of America, 1950.

Hunter College Archives

Wexler Library
Hunter College

Hunter College Bulletin.
The Wisterian

Board of Education, City of New York Collection

Special Collections
Milbank Library
Teachers College
Columbia University

Board of Education, City of New York, Office of the Superintendent of Schools. *Annual Reports of the Superintendent of Schools, City of New York, 1920–1934.*
———. *All the Children: Forty-First Report of the Superintendent of Schools, City of New York, 1938–39.* Brooklyn: Board of Education, 1939.
———. *All the Children: Forty-Third Report of the Superintendent of Schools, City of New York, 1939–40.* Brooklyn: Board of Education, 1940.
———. *All the Children: Thirty-Eighth Report of the Superintendent of Schools, City of New York, 1935–36.* Brooklyn: Board of Education, 1936.
———. *The First Fifty Years: A Brief Review of Progress, 1898–1948.* Brooklyn: Board of Education, 1948.
———. General Circulars, 1920–1940.
———. *Journal of the New York City Board of Education, 1920–1940.*
———. *Minutes of the Board of Education of the City of New York, 1920–1940.*
———. Miscellaneous circular issued by Associate Superintendent Jacob Greenburg, approved by Superintendent of Schools Harold G. Campbell, 21 January, 1936.
———. *Official Directory of the Board of Education of the City of New York, 1920–1940.*
———. "Program of In-Service Courses for Teachers Offered by Board of Superintendents of Public Schools of The City of New York." New York, n.p., 1939–1940.
———. *Proposed Requirements for Licenses for Teachers.* New York: n.p., May 1936.
———. *Report of Survey of Public School System, City of New York, 1924.* New York: Board of Education, 1929.
———. *A Survey of the Substitute Teachers in the Public Schools of the City of New York.* Prepared by Daniel Paul Higgins. New York: n.p., 1938.

Brooklyn Teachers Association, "Annual Reports, 1924–1929." Brooklyn: n.p., 1929.
New York State Department of Education. *Report of a Study of New York City Schools. Part I: The Administration-Supervisory Organization.* Prepared by Frank Pierrepont Graves. Albany: University of the State of New York Press, 1933.
————. *The Teacher's Handbook: A Guide for Use in the Schools of the City of New York.* 4th ed. New York: State Department of Education, 1928.
O'Shea, William J. *Progress of the Public Schools,* May 1, 1924–July 31, 1929. New York: Board of Education, 1929.
"Practical Suggestions for Teachers: Prepared for the Public School Teachers of the Bronx. " Bronx: n.p., 1926.
Principals of District 23 and 24, Bronx, New York. "Working Together: A Ten Year Report." New York: n.p., 1937.
Shiebler/Campbell Files.

Robert F. Wagner Labor Archives of the Tamiment Institute Library

Elmer Holmes Bobst Library
New York University

The Guild Teacher
Oral History of the American Left Collection
The Unemployment Committee of the New York Teachers Guild.
Teachers Stand in Line: Analysis and Forecast of Teacher Unemployment in the New York City School System. New York: n.p., 1936.

NEWSPAPERS

New York Sun — 1920–1940
New York Times — 1920–1940

CONTEMPORARY JOURNALS AND MAGAZINES

American Educational Digest
American School Board Journal
American Teacher
The Annals of The American Academy of Political and Social Sciences
Education
Educational Administration and Supervision
Educational Forum
Educational Record
Educational Research Bulletin
Elementary School Journal
Forum and Century
Grade Teacher
Guild Teacher
Harvard Educational Review
High Points
High School Teacher
Journal of Education
Journal of Educational Psychology
Journal of Educational Research
Journal of Educational Sociology
Journal of Experimental Education
Journal of the American Association of University Women
Journal of the National Education Association
Nation's Schools

BIBLIOGRAPHY

New Republic
New York State Education
New York Teacher
New York Teacher News
Primary Education—Popular Education
Review of Educational Research
School and Society
School Board Journal
School Executive Magazine
School Life
School Review
Secondary Education
Teachers College Record

BOOKS, PAMPHLETS, ARTICLES, AND DISSERTATIONS

Abelow, Samuel P."What New York City Teachers Do for Schools During Their Leisure Moments."
    School Life 15 (May 1930): 164–166.
Abzug, Bella. *Bella! Ms. Abzug Goes to Washington.* Edited by Mel Ziegler. New York: Saturday
    Review Press, 1972.
Alison, David. *Searchlight: An Exposé of New York City Schools.* New York: Teachers Center Press,
    1951.
Altbach, Philip G. *Student Politics in America: A Historical Analysis.* New York: McGraw-Hill ,
    1973.
———, and Peterson, Patti McGill. "Before Berkeley: Historical Perspectives on American Student
    Activism." *Annals of The American Academy of Political and Social Sciences* 395 (May
    1971): 1–14.
Banner, Lois W. *Women in Modern America: A Brief History.* New York: Harcourt Brace
    Jovanovich, 1974.
Baum, Charlotte; Paula Hyman; and Michel, Sonya. *The Jewish Woman in America.* New York:
    Dial, 1975.
Baxter, Annette K. "Virginia Crocheron Gildersleeve." In *Notable American Women: The Modern
    Period,* 273–275. Edited by Barbara Sicherman and Carol Hurd Green. Cambridge,
    Mass.: Belknap Press of Harvard University Press, 1980.
Bayor, Ronald Howard. *Neighbors in Conflict: The Irish, Germans, Jews and Italians of New York
    City, 1929–1941.* Baltimore: Johns Hopkins University Press, 1978.
Beale, Howard K. *Are American Teachers Free? An Analysis of the Restraints Upon the Freedom of
    Teaching in American Schools.* New York: Charles Scribner's Sons, 1936.
———. *A History of Freedom of Teaching in American Schools.* New York: Charles Scribner's
    Sons, 1941.
Benjamin, Paul L. "The Family Society and the Depression." *The Annals of The American Academy
    of Political and Social Science* 160 (March 1932): 135–143.
Bernstein, Victor H. "Teacher Goes Modern: Traditional 'School-marm' Type Gives Way to the
    Exponent of the New Freedom." *New York Times* 2 February, 1936 IX, 11.
Berrol, Selma Cantor. "Education and Economic Mobility: The Jewish Experience in New York
    City, 1880–1920." *American Jewish Historical Quarterly* 65 (March 1976): 257–271.
———. "From Compensatory Education to Adult Education: The New York City Evening Schools,
    1825–1935." *Adult Education* 26 (Summer 1976): 208–225.
———. "Immigrants at School: New York City, 1898–1914," Ph.D. diss., City University of New
    York, 1967.
———. "Julia Richman: Agent of Change in the Urban School." *Urban Education* XI (January
    1977): 357–374.
———. "Public Schools and Immigrants: The New York City Experience," 31–43 In *American
    Education and the European Immigrant, 1840–1940.* Edited by Bernard J. Weiss.
    Urbana: University of Illinois Press, 1982.

———. "School Days on the Old East Side: The Italian and Jewish Experience." *New York History* LVII (April 1976): 201–213.

———. "When Uptown Met Downtown: Julia Richman's Work in the Jewish Community of New York, 1880–1912." *American Jewish History* LXX (September 1980): 35–51.

Birnbaum, Norman, and Childers, Marjorie. "The American Student Movement." In *The Seeds of Politics: Youth and Politics in America*, 16–23. Edited by Anthony M. Orum. Englewood, N.J.: Prentice-Hall, 1972.

Boothe, Viva. "Gainfully Employed Women in the Family." *The Annals of the American Academy of Political and Social Science* 160 (March 1932): 75–85.

Bowers, C. A. *The Progressive Educator and the Depression: The Radical Years*. New York: Random House, 1969.

Brady, Kathleen. "The Depression and the Classroom Teacher." *Journal of the National Education Association* 22 (December 1933): 263–264.

Brax, Ralph S. *The First Student Movement: Student Activism in the United States During the 1930s*. Port Washington, N.Y.: Kennikat Press, 1981.

———. "When Students First Organized Against War: Student Protest During the 1930s." *New York Historical Society Quarterly* LXIII (July 1979): 228–255.

"Bricks Without Straw." *New York Teacher* IV (March 1939): 12.

Bronx Council of Social Agencies. *A Study of the Lower Bronx*. Bronx, N.Y.: The Bronx Council of Social Agencies, 1939.

Brooks, Thomas. "Teachers Divided: Teacher Unionism in New York, 1935–1940." In *Educating an Urban People: The New York City Experience*, 206–218. Edited by Diane Ravitch and Ronald K. Goodenow. New York: Teachers College Press, 1981.

———. *Towards Dignity: A Brief History of the UFT*. New York: United Federation of Teachers, Local 1, AFL-CIO, 1967.

Brown, Dorothy M. *Setting a Course: American Women in the 1920s*. Boston: Twayne, 1987.

Brumberg, Joan Jacobs, and Tomes, Nancy. "Women in the Professions: A Research Agenda for American Historians." *Reviews in American History* 10 (June 1982): 275–296.

Brumberg, Stephan F. *Going to America, Going to School: The Jewish Immigrant Public School Encounter in Turn-of-the-Century New York City*. New York: Praeger, 1986.

Campbell, Harold G. "America's Largest City School System." *The Journal of the National Education Association* 27 (September 1938): 178.

Cantor, Milton. *The Divided Left: American Radicalism, 1900–1975*. New York: Hill and Wang, 1978.

Caute, David. *The Great Fear: The Anti-Communist Purge Under Truman and Eisenhower*. New York: Simon and Schuster, 1978.

Chafe, William H. *The American Woman: Her Changing Social, Economic, and Political Role, 1920–1970*. New York: Oxford University Press, 1972.

Chamberlain, Leo M., and Meece, Leonard E. "Women and Men in the Teaching Profession." *Bulletin of the Bureau of School Service, College of Education, University of Kentucky* IX (March 1937): 1–60.

Chambers, M. M. "A Plea for Married Women Teachers." *School and Society* XXX (26 October 1929): 572–575.

Cohen, J. X. *Jews, Jobs and Discrimination: A Report on Jewish Non-Employment*. New York: American Jewish Congress, 1937.

———. *Towards Fair Play for Jewish Workers: Third Report on Jewish Non-Employment*. New York: American Jewish Congress, 1938.

Cohen, Miriam. "Changing Education Strategies Among Immigrant Generations: New York Italians in Comparative Perspective." *Journal of Social History* 15 (Spring 1982): 443–466.

Cohen, Robert P. *Revolt of the Depression Generation: America's First Mass Student Protest Movement, 1929–1940*. New York: Oxford University Press, 1993.

Cohen, Sol. *Progressives and Urban School Reform: The Public Education Association of New York City, 1895–1954*. New York: Teachers College Press, 1964.

Cole, Stephen. *The Unionization of Teachers: A Case Study of the UFT*. New York: Praeger, 1969.

Collier, Virginia MacMakin. *Marriage and Careers: A Study of One Hundred Women Who Are*

BIBLIOGRAPHY

Wives, Mothers, Homemakers and Professional Workers. New York: Channel Bookshop, 1926.

Costigan, Arthur T. "Even Socrates Couldn't Teach in N.Y.C. Schools." *New York Times,* 1 July 1989, 23.

Cott, Nancy F. *The Grounding of Modern Feminism.* New Haven: Yale University Press, 1987.

Coulton, Thomas Evans. *Struggle and Achievement at Brooklyn College, 1930–1955.* New York: Harper and Brothers, 1955.

Cowan, Neil M., and Cowan, Ruth Schwartz. *Our Parents' Lives: The Americanization of Eastern European Jews.* New York: Basic Books, Publishers, 1989.

Cremin, Lawrence A. *The Transformation of the School: Progressivism in American Education, 1876–1957.* New York: Random House, 1961.

Cuban, Larry. *How Teachers Taught: Constancy and Change in American Classrooms, 1890–1980.* White Plains, N.Y.: Longman, 1984.

Davis, Robert A. "The Teaching Problems of 1,075 Public School Teachers." *Journal of Experimental Education* IX (September 1940): 41–60.

DeMartini, Joseph R. "Student Activists of the 1930s and 1960s: A Comparison of the Social Base of Two Student Movements." *Youth and Society* 6 (March 1975): 395–422.

Denscombe, Martin. "The 'Hidden Pedagogy' and Its Implications for Teacher Training." *British Journal of Sociology of Education* 3 (1982): 249–265.

Donovan, Frances R. *The Schoolma'am.* New York: Frederick A. Stokes, 1938.

Draper, Hal. "The Student Movement of the Thirties: A Political History." In *As We Saw the Thirties: Essays on Social and Political Movements of a Decade,* 153–189. Edited by Rita James Simon. Urbana: University of Illinois Press, 1967.

Eagan, Eileen. *Class, Culture, and the Classroom: The Student Peace Movement of the 1930s.* Philadelphia: Temple University Press, 1981.

Elsbree, Willard S. *The American Teacher: Evolution of a Profession in a Democracy.* New York: American Book, 1939.

Ettinger, William L. "America Calls: Will *You* Answer the Call?" New York: BE, unpaged, ca. 1918–1924.

Evans, Sara. *Born for Liberty: A History of Women in America.* New York: Free Press, 1989.

Ewen, Elizabeth. *Immigrant Women in the Land of Dollars: Life and Culture on the Lower East Side, 1890–1925.* New York: Monthly Review Press, 1985.

Fass, Paula S. *Outside in: Minorities and the Transformation of American Education.* New York: Oxford University Press, 1989.

Feldstein, Stanley. *This Land That I Show You: Three Centuries of Jewish Life in America.* Garden City, N.Y.: Anchor/Doubleday, 1978.

Feuer, Lewis S. *The Conflict of Generations: The Character and Significance of Student Movements.* New York: Basic Books, 1969.

Flacks, Richard. "The Liberal Generation: An Exploration of the Roots of Student Protest." *Journal of Social Issues* XXIII (July 1967): 52–75.

Frazier, Benjamin W. "Comparing Typical Teachers." *School Life* 23 (March 1938): 261, 263.

Freedman, Samuel G. *Small Victories: The Real World of a Teacher, Her Students and Their High School.* New York: Harper and Row, 1990.

Garver, Paul N. "Legal Status of Married Women Teachers." *School and Society* 34 (24 October 1931): 571–576.

Gildersleeve, Virginia Crocheron. "A Dean's Portrait of the College Girl." *New York Times Magazine* (4 February 1934): 6–7.

Glazer, Nathan, and Moynihan, Daniel Patrick. *Beyond the Melting Pot: The Negroes, Puerto Ricans, Jews, Italians, and Irish of New York City.* Cambridge, Mass.: M.I.T. Press, 1963.

Glenn, Susan A. *Daughters of the Shtetl: Life and Labor in the Immigrant Generation.* Ithaca: Cornell University Press, 1990.

Goodier, Floyd F. "Another Conclusion Regarding the Married Woman Teacher." *Nation's Schools* 2 (December 1938): 51–52.

Gordon, Lynn D. "Annie Nathan Meyer and Barnard College: Mission and Identity in Women's

Higher Education, 1889–1950." *History of Education Quarterly* 26 (Winter 1986): 503–523.

———. "In the Shadow of SDS: Writing the History of Twentieth-Century College Students." *History of Education Quarterly* 26 (Spring 1986): 131–139.

Gordon, Milton M. *Assimilation in American Life: The Role of Race, Religion, and National Origins.* New York: Oxford University Press, 1964.

Gorelick, Sherry. *City College and the Jewish Poor: Education in New York, 1880–1924.* New Brunswick: Rutgers University Press, 1981.

Gornick, Vivian. *The Romance of American Communism.* New York: Basic Books, 1977.

Gould, Sidney C. "The Freedom of Teachers in New York City's Public Elementary and Secondary Schools From 1932–1952." Ph.D. diss., New York University, 1952.

Heirich, Max, and Kaplan, Sam. "Yesterday's Discord." In *The Berkeley Student Revolt: Facts and Interpretations*, 10–35. Edited by Seymour Martin Lipset and Sheldon S. Wolin. Garden City, N.Y.: Anchor Books, 1965.

Herbst, Jurgen. *And Sadly Teach: Teacher Education and Professionalization in American Culture.* Madison: University of Wisconsin Press, 1988.

Herbst, Margaret. "Reminiscences of the Depression Years." *Hunter Alumni Quarterly* (Spring 1970): 13.

Horowitz, Helen Lefkowitz. *Alma Mater: Design and Experience in the Women's Colleges from Their 19th-Century Beginnings to the 1930s.* New York: Alfred A. Knopf, 1984.

———. *Campus Life: Undergraduate Cultures from the End of the Eighteenth Century to the Present.* New York: Alfred A. Knopf, 1987.

Horowitz, Murray M. *Brooklyn College: The First-Half-Century.* Brooklyn: Brooklyn College Press, 1982

Howe, Irving. *A Margin of Hope: An Intellectual Autobiography.* New York: Harcourt Brace Jovanovich, 1982.

———. *Steady Work: Essays in the Politics of Democratic Radicalism, 1953–1966.* New York: Harcourt, Brace and World, 1966.

———. *World of Our Fathers.* New York: Simon and Schuster, 1976.

———, and Coser, Lewis. *The American Communist Party: A Critical History (1919–1957).* Boston: Beacon Press, 1957.

Hyman, Paula E. "Culture and Gender: Women in the Immigrant Jewish Community." In *The Legacy of Jewish Migration: 1881 and Its Impact*, 157–168. Edited by David Berger. Brooklyn: Brooklyn College Press, 1983.

Iverson, Robert W. *The Communists and the Schools.* New York: Harcourt, Brace, 1959.

Jersild, Arthur T. "Characteristics of Teachers Who Are 'Liked Best' and 'Disliked Most.'" *Journal of Experimental Education* IX (December 1940): 139–151.

Kaufman, Bel. *"Mihi Cura Futuri." The Hunter Magazine* 3 (April 1984): 4–9.

———. *Up the Down Staircase.* Englewood Cliffs, N.J.: Prentice-Hall, 1964.

Kempton, Murray. *Part of Our Time: Some Monuments and Relics of the Thirties.* New York: Dell, 1955.

Kenniston, Kenneth. "The Sources of Student Dissent." *Journal of Social Issues* XXIII (July 1967): 108–137.

Kessler-Harris, Alice. *Out to Work: A History of Wage-Earning Women in the United States.* New York: Oxford University Press, 1982

Kessner, Thomas. *The Golden Door: Italian and Jewish Immigrant Mobility in New York City, 1880–1915.* New York: Oxford University Press, 1977.

———. "Jobs, Ghettoes and the Urban Economy, 1880–1935." *American Jewish History* LXXI (December 1981): 231–238.

———. "The Selective Filter of Ethnicity: A Half Century of Immigrant Mobility." In *The Legacy of Jewish Immigration: 1881 and Its Impact*, 169–185. Edited by David Berger. Brooklyn: Brooklyn College Press, 1983.

Kidder, Tracy. *Among Schoolchildren.* New York: Houghton Mifflin, 1989.

Klehr, Harvey. *Communist Cadre: The Social Background of the American Communist Party Elite.* Stanford: Hoover Institute Press, 1978.

———. *The Heyday of American Communism: The Depression Decade.* New York: Basic Books, 1984.

Kramer, Sydelle, and Masur, Jenny, eds. *Jewish Grandmothers.* Boston: Beacon Press, 1976.

Landesman, Alter F. *Brownsville: The Birth, Development and Passing of a Jewish Community in New York.* New York: Bloch, 1969.

Lash, Joseph P. *The Campus Strikes Against War.* New York: Student League for Industrial Democracy, 1935.

Lee, Calvin B. T. *The Campus Scene: 1900–1970.* New York: David McKay, 1970.

Lee, Isabella J. W. "A History of the Labor Union Movement Among New York City Public School Teachers." Ph.D. diss., New York University, 1971.

Levine, David O. *The American College and the Culture of Aspiration, 1915–1960.* Ithaca: Cornell University Press, 1986.

Levinger, Lee J. *The Jewish Student in America.* Cincinnati: B'nai Brith, 1937.

Lewis, Celia. "On Your Guard: The Rapp-Coudert Resolution to Investigate the Schools." *New York Teacher* V (June 1940): 11.

———. "Schools for Tolerance," *New York Teacher* IV (December 1938): 10.

Limpus, Anne M. "Getting Ready for the New Class." *New York Sun* 16 September, 1931, 46.

———. "Getting Ready for New Term." *New York Sun,* 11 September, 1933, 34.

Lobaugh, Dean. "Men Must Teach." *Nation's Schools* 19 (January 1937): 33–35.

Lortie, Dan C. *School-Teacher: A Sociological Study.* Chicago: University of Chicago Press, 1975.

Lynd, Robert S., and Lynd, Helen Merrell. *Middletown in Transition: A Study in Cultural Conflicts.* New York: Harcourt, Brace, 1937.

McGill, Kenneth H. "The School-Teacher Stereotype." *Journal of Educational Sociology* IV (June 1931): 642–650.

McGill, Nettie Pauline. "Some Characteristics of Jewish Youth in New York." *The Jewish Social Service Quarterly* XXIV (December 1937): 251–272.

———, and Matthews, Ellen Nathalie. *The Youth of New York City.* New York: Macmillan, 1940.

McGuffey, Verne. "Some Elements in the Cultural Background of Students in One of the New York City Training Schools for Teachers." *Educational Administration and Supervision* 14 (April 1928): 279–282.

Maller, J. B. "A Study of Jewish Neighborhoods in New York City." *The Jewish Social Service Quarterly* 10 (1934): 271–276.

Mallon, Arthur. "The Development of the Municipal Teacher Training Colleges in New York City." Ph.D. diss., New York University, 1935.

Mangano, Ronald, and Casebeer, Arthur L. "Alarming Parallels in Student Anti-War Activism of the Thirties and the Sixties." *National Association of Student Personnel Administrators Journal* 9 (October 1971): 119–125.

Mann, Georg. "Two Lefts: A Look across the Generation Gap." *South Atlantic Quarterly* 69 (Summer 1967): 431–445.

Miller, Michael Henry. "The American Student Movements of the Depression, 1931–1941: A Historical Analysis." Ph.D. diss., Florida State University of Education, 1981.

Moffett, M'Ledge. *The Social Background and Activities of Teachers College Students.* New York: Teachers College, Columbia University, 1929.

Moore, Deborah Dash. *At Home in America: Second Generation New York Jews.* New York: Columbia University Press, 1981.

Muraskin, Lana D. "The Teachers Union of the City of New York From Inception to Schism, 1912–1935." Ph.D. diss., University of California, Berkeley, 1979.

Murphey, Kathleen. "Boston Teachers Organize, 1919–1965." Ph.D. diss., Harvard University, 1981.

Murphy, Marjorie. *Blackboard Unions: The AFT and the NEA, 1900–1980.* Ithaca: Cornell University Press, 1990.

———. "From Artisan to Semi-Professional: White Collar Unionism Among Chicago Public School Teachers, 1870–1930." Ph.D. diss., University of California, Davis, 1981.

"My Day: By a Junior High School Teacher." *New York Teacher* IV (December 1938): 26–27.

Naison, Mark. *Communists in Harlem During the Depression.* Urbana: University of Illinois Press, 1983.

Nasaw, David. *Schooled to Order: A Social History of Public Schooling in the United States.* New York: Oxford University Press, 1979.

National Education Association. "Requirements Affecting Appointment, Retention and Promotion of Teachers." *Research Bulletin 6* (September 1928): 221–244.

———. "The Status of the Teaching Profession." Prepared by E. S. Evenden. *Research Bulletin 18* (March 1940): 51–79.

———. "The Teacher Looks at Teacher Load." *Research Bulletin 17* (November 1939): 223–270.

Newcomer, Mabel. *A Century of Higher Education for American Women.* New York: Harper and Brothers, 1959.

Notable American Women, 1607–1950: A Biographical Dictionary. Edited by Edward T. James. Cambridge, Mass.: Belknap Press of Harvard University Press. 1971.

Notable American Women: The Modern Period. Edited by Barbara Sicherman and Carol Hurd Green. Cambridge, Mass.: Belknap Press of Harvard University Press, 1980.

Olneck, Michael R., and Lazerson, Marvin. "The School Achievement of Immigrant Children: 1900–1930." *History of Education Quarterly* XIV (Winter 1974): 453–482.

Oren, Dan A. *Joining the Club: A History of Jews and Yale.* New Haven: Yale University Press, 1985.

Patterson, Samuel White. *Hunter College: Eighty-Five Years of Service.* New York: Lantern Press, 1955.

Perlmann, Joel, and Margo, Robert. "Who Were America's Teachers? Toward a Social History and a Data Archive." *Historical Methods* 22 (Spring 1989): 68–73.

Peterson, Patti McGill. "Student Organizations and the Antiwar Movement in America, 1900–1960." *American Studies* XIII (Spring 1972): 131–147.

Quindlen, Anna. "Brooklyn College's Class of '33 Relives the Honor." *New York Times,* 8 June 1983, 14.

Ravitch, Diane. *The Great School Wars: New York City, 1805–1973: A History of the Public Schools as Battlefield of Social Change.* New York: Basic Books, 1974.

Rawick, George Philip. "The New Deal and Youth: The Civilian Conservation Corps, the National Youth Administration, and the American Youth Congress." Ph.D. diss., University of Wisconsin, 1957.

Rischin, Moses. *The Promised City: New York's Jews, 1870–1914.* Cambridge, Mass.: Harvard University Press, 1962.

Rose, Louise Blecher. "The Secret Life of Sarah Lawrence." *Commentary* (May 1983): 52–56.

Rudolph, Frederick. "Neglect of Students as a Historical Tradition." In *The College and the Student: An Assessment of Relationships and Responsibilities in Undergraduate Education by Administrators, Faculty Members, and Public Officials,* 47–58. Edited by Lawrence E. Dennis and Joseph F. Kauffman. Washington, D.C.: American Council on Education, 1967.

Rupp, Leila J. "Reflections on Twentieth-Century American Women's History." *Reviews in American History* 9 (June 1981): 275–284.

Scharf, Lois. *To Work and to Wed: Female Employment, Feminism, and the Great Depression.* Westport, Conn.: Greenwood, 1984.

Schwager, Sally. "Educating Women in America." *Signs* 12 (Winter 1987): 333–372.

Sears, William P., Jr. "The Schools and the Depression." *Education* LIII (April 1933): 501–503.

Seller, Maxine. "The Education of the Immigrant Woman, 1900–1935." *Journal of Urban History* 4 (May 1978): 307–331.

Shaffer, Robert. "Women and the Communist Party, USA, 1930–1940." *Socialist Review* 9 (May–June 1979): 73–118.

Shuster, George N. *The Ground I Walked On: Reflections of a College President.* New York: Farrar, Straus and Giroux, 1961.

Sicherman, Barbara, and Green, Carol Hurd, eds. *Notable American Women: The Modern Period.* Cambridge, Mass.: Belknap Press of Harvard University Press, 1980.

Silberman, Charles. *Crisis in the Classroom: The Remaking of American Education.* New York: Random House, 1970.

Simon, Kate. *Bronx Primitive: Portraits in a Childhood.* New York: Harper and Row, 1982.

————. *A Wider World: Portraits in an Adolescence.* New York: Harper and Row, 1986.

Snedden, David. "Personnel Problems in Educational Administration: Married Women as Public School Teachers." *Teachers College Record* XXXVI (April 1935): 613–621.

Solomon, Barbara. *In the Company of Educated Women: A History of Women and Higher Education in America.* New Haven: Yale University Press, 1985.

Sowell, Thomas. *Ethnic America.* New York: Basic Books, 1981.

Steinberg, Stephen. *The Academic Melting Pot: Catholics and Jews in American Higher Education.* New York: McGraw-Hill, 1974.

————. "The Rise of the Jewish Professional: Case Studies of Intergenerational Mobility." *Ethnic and Racial Studies* 9 (October 1986): 502–513.

Stern, Elizabeth Vera Loeb. "A History of Hunter's Splendid Century." *Hunter Alumni Quarterly* (Winter 1970): 13–20.

Strober, Myra, and Tyack, David. "Why Do Women Teach and Men Manage? A Report on Research on Schools." *Signs* 5 (Spring 1980): 494–503.

Synott, Marcia Graham. "Anti-Semitism and American Universities: Did Quotas Follow the Jews?" In *Anti-Semitism in American History*, 233–271. Edited by David A. Gerber. Urbana: University of Illinois Press, 1986.

————. *The Half-Opened Door: Discrimination at Harvard, Yale, and Princeton, 1900–1970.* Westport, Conn.: Greenwood, 1979.

Taffel, Helen Hochfelder. "Reminiscences of the Depression Years." *Hunter Alumni Quarterly* (Spring 1970): 13.

Taft, Philip. *United They Teach: The Story of the United Federation of Teachers.* Los Angeles: Nash, 1974.

"Teacher or Factory Hand?" *Journal of the National Education Association* VXIX (June 1930): 171–172.

Tenenbaum, Samuel. "Supervision: Theory and Practice." *School Executive* 59 (March 1940): 28–29.

Tentler, Leslie Woodcock. *Wage-Earning Women: Industrial Work and Family Life in the United States, 1900–1930.* New York: Oxford University Press, 1979.

Tyack, David. *The One Best System: A History of American Education.* Cambridge, Mass.: Harvard University Press, 1974.

————, and Hansot, Elisabeth. *Managers of Virtue: Public School Leadership in America, 1820–1980.* New York: Basic Books, 1982.

————; Lowe, Robert; and Hansot, Elisabeth. *Public Schools in Hard Times: The Great Depression and Recent Years.* Cambridge, Mass.: Harvard University Press, 1984.

U.S. Bureau of the Census. *Abstract of the Fourteenth Census of the United States.* Washington, D.C.: GPO, 1923.

————. *Education of the American Population: A 1960 Census Monograph.* Prepared by John K. Folger and Charles B. Nam. Washington, D.C.: GPO, 1967.

————. *Fifteenth Census of the United States: 1930. Vol. 5: Population, General Report on Occupations.* Washington, D.C.: GPO, 1935.

————. *Thirteenth Census of the United States: 1910. Vol. 3: Population.* Washington, D.C.: GPO, 1913.

U.S. Office of Education. *Biennial Survey of Education in the United States: Statistical Summary of Education, 1939–40*, vol. 2. Washington, D.C.: GPO, 1943.

————. *National Survey of the Education of Teachers, Summary and Interpretation*, bulletin No. 10. Prepared by E. S. Evenden. Washington, D.C.: GPO, 1933.

Urban, Wayne J. *Why Teachers Organized.* Detroit: Wayne State University Press, 1962.

Van Denburg, Joseph King. *Causes of the Elimination of Students in Public Secondary Schools of New York City.* New York: Teachers College, Columbia University, 1911.

Ware, Susan. *Holding Their Own: American Women in the 1930s.* Boston: Twayne, 1982.

Warren, Donald, ed. *American Teachers: Histories of a Profession at Work.* New York: Macmillan, 1989.

Wattenberg, William W. *On the Educational Front: The Reactions of Teachers Associations in New York and Chicago.* New York: Columbia University Press, 1936.

Wechsler, Harold S. *The Qualified Student: A History of Selective College Admission in America.* New York: John Wiley and Sons, 1977.

————. "The Rationale for Restriction: Ethnicity and College Admission in America, 1910–1980," *American Quarterly* 36 Winter 1984): 643–667.

Wechsler, James. *Revolt on the Campus.* New York: Covici-Friede, 1935.

Weinberg, Sydney Stahl. *The World of Our Mothers: The Lives of Jewish Immigrant Women.* Chapel Hill: University of North Carolina Press, 1988.

Wittner, Lawrence. *Rebels Against War: The American Peace Movement, 1933–1983.* Philadelphia: Temple University Press, 1984.

Woods, Elizabeth L. "When Wives Teach School: Should Eugenicists Demur?" *Eugenics* 4 (February 1931): 61.

Woody, Thomas. *A History of Women's Education in the United States.* 2 vols. New York: Science Press, 1929.

Wouk, Herman. *Marjorie Morningstar.* Garden City, N.Y.: Doubleday and Company, 1955.

Zborowski, Mark, and Herzog, Elizabeth. *Life is With People: The Jewish Little-Town of Eastern Europe.* New York: International Universities Press, 1952.

Zinn, Howard. "A Comparison of the Militant Left of the Thirties and the Sixties." In *The Thirties: A Reconsideration in the Light of the American Political Tradition,* 27–43. Edited by Morton J. Frisch and Martin Diamond. DeKalb: Northern Illinois University Press, 1968.

Zitron, Celia Lewis. *The New York City Teachers Union, 1916–1954: A Story of Educational and Social Commitment.* New York: Humanities Press, 1968.

Zysman, Dale. "Dear Sir: An Extract from an Open Letter to Superintendent Bayne." *New York Teacher* IV (March 1939): 20–22.

INDEX

Board of Examiners (*continued*)
and radical students, 77; survey of
applications, 89; and teaching licenses, 76,
77, 78. *See also* Gertrude Epstein; teaching
licenses
Board of Higher Education, 60; proposes
tuition, 48
Board of Superintendents, 165
Bronx Boro-Wide Teachers Association, 129
Brooklyn College, 8, 19, 24, 25, 26, 27, 51, 52,
53, 54; economic survey, 28; education
students, 29–30, 177; faculty-student
conflict, 37; Jewish enrollment, 21, 42;
newspaper, 43; percentage of Jewish
women, 30; sanctions against activists, 60–
62; student activism, 43, 47, 48, 71; student
polls, 29; yearbook, 21, 43, 72
Brooklyn Teachers Association, 107, 125;
officers, 129
Brooklyn Training School, 185n6
Browder, Earl, 48
Brumberg, Joan Jacobs, 3

Campbell, Harold G., 119, 120, 159, 160
Catholic Teachers Association of New York,
159
Caute, David, 169
Childs, John L., 103
Chomsky, Anna, 81
Citron, Alice, 179; and activism, 164–166; and
African Americans, 170; and Isadore Begun,
202n62; removal from teaching, 166;
sanctioned by administration, 165;
supporters of, 166, 167. *See also* Communist
party; McCarthyism; public schools
City College of New York (CCNY), 19,
187n79; Jewish enrollment, 19, 21;
sanctions against activists, 57; student
activism, 57
Class, Culture, and the Classroom (Eagan), 41
clubs and organizations (junior and senior high
school), 99, 100, 120; membership, 121;
national, 120; religious, 152
clubs and organizations (college): Barnard
College, 64; Brooklyn College, 44;
Columbia University, 63; Hunter College,
44, 45, 47, 55, 58, 60; national, 44–46;
religious, 39. *See also* American Student
Union
Cohen, Morris, 35
Cohen, Sol, 114
Cole, Stephen, 181–182n3
college admission quotas, 41; at Barnard
College, 70, 184–185n1; at medical schools,
2; at NYC private colleges, 18

college publications: newspapers, 39, 43–44; in
NYC, 70; in the U.S., 43; yearbooks, 39, 43.
See also Barnard Bulletin; *individual
colleges*
Collier, Virginia MacMakin, 144, 145
Colligan, Eugene, 57–58, 62
Columbia University, 41, 81; publications, 63,
70; radical students, 64. *See also* Gertrude
Epstein
Committee on Academic Freedom, 167
common schools, 10, 133
Communist party, 48, 50, 53, 54, 64, 67, 68; and
African Americans, 170; and Board of
Education, 78; and Devany Law, 78; and
Harlem teachers, 163, 165; and Jewish
teachers, 168; members of Teachers Union,
169; teacher-members of, 158, 163, 168,
169, 170. *See also* anti-Communism;
McCarthyism; radical movements; Young
Communist League
Compulsory Education Law of 1936, 108
Cott, Nancy F., 171
Coughlin, Charles E., 47, 161
Council of Bedford-Stuyvesant-Williamsburg,
166
Counts, George S., 103
Cremin, Lawrence A., 194n34
Cuban, Larry, 102, 194n34

Daily Worker, 53–54; and Gertrude Epstein, 64,
65, 67
Daughters of the American Revolution, 153
Daughters of the Shtetl (Glenn), 9
Department of Health, NYC, 118
Devany Law, 178. *See also* Communist party
Dewey, John, 101, 194n27. *See also* educational
theories; progressive education
Dodd, Bella Visconti, 169
Doty, Katharine S., 63–66, 68. *See also*
Gertrude Epstein
Draper, Hal, 43, 72
Dual Job Law, 126–127, 140

Eagan, Eileen, 37, 41
Eastern Europe, 4; education in, 4, 5, 7, 70–71
education, U.S.: early nineteenth century, 10.
See also educational theories; feminization
of teaching
Education Discussion Group, *see* American
Education Association
Education Signpost, see American Education
Association
educational theories, 101–104; Activity
Program, 101, 102, 124, 130–131; and
Board of Education, 102, 103–104; in high